=1●1=
BASEBALL PLACES
TO SEE BEFORE YOU STRIKE OUT

Noel ~

To a great coach!

Happy Birthday!

Linda

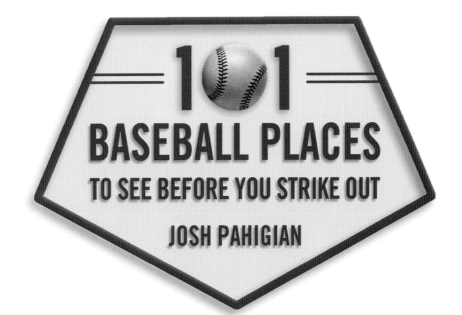

101
BASEBALL PLACES
TO SEE BEFORE YOU STRIKE OUT

JOSH PAHIGIAN

The Lyons Press
Guilford, Connecticut

An imprint of The Globe Pequot Press

To buy books in quantity for corporate use
or incentives, call **(800) 962–0973**
or e-mail **premiums@GlobePequot.com**.

Copyright © 2008 Joshua Pahigian

ALL RIGHTS RESERVED. No part of this book may be reproduced or transmitted in any form by any means, electronic
or mechanical, including photocopying and recording, or by any information storage and retrieval system, except as
may be expressly permitted in writing from the publisher. Requests for permission should be addressed to The Lyons
Press, Attn: Rights and Permissions Department, P.O. Box 480, Guilford, CT 06437.

The Lyons Press is an imprint of The Globe Pequot Press.

10 9 8 7 6 5 4 3 2 1

Printed in China

Designed by LeAnna Weller Smith

ISBN 978-1-59921-251-7

Library of Congress Cataloging-in-Publication Data is available on file.

CONTENTS

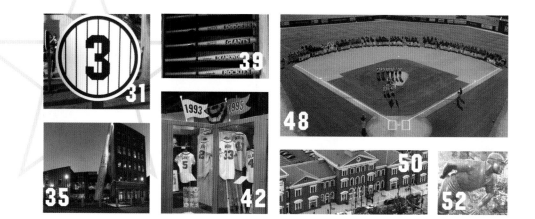

INTRODUCTION

Baseball is "America's Game." It is our "National Pastime." It transcends generations and brings together Americans from all walks of life to play, watch, and celebrate as one. The culture of the game—too mainstream to be called a *sub*culture—is as rich and varied as the fabric of American society itself, and it can be found on all corners of the American continent. Yes, other sports have made inroads into America's sporting consciousness through the years and at various times have laid their respective claims to being the country's most popular game, but make no mistake, baseball is still king.

The book you hold in your hands will reassure you of this. It will remind you of all those special qualities that make the game we play and watch at so many levels such a unique American phenomenon. It will recall how baseball has stood the test of time as our country has grown. It will explain how, unlike any other sport, the story of baseball's evolution is inextricably intertwined with the story of America's own coming of age. It will explain how baseball has helped break down all of those unfortunate barriers to peace, prosperity, and brotherhood that have at times divided us as a nation: differences of race, religion, economic status, and politics. It will explain how baseball, above all other sports and above all other forms of American entertainment, has brought us together, acting as a great unifier. And it will do all of this within a structural framework that introduces you to 101 favorite baseball places spread across the country.

For traveling fans, whose leisure or business excursions take them frequently to far-from-home places around the country, this book will serve as a guide, leading to their own special experiences. For homebodies, the book will capture the spirit of each location, allowing them to gain, right from the comfort of their own easy chairs, a better appreciation of whatever aspect of the game's past or present is rooted at each site.

While all of this may seem a bit grandiose and ambitious, in truth this was not an exceedingly difficult book for your humble author to write. As writer, my charge was simply to tell baseball's story, or rather its *stories*, and to let readers arrive at whatever conclusions they might regarding the scope of the game's reach and the extent to which it has impacted and continues to impact American life. The book is meant to be a celebration of the game's players, fans, and ballparks at all levels and of the tradition it has amassed through the years in small towns, big cities, and all of the communities in between.

Among the places profiled within these pages, readers will find more than twenty baseball museums—ranging from well-known haunts like the National Baseball Hall of Fame and the Negro Leagues Baseball Museum to lesser-known sites like the Ty Cobb Museum and Cy Young Museum. There are also entries devoted to gravesites and monuments spread across the country that pay tribute to some of the game's most revered and influential figures. Sites related to baseball history and pop culture also receive their just due, as places like the Chicago courthouse where baseball lore holds that Joe Jackson refused to tell a young

fan it "wasn't so" and the *Field of Dreams* movie site are detailed. Places that figure prominently in baseball myth, like the Chicago Cubs' "Curse of the Billy Goat" also receive treatment, as do more than a dozen baseball-themed bars and restaurants, a car wash owned by a former big leaguer, and an amusement park owned by another.

And what would a book like this be worth if it didn't afford proper page space to the fields where baseball players of all ages and skill levels play the game they love? The book includes entries devoted to select major-league, minor-league, spring-training, college, high school, and youth ballparks that are a cut above the rest, and there's even a section about one very special Wiffle Ball field. There are also chapters related to the old ballpark sites that fans can visit to discover the remnants of famous hardball cathedrals of yesteryear. It's pretty mind-blowing to stand in the exact spot from which more than a century ago Cy Young delivered the very first pitch of the very first World Series game, or to dig in beside a home plate that lies in the exact spot as when Bill Mazeroski stepped into the batter's box and belted his walk-off homer to propel the Pirates past the Yankees in the 1960 World Series. I dare say it's impossible not to get goose bumps as you confront baseball history at places like these. And in the end, that's what this book is about: goose bumps. It introduces readers to all of the diverse places across America (and that includes Alaska, Hawaii, and Canada, too) that are sure to evoke an emo-

Stature of Shoeless Joe Jackson in Greenville, South Carolina

tional response from anyone who loves the game. Some are fun—like the St. Paul Saints' Midway Stadium, some are solemn—like the laboratory where mad chemist Victor Conte perfected the Human Growth Hormone that would fuel baseball's Steroid Era, some are educational—like the Yogi Berra Museum and Learning Center, some are majestic—like Yankee Stadium's Monument Park, some are mysterious—like the spot where every glob of mud that's been rubbed on every big league ball since the 1950s has been mined, and some are just plain silly—like the Milwaukee brewery that houses Bernie Brewer's old slide and chalet from County Stadium. As author, my hope is that by reading about or visiting all of these places, you will come to know the most magical game of all a bit more intimately. And you'll fall in love with baseball a bit more deeply. Enjoy!

=1●1=
BASEBALL PLACES
TO SEE BEFORE YOU STRIKE OUT

Plaque Gallery at the National Baseball Hall of Fame in Cooperstown

★ ★ ★

=1=

THE NATIONAL BASEBALL HALL OF FAME AND MUSEUM

25 Main Street | Cooperstown, New York

When it comes to baseball landmarks, few would argue that the Hall of Fame is not the granddaddy of them all. This perfect tribute to the game's history is located in the perfect setting for it. And while this bucolic little village in central New York State may not, in fact, be the place where the game magically emerged from the primordial soup of the other bat-and-ball games that preceded it, it plays the part of baseball's Garden of Eden perfectly. Its small-town ethos and country charm symbolize all of the pastoral communities across the land that contributed, each in their own way, to baseball's evolution during the 1800s.

The story of how baseball's home came to reside at Cooperstown is one that involves some shoddy research, fortunate timing, generosity, and serendipitous forward thinking on the part of both the village fathers and the baseball establishment. In the

early 1930s, three decades after the Mills Commission had erroneously concluded that Abner Doubleday invented baseball in Cooperstown in 1839, baseball began making preparations for its one hundredth birthday party. It seemed only natural that the game's centennial celebration should take place in the town from which it had supposedly originated, and baseball commissioner Kenesaw Mountain Landis, National League president Ford Frick, and American League president William Harridge all arranged to be on hand.

Around the same time that these preparations were getting under way, an ancient cloth-stuffed baseball was discovered in the attic of a farmhouse just a few miles outside Cooperstown. The withered artifact, immediately dubbed "the Doubleday Baseball," lent further credence, or so the locals said, to the notion that the National Game had been invented in Cooperstown. Recognizing the significance of the find, prominent Cooperstown philanthropist Stephen C. Clark purchased the ball for five dollars in 1934 and began displaying it in the Cooperstown municipal offices. Soon other locals came forward with mementos from baseball's past, helping Clark build a small one-room shrine in the village office building. Inspired by the pride that his fellow villagers took in celebrating Cooperstown's role in the invention of baseball, Clark and his friend Alexander Cleland began exploring the idea of establishing a National Baseball Museum. This idea was blossoming at precisely the time when Frick, the National League president, had begun campaigning for the creation of a baseball Hall of Fame. The two parties eventually merged their interests, thus conceiving the National Baseball Hall of Fame and Museum, which officially opened on June 12, 1939. Twenty-five baseball legends were inducted into the Hall during baseball's one-hundredth-birthday bash, including the five players—Ty Cobb, Babe Ruth, Honus Wagner, Christy Mathewson, and Walter Johnson—who had been elected by the baseball newspaper writers of the day on the very first ballot in 1936. Also inducted at that time were the twenty others who had been elected in three subsequent votes.

Through the decades this awe-inspiring baseball repository has undergone several expansions to accommodate the hundreds and hundreds of donations it has received from private collectors, players, teams, fans, and generous others who have contributed to its collection of baseball treasures. Today the 350,000 visitors who make the pilgrimage to Cooperstown each year find more than 260 bronze plaques hanging in the Hall's plaque gallery to honor the players, coaches, executives, umpires, journalists, and other individuals who have made the most profound contributions to the game. In addition visitors find an artifact-laden timeline of the game's history that begins in the 1800s and continues all the way to the present. There are also exhibits dedicated to Babe Ruth; the no-hitters and perfect games; every World Series since 1903; baseball cards; baseball records; U.S. presidents and their involvement in the game; youth baseball; the minor leagues; the Negro Leagues; women in baseball; old-time ballparks; the thirty teams currently composing the major leagues; the Cy Young Award, MVP Award, and Gold Glove Award; baseball's international presence; baseball art; baseball in the movies; and much more. In total there are more than 35,000 three-dimensional items on display and more than 130,000 baseball cards and photos, and that's not even counting the items housed at the adjoining Hall of Fame Library, which opened in 1968 to serve the needs of baseball historians, writers, filmmakers, and trivia buffs.

The Hall's trademark annual event is its Hall of Fame Weekend and Induction Ceremony, which takes place over four days in the latter half of July. During this special time, tens of thousands of fans, many of the Hall's living members, and the national baseball media descend on Cooperstown to pay tribute to whichever individuals are about to be immortalized. Although Cooperstown is the most crowded and most vibrantly decorated during this time of year, the museum and village attract a steady stream of visitors throughout the rest of the year as well. Just as every child dreams of one day going to Disneyland, every true baseball fan dreams of one day visiting the Hall of Fame. But unlike the former attraction, which many find over-hyped, over-crowded, and over-commercialized, the museum in sleepy little Cooperstown always delivers a satisfying, enriching, and altogether mesmerizing experience.

The Hall is open every day of the year except for Thanksgiving, Christmas, and New Year's Day. From Memorial Day through Labor Day, its hours are 9:00 A.M. to 9:00 P.M. seven days a week. The rest of the year it is open from 9:00 A.M. to 5:00 P.M. Admission costs $14.50 for adults, $9.50 for senior citizens and children aged seven through twelve, and $5.00 for children under seven.

★ ★ ★

= 2 =
THE *FIELD OF DREAMS* MOVIE SITE
Lansing Road | Dyersville, Iowa

Fans of the classic baseball movie *Field of Dreams* will remember that throughout the film Joe Jackson's ghost implores main character Ray Kinsella to turn his unprofitable Iowa cornfield into a baseball diamond. "If you build it, he will come," the ghost's voice echoes, and Ray gets to work, turning under his crop, laying sod, and spreading infield clay in the hope that his magical field will somehow afford him the chance to play one last game of catch with his deceased father.

By movie's end, "*he* will come" has evolved into "*they* will come," and more than reconnecting Ray with his father, the baseball diamond in the middle of nowhere has also provided Ray with an income source that will allow him to pay his mortgage and "save" his family's home. As the movie concludes, an unending stream of cars wends its way along the dirt road leading to the field, as tourists flock to the diamond to marvel at its uniqueness and watch Ray's ghost players.

In a case of life imitating art, the field used in the filming of the movie—which exists on two abutting plots owned by two different Iowa families—has drawn more than one hundred thousand visitors since Universal Studios released *Field of Dreams* in 1989. The Lansing family owns the infield and

Field of Dreams movie site

rightfield portions of the diamond and lives in the same white farmhouse that visitors will remember from the movie. The Ameskamp family owns the leftfield and centerfield portions of the diamond. The field and house appear exactly as they did in the film, with the exception of the power lines that bisect the field—running from behind third base out through centerfield.

Don Lansing, the elderly gentleman who has lived in the farmhouse since his childhood, is happy to recount for visitors his initial reaction on being approached by a Universal Studios executive bent on turning under Don's soybean and tobacco crops, building a baseball field, and planting corn-

stalks across the "outfield" portion of Don's land. "You want to build a ballfield here?" Don recalls asking. "Why?" If that sounds a lot like the response Ray Kinsella got from his friends and family members in the movie, you're right, it is.

In any case, Don stopped asking questions when Universal cut him a check, and then he watched in amazement as his land was leveled, sod was laid, and light towers were erected, all in a span of a few short days. After the movie was shot—including the dramatic final scene that included some 1,500 local citizens and their cars, making their way up Don's driveway—Don decided to maintain the baseball field for visitors to use. Never did he imagine it would become a site of national tourist interest. But it did . . . just like in the movie.

The field is open during daylight hours from April through November, and best of all, it is completely free. Don runs a small souvenir shop on the Lansing side of the diamond and mows his portion of the lawn, while the Ameskamps operate a larger souvenir store in leftfield foul territory and mow their portion of the outfield grass. At the Ameskamp family's Left & Center Field of Dreams gift shop, visitors find a map of the United States upon which baseball travelers place pushpins to signify their states of origin. There are also business cards left by international travelers tacked to the board, connecting the field to such faraway places as Australia, Chile, England, France, Germany, Holland, Japan, Norway, Spain, Scotland, and Switzerland.

So, bring a ball, bring a mitt, and most important, bring your imagination. Have a catch on the Field of Dreams. The experience may just be magical.

=3=
THE NEGRO LEAGUES BASEBALL MUSEUM

1616 East 18th Street | Kansas City, Missouri

After Moses Fleetwood Walker played his last game for the Toledo Blue Stockings in 1884, a long era of segregated baseball began in Major League Baseball that would not be challenged until Jackie Robinson took the field with the Brooklyn Dodgers in 1947. Spanning the decades in between, regional teams of black stars formed across the United States and barnstormed around the country playing one another. In the early 1900s several efforts were made to unite these teams under the umbrella of a central league but with little success. Finally, Rube Foster—a former player, manager, and owner of the Chicago American Giants—brought together representatives from several prominent Midwest teams and formed the Negro National League in 1920. The league stuck.

Today the pioneering spirit, immense talent, and unfailing love for the game of baseball—even in the face of so much adversity—that helped the Negro Leagues survive for more than four decades is reflected at the Negro Leagues Baseball Museum. This amazing baseball attraction was born in the early 1990s, when a group of Kansas City businessmen, historians, and former Negro

Field of Legends at the Negro Leagues Museum

Leagues players opened a small museum in the city's Lincoln Building. The museum quickly expanded, buoyed by a renewed interest in the Negro Leagues brought on by the Ken Burns documentary *Baseball*. The PBS miniseries introduced the nation to Buck O'Neil, a former Kansas City Monarch, who captivated viewers with his vivid memories of black baseball's Golden Age. Over the next few years Kansas City contributed more than $20 million to build a new 50,000-square-foot home for the Negro Leagues Baseball Museum and for the adjoining American Jazz Museum. The two museums opened in 1997 in Kansas City's Historic District.

The Negro Leagues Baseball Museum offers a self-guided tour that traces the history of the game and of American race relations. The photograph- and artifact-laden chronology begins with an exhibit devoted to baseball's earliest days immediately following the Civil War. Then it examines the experiences of a largely unknown cast of African-American pioneers that integrated baseball at the semipro, college, and professional levels in the 1880s and 1890s. Next comes an exhibit related to the "gentlemen's agreement" that unofficially banned blacks from the major leagues at the turn of the century and to the barnstorming teams of black stars that formed as a result.

The next section of the museum, devoted to the founding and four-decade history of the Negro Leagues, is the largest. It tells the stories of how the Negro National League was born, how night baseball debuted in the Negro Leagues in the 1930s, how the Negro Leagues experienced a renaissance during the Great Depression, how Satchel Paige became the most famous Negro Leagues star of all, how black baseball spread to Mexico, and more. Next are exhibits related to the integration of the major leagues and to the eventual dissolution of the Negro Leagues.

After learning about the founders and great stars of the Negro Leagues, visitors end the tour by spilling out onto a replica of a baseball diamond. The Field of Legends is home to twelve life-size statues that portray some of the best Negro Leaguers ever to play the game. The bronze likenesses include Foster, O'Neil, Paige, Josh Gibson, Buck Leonard, Pop Lloyd, Judy Johnson, Ray Dandridge, Cool Papa Bell, Oscar Charleston, Leon Day, and Martin Dihigo. Among this group, O'Neil is the only player not also honored with a plaque at the National Baseball Hall of Fame at Cooperstown. Many within the baseball establishment consider this oversight a travesty, but O'Neil, who passed away in 2006, never shed any tears on his own behalf. He was happy to keep telling stories about the great Negro Leagues players and the teams, and he turned out at the Negro Leagues Baseball Museum regularly to share his love of the game with others.

The museum is open Tuesday through Saturday from 9:00 A.M. to 6:00 P.M. and on Sunday from noon to 6:00. Admission costs $6.00 for adults and $2.50 for children.

= 4 =

MONUMENT PARK

Yankee Stadium | East 161st Street and River Avenue | Bronx, New York

No big-league team goes to greater lengths to honor its legendary players, managers, and executives at its stadium than do the New York Yankees. And for good reason. The Bronx Bombers can lay claim to an all-time roster that easily trumps the best performers that any two— or maybe even three—other franchises combined can muster.

Yankee Stadium's Monument Park has steadily grown in size ever since its first slab of granite was erected in 1932, when the likeness of longtime Yankees skipper Miller Huggins was emblazoned in bronze on a monument and set in front of the centerfield flagpole. A monument honoring Lou Gehrig was added in 1939 and then a year later a plaque on the outfield wall honoring Yankees owner Jacob Ruppert. In 1949 a third monument, this one honoring Babe Ruth, was placed beside Huggins's. Together the three monuments stood in the field of play some 450 feet from home plate and remained there until Yankee Stadium was renovated during the 1974 and 1975 seasons. As part of the remodeling, the left-centerfield fence was brought about 30 feet closer to home plate, relegating the monuments to the no-man's-land between the playing field and the bleachers.

Today this unique area offers visitors year-round access to the monuments and plaques that pay tribute to the very best players to have worn the uniform of the game's very best team. On game day ticket-bearing fans (except those with bleacher seats) can access Monument Park, beginning when the stadium gates open and continuing until forty-five minutes before the first pitch. On weekdays throughout the season and during the off-season, the park is also accessible to fans who take the Yankee Stadium Tour, which begins daily at noon. The tour costs $14.00 for adults and $8.00 for children.

. Within the park fans find the original three monuments, as well as ones honoring Mickey Mantle and Joe DiMaggio, which were added in 1996 and 1999 respectively, and one paying tribute to the victims and rescue workers of the September 11, 2001, terrorist attacks on New York's World Trade Center. There is also a monument honoring Jackie Robinson, which was added in 2007 on the sixtieth anniversary of Robinson's breaking baseball's color barrier.

Monument Park also features a corridor that displays the sixteen retired numbers in Yankees history, which appear on pinstriped plaques. These include number 1 for

HENRY LOUIS GEHRIG
JUNE 19TH 1903 — JUNE 2ND 1941

A MAN, A GENTLEMAN
AND
A GREAT BALL PLAYER
WHOSE AMAZING RECORD
OF 2130 CONSECUTIVE GAMES
SHOULD STAND FOR ALL TIME.

THIS MEMORIAL IS A TRIBUTE
FROM THE
YANKEE PLAYERS
TO THEIR BELOVED CAPTAIN AND TEAM MATE

JULY THE FOURTH
1941

Lou Gehrig monument at Yankee Stadium's Monument Park

Billy Martin, number 3 for Ruth, number 4 for Gehrig, number 5 for DiMaggio, number 6 for Roger Maris, number 7 for Mantle, number 8 for Bill Dickey, another number 8 for Yogi Berra, number 10 for Phil Rizzuto, number 15 for Thurman Munson, number 16 for Whitey Ford, number 23 for Don Mattingly, number 32 for Elston Howard, number 37 for Casey Stengel, number 44 for Reggie Jackson, and number 49 for Ron Guidry. Below the numbers are placards that offer biographical information about each retiree. Not far away, hanging on the back wall of Monument Park, fans find plaques that pay tribute to slightly lesser stars in Yankees history like Lefty Gomez, Allie Reynolds, and Red Ruffing, as well as to the major stars also honored elsewhere in the park with retired numbers and monuments.

Finally, although many aspects of the fan experience in the Bronx will likely change when the new Yankee Stadium opens in 2009, one thing will stay more or less the same. The Yankees have assured fans throughout the design and construction phases of their new home that Monument Park will be transported to the new stadium.

Lamade Stadium in Williamsport, Pennsylvania, home of the Little League World Series

★ ★ ★

THE LITTLE LEAGUE INTERNATIONAL COMPLEX

539 Route U.S. Highway 15 | South Williamsport, Pennsylvania

The home of Little League Baseball offers wanderers a wealth of opportunities to connect with the game's past, present, and future, whether during August, when the annual Little League World Series takes place, or any other time of year. The 66-acre complex, which sits just across the Susquehanna River from where Little League Baseball originated in Williamsport more than seven decades ago, includes Howard J. Lamade Stadium, the recognizable ballpark beneath the grassy green hillside where the Little League World Series championship game is played; Volunteer Stadium,

101 BASEBALL PLACES TO SEE BEFORE YOU STRIKE OUT

where early-round and consolation games are played; and the Peter J. McGovern Little League Museum, which celebrates the history of Little League Baseball and Softball and honors Little League alums who have distinguished themselves in a variety of fields.

Little League Baseball and Softball, today played by more than 2.6 million children in more than seventy countries on six continents annually, was born in the late 1930s as the brainchild of a Williamsport clerk named Carl E. Stotz. Although Mr. Stotz didn't have any children of his own, he enjoyed throwing batting practice to his young nephews. More than just practicing with his young friends, though, he wanted them to experience the excitement of actual competition. And so, in the winter of 1938–1939, he got to work, envisioning a scaled-down version of the sport that would allow youngsters opportunities to learn the finer points of the game and to learn the value of good sportsmanship.

The very first Little League fielded three teams in Williamsport in the spring of 1939. The first game was played on June 6, at a field on West Fourth Street that would serve as a template for miniature diamonds across Pennsylvania in the years to follow. By 1947 Little League had expanded outside Pennsylvania, emigrating first to Hammonton, New Jersey. By 1950 Little League had spread outside the United States, establishing a circuit in Panama.

As for the first Little League World Series, it took place in 1947, when a team from Williamsport defeated one from Lock Haven 16–7. After the first twelve World Series were played on West Fourth Street at the field now known as Memorial Park, the tournament had grown too big for the little diamond, so Williamsport's Little League officials moved the World Series across the Susquehanna. Although Lamade Stadium has undergone many renovations since opening in 1959, it retains its old-time charm. The grandstand runs along both foul lines and is covered by a low roof. The trademark outfield hill hovers above the 225-foot-deep home-run fence and provides a comfortable place for fans to recline and watch the game. Adjacent **Volunteer Stadium**, which was added in 2001, is also a cozy place to watch a game. Admission to both parks is absolutely free during the annual tourney.

The Little League World Series begins on July 1 at sites around the world and involves more than 7,000 entrants. By early August the field has been whittled to just sixteen teams that report to South Williamsport for the thirty-two-game World Series finale. The tournament culminates in a championship game that is witnessed by the nearly 40,000 fans who cram into Lamade and by a worldwide television audience. In recent years future major leaguers like Gary Sheffield (1980), Jason Varitek (1984), Jason Bay (1990), Jason Marquis (1991), and Lastings Milledge (1997) have gotten their first taste of the national spotlight at Lamade.

Another popular attraction at the Little League complex is the **museum**, which offers artifacts from the league's earliest games. It also provides interactive exhibits like batting and pitching cages and trivia games and features an expansive collection of autographed balls and baseball cards. The highlight, though, is the Hall of Excellence, which honors people like George W. Bush, Kevin Costner, Tom Selleck, George Will, Kareem Abdul-Jabbar, Bruce Springsteen, Mike Schmidt, Cal Ripken Jr., Dale Murphy, Jim Palmer, Nolan Ryan, Tom Seaver, and other famous Americans who have played Little League. Between Memorial Day and Labor Day, the museum is open Monday through Saturday from 10:00 A.M. to 7:00 P.M.

and Sunday from noon to 7:00. During the off-season, it is open Monday, Thursday, and Friday from 10:00 A.M. to 5:00 P.M. and Saturday from noon to 4:00. Admission costs $5.00 for adults and $1.50 for children.

Two miles north of the complex, a historic marker honors "the founder of Little League Baseball," Mr. Stotz, at **Memorial Park**. Right nearby, fans will also find **Bowman Field** (1700 West Fourth Street), a full-size professional diamond that dates back to 1923. One of the oldest working minor-league ballparks in the country, Bowman currently serves as the home of the New York–Penn League Williamsport Crosscutters.

=6=

RICKWOOD FIELD

1137 Second Avenue West | Birmingham, Alabama

Part museum and part working ballpark, Rickwood Field offers baseball wanderers the chance to step back in time and explore the oldest standing professional ballpark in the country. Built in the Classic Era of stadium construction, Rickwood opened in 1910, two years before Fenway Park. It would serve as Birmingham's minor-league hub for nearly eight decades and as the home of the Birmingham Black Barons of the Negro National League from 1923 through 1950. In 1988 it was

semiretired when the Southern League Birmingham Barons moved to a new stadium in the nearby city of Hoover, but a group of local volunteers continues to ensure that the park is preserved. Since the early 1990s the "Friends of Rickwood" have contributed more than $2 million toward the restoration of this National Historic Landmark and have helped organize the annual "Rickwood Classic," a throwback game played each summer between the Barons and one of their Southern League opponents. The old

Entrance to Rickwood Field

park is also used for a variety of amateur games and sees occasional use as a film site, having provided the primary setting for movies like *Cobb* and *Soul of the Game*.

While the Rickwood Classic should rate high on any fan's list of must-see games, baseball junkies unable to land themselves in Birmingham on this one special day per year should not despair. Rickwood Field is open to fans year-round during daylight hours and even offers a self-guided tour that leads through the stands, into the dugouts, onto the field, and behind the outfield fences, providing plenty of historic information along the way.

Rickwood Field was designed to look like Forbes Field, which opened a year earlier in Pittsburgh. The country's first minor-league park to be constructed of concrete and steel, it was built at a cost of $75,000, provided by Barons owner and eventual stadium namesake A. H. "Rick" Woodward. The park opened on August 18, 1910, when the first of many sellout crowds to pass through its gates watched the home team down the Montgomery Climbers 3–2 on a walk-off hit in the ninth inning. During the 1920s the Southern Association Barons drew more than 160,000 fans in eight different seasons, including a high-water mark of 299,000 in 1927. After the lean baseball years brought on by the Great Depression and World War II, attendance spiked again in Birmingham in the 1940s when the Barons and Black

Barons shared Rickwood. In 1948 the Barons, who were then a Boston Red Sox affiliate, set a franchise record, drawing 445,926 fans. That same year, the Black Barons won the National Negro League pennant, sparked by seventeen-year-old centerfielder Willie Mays.

In addition to Mays, Birmingham was also home at various points to other baseball immortals, like Satchel Paige, Burleigh Grimes, Pie Traynor, Rube Marquard, Reggie Jackson, Rollie Fingers, Catfish Hunter, and Vida Blue.

Fans who visit Rickwood Field today find the ballpark looking much like it did in the 1930s and 1940s, save for some metal bleachers and plastic seats that were added in the early 1980s to replace the old wooden ones. From the street outside, the upper level offers a pale green facade, while the lower level takes on a light cream hue. Fans pass through several square "arches" to enter the park, then spill into a grandstand, the back two-thirds of which is covered by a low roof that extends from the rightfield foul pole to the home-plate area and then out to third base. The advertisements on the outfield fences and the manually operated scoreboard in left are period-specific replicas that were added by Hollywood set designers during the filming of *Cobb*. The unique tiled-roof gazebo that sits atop the grandstand behind home plate once provided a place for the public-address announcer to sit and watch the game. The light banks thrust forward off the grandstand roof on metal staging so that the lights seem to hang right out over the field.

After spending a few minutes poking around this enchanting old yard, it seems possible, even probable, that Willie Mays and some of his contemporaries might emerge from the home dugout at any moment and trot out to their positions on the field.

★ ★ ★

=7=

THE GREEN MONSTER

Fenway Park, Lansdowne Street | Boston, Massachusetts

The most famous wall in all of sports stands at Fenway Park in Boston. The looming Green Monster begins its ascent just 310 feet from home plate in leftfield and rises 37 feet, 2 inches into the Boston sky. It is one of the chief attractions that draw fans to Boston's "little lyrical bandbox of a ballpark," as John Updike once described it, and is one of the reasons the Red Sox sell out every one of their home games year after year.

Fans who have followed the game for any

The Green Monster at Fenway Park

length of time have surely observed that "the Wall" is an ever-evolving edifice. While some aspects of it have remained the same, others have changed with time. What fans may not know is that when Fenway Park originally opened in 1912, the Wall was not part of the ballpark design. Rather, a steep hill rose at the back of Fenway's leftfield lawn, and atop the hill stood a 25-foot-high fence that separated the field from the city outside. In these early days, Red Sox leftfielder Duffy Lewis learned to adroitly scale the hill while pursuing fly balls, and the hill came to be known as "Duffy's Cliff."

With the advent of the lively ball, the Red Sox leveled the hill in 1934 and constructed a 200-foot long, 37-foot-high wall, using more than 15 tons of iron. The manual scoreboard that appears on the Wall today also debuted in 1934, although the Wall's trademark green paint would not appear until 1947. Originally, the Wall was plastered with advertisements for products like soap, shaving creams, razors, shoes, cigarettes, and clothes. In 1936 a 23-foot-high screen was added at the top to protect pedestrians and motorists on Lansdowne Street from outgoing balls. The screen stood above Lansdowne collecting homers until 2003, when the Red Sox added 294 seats in its place. For old time's sake, the Red Sox left on the face of the Wall the ladder that members of the ground crew had used for decades to scale the Monster and retrieve the home-run balls after games. Today any player who hits the ladder with a batted ball is awarded a ground-rule triple.

Through the years, the Green Monster has played a leading role in the evolution of Red Sox mythology, and during the Red Sox' long championship drought, some fans and pundits blamed it for the team's many failures. Though modern statistical analysis has since proven otherwise, for generations the popular wisdom dictated that right-handed hitters would flourish at Fenway, and left-handed pitchers would flounder. Thus, Red Sox management traditionally overvalued the former and undervalued the latter, resulting in teams that consistently lacked balance in the lineup and rotation.

The Wall also played a role in two of the most dramatic moments in Red Sox history. In Game Six of the 1975 World Series, Carlton Fisk swatted a twelfth-inning homer that clanked off the foul pole above the Monster to give the Red Sox a 7–6 win against the Reds. The classic image of Fisk waving

at the ball to stay fair along the first-base line was captured on film thanks to a rat inside the Monster. According to legend, a massive rodent startled an NBC cameraman stationed inside the leftfield scoreboard. Instead of following the flight of the ball, the frightened cameraman left his lens fixed on the first-base line, where Fisk did his impromptu dance. The Wall made its presence known before a national television audience again in 1978, when the New York Yankees traveled to Boston for a one-game playoff to decide the American League East title. With the Red Sox leading 2–0 in the seventh inning, light-hitting Yankees shortstop Bucky Dent lofted a fly ball to leftfield that would have been a routine fly out in any other big-league park but settled into the net atop the Wall for a three-run homer. The dinger propelled the Yankees to victory.

Today fans linger on Lansdowne Street before the Fenway gates open, waiting for batting-practice homers to fly over the Monster Seats and into the street, while they eat grilled sausages provided by vendors who set up along the sidewalks. Once the ballpark gates open, a steady stream of first-time and fiftieth-time visitors alike make their way out to Section 33 of the leftfield grandstand to pose for pictures in front of the Wall, touch the Wall, or simply watch batting-practice balls clang against its green facade. And once the game begins, some 294 lucky fans watch the game from a vantage point unlike any other in baseball, perched high above field level.

Babe Ruth's grave

= 8 =

BABE RUTH'S GRAVE

Gate of Heaven Cemetery | 10 West Stevens Avenue | Hawthorne, New York

Twenty-five miles north of New York City, the greatest baseball player ever to don Yankees pinstripes—or any uniform, for that matter—lies buried. In addition to serving as the final resting place of Babe Ruth, Gate of Heaven Cemetery also provides a peaceful sanctuary of repose for longtime on-again/off-again Yankees man-ager Billy Martin and former major-league umpire John McSherry.

Of the three baseball headstones in the sprawling graveyard, Ruth's (Section 25, Plot 1115, Grave 3) is the most impressive. His white monument depicts a life-size image of Jesus resting a guiding hand on the shoul-der of a young boy. The epitaph to the left reads, MAY THE DIVINE SPIRIT THAT ANIMATED BABE RUTH TO WIN THE CRUCIAL GAME OF LIFE INSPIRE THE YOUTH OF AMERICA. The letters on the right read, GEORGE HERMAN RUTH 1895–1948 AND CLAIRE RUTH 1900–1976.

The many baseball pilgrims who visit the Bambino's grave leave behind a multitude of mementos the slugger would surely appreciate. On any given day, visitors are apt to find Ruth's monument decorated with empty, half-empty, and full beer bottles, half-eaten hot dogs, baseballs, baseball bats, baseball cards, Yankees hats, Yankees pennants, and other pieces of pinstriped memorabilia.

Ruth died at the age of fifty-three, after a two-year bout with throat cancer. He made his final appearance at Yankee Stadium on June 13, 1948, putting on a Yankees uniform one last time to appear on the field as part of a pregame ceremony commemorating the twenty-fifth anniversary of the stadium's opening. Ruth was admitted to New York's

Memorial Sloan-Kettering Hospital shortly thereafter and passed away on August 16. His body lay in state at Yankee Stadium for two days before being transferred to Manhattan's Saint Patrick's Cathedral for funeral services.

Martin's headstone (Section 25, Plot 21, Grave 3) is less than 200 feet from Ruth's. Its gray granite offers a large engraved cross in the center, a depiction of Saint Jude on the left, and a quote from the deceased skipper on the right, reading, I MAY NOT HAVE BEEN THE GREATEST YANKEE TO PUT ON THE UNIFORM BUT I WAS THE PROUDEST. The number 1—Martin's old uniform number—is chiseled into the right and left sides of the stone.

McSherry's stone (Section 44, Plot 480, Grave 3) features the National League logo of an eagle spreading its wings with a baseball superimposed in the foreground. McSherry died of a heart attack that he suffered in the top of the first inning of the Reds season opener against the Expos on April 1, 1996.

★ ★ ★

= 9 =

JOHNNY ROSENBLATT STADIUM

1202 Bert Murphy Avenue | Omaha, Nebraska

Ranking right up there with the Little League World Series and National Baseball Congress, the College World Series is one of the most exciting amateur baseball events. Since 1950, when the University of Texas defeated Washington State 3–0 in the championship game, the College World Series has been held at Johnny Rosenblatt Stadium. Previously, the first three series had taken place elsewhere—in

Johnny Rosenblatt Stadium, home of the College World Series

Kalamazoo, Michigan, in 1947 and 1948 and in Wichita, Kansas, in 1949.

The NCAA Division I Baseball tournament begins with a field of sixty-four teams that play opening-round games at sites across the country. Then the eight Super-Regional winners advance to Omaha for the World Series, which takes place over ten days in the latter half of June. The finale is a best-of-three-games series that attracts standing-room-only crowds of 28,000 fans or more and a national television audience on ESPN. Over the ten days, the World Series attracts more than 260,000 fans, including many who camp out in RVs in a parking lot beside Rosenblatt Stadium. The fans are baseball-happy collegians, who bring an enthusiasm to the diamond that is more commonly observed at college basketball courts; scouts and player agents; school alumni; and seam-heads with no direct connections to the schools who simply want to watch some great baseball and see the next wave of big-league stars before they report for their Rookie League assignments.

The story of how the College World Series arrived in Omaha is the story of Johnny Rosenblatt, a local semipro player who entered politics after his playing days and as the mayor of Omaha championed the cause of building the stadium that now bears his name. The ballpark was originally called "Municipal Stadium" until it was renamed in honor of Mr. Rosenblatt in 1964. It opened as the home of the Western League Omaha Cardinals in 1949 and attracted the College World Series a year later. While Omaha has remained a minor-league outpost through the decades, it is better known as the site of the college championship and rightfully so. This is where most fans first heard about future big-league stars like Sal Bando (1965), Barry Bonds (1983 and 1984), Roger

Clemens (1983), Nomar Garciaparra (1994), Todd Helton (1995), Bob Horner (1977), Tim Hudson (1997), Huston Street (2002, 2003, and 2004), Mike Mussina (1988 and 1990), Dave Winfield (1973), and scores of others college stars who went on to enjoy successful big-league careers.

Rosenblatt Stadium has been frequently renovated and expanded through the decades to bring it to its current seating capacity of 24,000. The exterior features red brick at ground level and bright red and blue beams that support the blue press box above. A statue entitled *The Road to Omaha* stands outside the main entrance, greeting fans with a victorious quartet of players celebrating a title. Inside, the seating bowl offers bright blue, gold, and red seats, while bleachers run across the outfield. A historic display on the concourse celebrates Nebraska baseball history, offering the chance to learn about

the five Nebraskans—Grover Cleveland Alexander, Richie Ashburn, Wade Boggs, Sam Crawford, and Bob Gibson—enshrined at the National Baseball Hall of Fame, as well as about the playing and political careers of Johnny Rosenblatt, whose old mitt and bat are on display in a locker that also includes a team photo of Mr. Rosenblatt posing beside Babe Ruth and Lou Gehrig, who stopped by Omaha on a barnstorming tour.

The preferred time to visit "The 'Blatt" is during the World Series, of course, when the ballpark is packed with rabid fans, but it is also worth making the trip to Omaha during the Pacific Coast League season, when the top farm club in the Kansas City Royals chain takes the field before smaller crowds. The Omaha Royals, who have played at the ballpark since 1969, block off a healthy portion of the outfield and upper-level seats to create a more intimate environment for bush-league fans.

★ ★ ★

= 10 =

DODGERTOWN

4101 26th Street | Vero Beach, Florida

The most famous spring-training site of all, Dodgertown originated as the brainchild of baseball visionary Branch Rickey and developed through the years as the pet project of Dodgers owner Walter O'Malley. At a time when most

major-league teams were affiliated with upwards of twenty-five farm clubs, Rickey envisioned a "baseball college" where he could bring together all 600 players in the Dodgers system and teach them how to play "Dodgers baseball." Rickey also wanted to create a

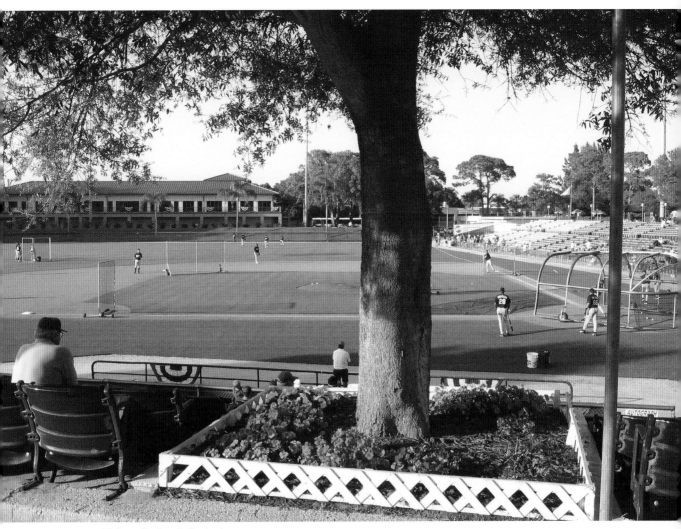

Holman Stadium in Dodgertown

safe environment for emerging African-American stars like Jackie Robinson, Don Newcombe, and Roy Campanella, who were unable to play and practice with their white teammates throughout much of the Jim Crow South.

In 1949 Rickey brokered a deal with Vero Beach mayor Bud Holman to rent a decommissioned naval air base in the small seaside town. Under Holman's direction, Vero Beach hastily chiseled ball fields into its abandoned airstrips and converted the old military barracks into dormitories for baseball players. Over the ensuing decades O'Malley turned this initially Spartan site into a posh resort, building a movie theater, tennis courts, basketball courts, two golf courses, and a swimming pool for his players. He also added such decorative flourishes to the 110-acre complex as baseball-shaped streetlights, orange groves, and a heart-shaped pond that he presented to his wife one year on Valentine's Day. Other aspects of the complex developed more organically, like the backfield off Don Drysdale Way, which grew to be known as Campy's Bullpen, owing to the work a wheelchair-bound Campanella did there with young Dodgers catchers in his later years. A blue and white sign marks the spot where Campy used to sit in the shade and bark out instructions to young backstops.

But the centerpiece of Dodgertown was, and still is, Holman Stadium—one of the most delightful little ballparks in professional baseball, simply because there is so little about it that resembles a professional ballpark. The field is surrounded not by the walls of a stadium but rather by a manmade hill that traces the perimeter of the diamond. Behind home plate and along the baselines, stadium chairs are laid right into the hillside. Many fans sit in the shade of live oak trees that grow between the seats, while the players sit on uncovered benches at field level along the baselines. The wooden press box is barely big enough to hold a dozen people but squeezes in a few more when Vero Beach icon Tommy Lasorda is holding court. There is no flashy scoreboard in the outfield, just a grassy incline where fans can set up lawn chairs and watch the game. For years there wasn't even an outfield wall, but today there is a low chain-link fence, like the kind at Little League parks across the country.

From the main ballpark, visitors in February and March can follow the player-named streets and footpaths to practice fields where minor leaguers take batting practice, shag flies, and scoop up grounders. Visitors can also tee it up at Dodger Pines Golf Club or Dodgertown Country Club, both of which are open to the public year-round.

As idyllic as this setting is, it may not last much longer, so it's a site that fans should plan to visit ASAP. In 2007 the Dodgers pulled their Florida State League team out of Vero Beach, relocating their Class-A prospects to the California League. Fortunately for fans a Tampa Bay Devil Rays farm club quickly moved in to Dodgertown to ensure summer baseball would continue to be played at quaint little Holman Stadium. As for spring baseball, though, the Dodgers are planning to pull their big leaguers out of Vero Beach in 2009, when they will relocate them to a spring camp in Glendale, Arizona. At that time hopefully some other team will swoop in to claim Vero Beach as its spring base—possibly the Baltimore Orioles, who have reportedly grown discontented in recent years with their Grapefruit League digs in Fort Lauderdale—but Dodgertown won't be quite the same without the Dodgers, who may draw 15,000 fans per game to their new park in the Cactus League but won't enjoy a spring experience nearly as magical as the one Branch Rickey and Walter O'Malley envisioned and then made into reality so many decades ago.

★ ★ ★

= 11 =
THE CAPE COD LEAGUE
Barnstable County | Massachusetts

A haven for top-tier college players and baseball's legion of weather-beaten scouts, the Cape Cod League also attracts a wide range of fans to its ten ballparks spread across the peninsula that is New England's vacation mecca each summer. The players who arrive on the Cape to take part in the invitation-only summer circuit play a 44-game schedule that begins in mid-June and concludes in mid-August. They live with local families who are eager to welcome them into their homes. They work part-time jobs during the day, often in support of the Cape's thriving beach-tourism industry. They swim in the Cape's warm waters and sun themselves on its sandy beaches. But first and foremost, they test their skills each night against the very best amateur competition in the land. For many players, this is the first time they are required to use wooden bats in competition instead of the lighter metal models still favored in the college game.

And it shows. Pitchers duels are much more common than slugfests. And when a hitter does demonstrate that he can get around on a 90-mile-per-hour fastball using a heavier bat than he's accustomed to, the

scouts take notice. With a good showing on the Cape, a college player whose skills might previously have been under-appreciated can monumentally improve his status in the estimation of the baseball establishment and markedly improve his ranking in the next year's amateur draft.

In recent decades, the Cape's cozy fields have served as important proving grounds in the development of up-and-comers like Jeff Bagwell, Albert Belle, Will Clark, Nomar Garciaparra, Todd Helton, Ben Sheets, Frank Thomas, Jason Varitek, and Barry Zito. But those are just a handful of the recent success stories. The Cape League actually dates back to 1885. It was a "town league" in those early days and wouldn't become a "college league" until 1963. As early as 1919, though, future Hall of Famer Pie Traynor was lacing up his spikes for the club in Falmouth. And in 1967 Thurman Munson batted .420 for Chatham, a record that would stand until 1976, when a youngster named Buck Showalter batted .434 for Barnstable.

Today, during a typical major-league season about 200 former Cape alumni appear in major-league uniforms, or to put it another

The Cotuit Kettlers in Lowell Park in the Cape Cod League

way, one in every seven big leaguers today spends a summer on the Cape. As you might expect, then, the games are highly competitive. Not only do they showcase some of the heaviest hitters and hardest throwers from the college ranks, but they do so against the backdrop of incredibly intimate little ballparks, most of which double as high school fields during the rest of the year. Fans turn out for games that begin between 5:00 and 7:00 P.M., stopping to make small donations at the gate before finding places to sit on the bleachers or stand along the fence. Even at ballparks like Cotuit's sixty-year-old Lowell Park, which has an official seating capacity of only 600, gatherings of 1,000 or even 1,500 people are common.

These spectators are parents and friends of the players, who come to the Cape for a few days' vacation and to check in on their budding baseball star; local families, who root especially hard for whichever player has been sleeping in their spare room and mowing their lawn for the past few weeks;

local retirees; schoolteachers; youth coaches; Little Leaguers; summer vacation-goers; and anyone else who appreciates the crack of the bat or the thud of a heavy fastball smacking into a catcher's mitt on a glorious summer night.

The league's ten fields are all located within 50 miles of each other. Ask ten locals which is their favorite park, and you're apt to get ten different answers, although most will agree that three of the league's finest fields are the pine-enveloped **Lowell Park** (Lowell Street); Orleans' **Eldredge Park** (Route 28), which provides seating on a grassy hillside; and Chatham's **Veteran's Park** (Route 28), which showcases stunning pink sunsets all summer long. Every one of the Cape Cod League parks is special, though, and worth visiting. For information about and directions to all of the ballparks on the Cape and for a current schedule, readers should visit www.capecodbaseball.org.

Sluggers, a Wrigleyville fixture

★ ★ ★

= 12 =

WRIGLEYVILLE

North Clark Street and West Addison Street | Chicago, Illinois

This book would not be complete without offering an appreciative nod to the unqualified "best ballpark neighborhood" in baseball. Whether fans find themselves passing through Chicago during the heat of summer, when bleacher seats to Wrigley Field afternoon games fetch several times face value on the black market, or during the chill of winter, when dreams of spring training are about all fans have to keep them going, a trip to the festive baseball wonderland surrounding Wrigley is in order. What this maze of North Side streets lacks in public-parking spots it more than makes up for in sports bars, saloons, restaurants, and clubs that embrace the ethos of baseball's most lovable losers.

The Cubby Bear Lounge and Murphy's Bleachers are the two most famous Wrigleyville watering holes. But there are dozens of other joints equally worthy of fan attention that all display their own collections of Cubs memorabilia and feature menus with items creatively named after the most famous players in neighborhood history.

The Cubby Bear has welcomed thirsty fans to the corner of Addison and Clark—kitty-corner to Wrigley Field's distinctive red marquee—since opening as the Cubs Pub in 1946. It has gradually expanded to the point where it now offers six bars and a gift shop in its 30,000 square feet of space. When the Cubs are playing a day game, the Cubby Bear begins selling cans of Old Style, bottles of Cubby Bear Root Beer, and authentic Chicago-style hot dogs at 10:00 A.M.

Named after the goat that was denied entrance to Wrigley Field during the 1945 World Series, **Murphy's Bleachers** hasn't been around quite as long as the Cubby Bear, but it attracts its own swelling game-day crowds at the corner of Waveland and Sheffield Avenue, just outside the gates to the bleachers. As game time approaches, Murphy's is a great place to watch the ballpark crowd gather or to score tickets from fellow patrons who decide they'd just as soon spend the next few hours right here,

where the beer flows more freely and the women are easier to talk to, than within the friendly confines of the ballpark across the street.

Fans looking to shake the dust off their lumber and to take a few swings, no matter the time of year or time of day, can visit this author's favorite Wrigleyville location, **Sluggers** (3540 North Clark Street). On the second floor above the festive barroom, this joint offers indoor batting cages within a large game room. According to legendary Cubs fan Ronnie Woo Woo, who can often be seen cutting a rug at Sluggers after home games, local son John Cusack used to take batting practice upstairs before he made it big in Hollywood. And through the years Sluggers has featured such celebrity bartenders as Andre Dawson, Rick Sutcliffe, Goose Gossage, and Minnie Minoso.

Just across the street from Sluggers on Clark Street, fans will find an impressive baseball mural inside the **Goose Island Brew Pub**. This baseball art depicts several of the game's all-time greats playing the game they loved. While marveling at the likenesses of Hank Aaron, Joe Jackson, Walter Johnson, and Babe Ruth, fans can sip pints of Ryne 23, a wheat-and-pale malt named after Cubs Hall of Famer Ryne Sandberg.

But these are just a handful of the more than three dozen watering holes that patrons will find in Wrigleyville, so thirsty fans should be sure to allot ample time to explore the rest of this incredible seam-head haven too.

Lawrence-Dumont Stadium sign at the National Baseball Congress

THE NATIONAL BASEBALL CONGRESS/HALL OF FAME

Lawrence-Dumont Stadium | 300 South Sycamore Street | Wichita, Kansas

The Little League World Series and College Baseball World Series may be baseball's most widely publicized amateur tournaments, but the National Baseball Congress (NBC) World Series is an event no less worthy of fan attention. It welcomes more than forty teams to Wichita each summer for a two-week extravaganza that features more than eighty games. And for three days in the middle of the tourney, one of baseball's unique spectacles—a fifty-six-hour marathon called "Baseball Around the Clock"—treats fans to seventeen consecutive games. This rivals and perhaps exceeds the surreal experience of watching a game in the middle of the night offered by the Alaska Summer League's "Midnight Sun Game," since in Wichita the games just keep coming, day after day after day. Some fans slump down in their stadium seats or sprawl out in the aisles of historic Lawrence-Dumont Stadium to catch a few Zs during the darker hours of the late games, while others sip coffee and pop M&Ms, refusing to miss a single pitch, and others grudgingly retire to the small village of tents on the grassy knoll outside the stadium.

The teams that compete in this unique baseball bonanza are composed of the nation's top college baseball stars in some cases and also of aging semipro players who simply want the experience of competing at the highest level they can. Other teams include former major leaguers looking to rekindle the glory of their youth.

The heroics of the more than 600 future or former major leaguers who have played in the NBC World Series are celebrated at the NBC Hall of Fame behind the outfield fence. The concourse behind the seats also offers a wealth of plaques and old photographs for fans to peruse. Both the hall and the concourse are open year-round, Monday through Friday from 10:00 A.M. to 5:00 P.M., and admission is always free. This is a great place to learn about the exploits of NBC heroes like Barry Bonds, Joe Carter, Roger Clemens, Ron Guidry, Tony Gwynn, Whitey Herzog, Ralph Houk, Billy Martin, Mark McGwire, John Olerud, Tom Seaver, Ozzie Smith, Don Sutton, Dave Winfield, and many others.

Satchel Paige was the star of the very first NBC World Series, which was played in 1935. The NBC was formed by local sporting-goods salesman Raymond "Hap" Dumont, who dreamed of creating a national tournament that would bring the country's best semipro and barnstorming teams to Wichita. Dumont had previously run a state-wide event in Wichita at a ballpark on the banks of the Arkansas River, and after that park burned down, he convinced the city to build him a new park using WPA funding. The park was named after Robert Lawrence, a prominent local citizen who had died the year before. To headline the first NBC World Series, Dumont lured Paige to town with the promise of a $1,000 payday. And Paige didn't disappoint. The great hurler won four games, striking out sixty batters along the way, and led his team from Bismarck, North Dakota, to the title.

Fans of today's World Series file into the same ballpark where Paige once dazzled their grandparents and great-grandparents. The delightfully old-timey ballpark, which was re-named Lawrence-Dumont Stadium in 1972, is notable for its many pillars that rise up from the grandstands to support the press box. The one downer at this otherwise charming facility is its artificial turf on the infield. But even this sacrilege is forgivable, considering the wear and tear the field faces each year during the seemingly unending tournament.

The World Series begins in the last week of July and ends in the second week of August. Despite daytime temperatures that soar over 100 degrees, attendance averages more than 5,000 fans per day over the two weeks. A ticket for the entire tournament costs between $60.00 and $115.00, depending on the seating level, while single-day tickets cost $5.00 for a three-game morning session or $5.00 to $10.00 for a three-game evening session. Fans who enter the Baseball Around the Clock contest must check in with ballpark staff at least once per game at a random time that is announced over the PA system, then at the end, the bleary-eyed few who succeed in staying awake for all seventeen games win a free tee shirt, a free pass to the rest of the tournament, and gifts from the tournament's local sponsors.

★ ★ ★

= 14 =

DOUBLEDAY FIELD

Elm Street and Main Street | Cooperstown, New York

From April through October no baseball diamond in America sees as much or as varied use as Cooperstown's Doubleday Field. The ballpark, which is owned and operated by the Village of Cooperstown, lies on the very site where baseball mythology says the very first baseball game was played in 1839. At a charge of

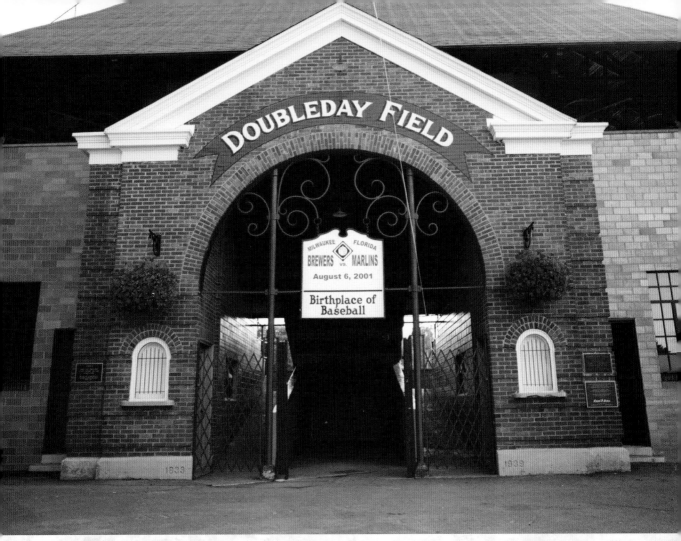

Doubleday Field

$300 per game, the field hosts three contests per day, seven days a week, during baseball season, offering youth, high school, college, minor-league, major-league, and senior-league players the chance to flash their leather and swing their hardwood on the plot that in 1907 was declared the birthplace of baseball by the Mills Commission.

The Mills Commission was formed in 1905 by sports-equipment pioneer Albert Spalding, who sought to determine the inventor of America's rapidly growing National Pastime. After more than two years of not-so-exhaustive research, the commission returned the verdict that Spalding and others eager to promote baseball as the National Game had hoped for. The report said baseball was a uniquely American phenomenon, a game derivative of none other that had emanated from the nation's pastoral countryside. The commission based its finding on the testimony of an elderly man named

Abner Graves, who recalled playing baseball when he was five years old in Cooperstown. Graves credited a young army officer named Abner Doubleday with introducing him and his friends to the game they played during the summer of 1839 at Elihu Phinney's cow pasture.

And so sleepy little Cooperstown—a town so quaint and cozy and quintessentially American that it practically bled red, white, and blue—was suddenly thrust into the national spotlight as the birthplace of baseball. Never mind that Doubleday, a Civil War hero who had left behind a lifetime's worth of letters and papers when he died in 1893, had never once claimed to have played a role in the invention of the game. Never mind that his obituary in the *New York Times* made no mention of any link between him and baseball. Never mind that he spent the entire summer of 1839 at West Point, not Cooperstown. Never mind that shortly after convincing the Mills Commission that Cooperstown was the birthplace of baseball Abner Graves murdered his wife and was sent to an insane asylum.

Over the next half century, these and other concerns would eventually cast doubt upon the Mills Commission's findings, but by the time Congress would declare Hoboken, New Jersey, the true birthplace of baseball in 1953, Cooperstown had already cemented its place as a baseball landmark nonparallel. Even if the likelihood that Cooperstown was the birthplace of baseball seemed remote, the idyllic town had

played the part so well that those associated with the game were happy to continue playing along with the myth.

The story of how Cooperstown embraced baseball, and of how baseball embraced it back, goes something like this. After the Mills Commission's finding, National League president John Tener made the pilgrimage to the village in 1916 to visit the Phinney pasture. Shortly thereafter, the Cooperstown Playground Committee entered into a lease agreement with the Phinney family and converted a parcel of their farmland into an actual baseball field. The first game at "Doubleday Field" was played between amateur teams representing Cooperstown and nearby Milford on September 6, 1920. Three years later, the Village of Cooperstown purchased the field from the Phinneys and in 1924 a wooden grandstand was built. The 1930s saw the gradual expansion of the playing field and the erection of a cement grandstand, thanks to a pair of Works Progress Administration initiatives, while just a block away the National Baseball Hall of Fame was constructed. Both the renovated field and the Hall of Fame opened in 1939 to commemorate the one-hundredth anniversary of baseball's invention. On the date of the Hall's grand opening, June 12, 1939, locals were treated to a six-inning exhibition at Doubleday Field between teams of American League and National League All-Stars. The next summer Cooperstown hosted its first "Hall of Fame Game," when the Boston Red Sox and Chicago Cubs traveled to upstate New York to play.

Today, the annual tradition of playing a Hall of Fame Game continues, as two big-league teams travel to Cooperstown each May or June to play each other. Usually the regulars take one turn at the plate and then give way to minor-league call-ups, who fill out the rosters. Whether fans are fortunate enough to be in Cooperstown for this special event when the pros come to town or whether they stop by Doubleday Field to watch an amateur game, they are sure to find their time spent at the park enjoyable. Though it may not be the first place where baseball was played, it is still a special old field steeped in charm. The arched, redbrick entrance appears much as it did in 1939, the pastoral outfield view consists of cozy little homes and lush green trees, and the small town atmosphere is nothing short of delightful. Doubleday Field is also the site of one minor-league game per year, a contest between the Oneonta Tigers and one of their New York–Penn League rivals.

★ ★ ★

= 15 =

DURHAM ATHLETIC PARK

500 West Corporation Street | Durham, North Carolina

Not to be confused with Durham Bulls Athletic Park—the stadium that replaced it as the home of the local minor-league team in 1995—Durham Athletic Park is one of the most recognizable ballparks in America, thanks to the starring role it played in the 1988 film *Bull Durham*. The ballpark that provided the backdrop for the bush-league antics of washed-up slugger Crash Davis, rising star Nuke LaLoosh, and baseball groupie Annie Savoy still looks the same as it did when the movie was filmed in 1987. And it still sees use as an amateur field.

The trademark feature is the park's cylindrical orange ticket office, which is topped by a cone-shaped roof. The structure makes the ballpark look like an oddly colored castle. Inside, the pale blue roof covers the infield grandstand, making for a cozy atmosphere. Don't bother looking for the snorting blue bull that blew smoke out its nose in the movie, though; it now resides a mile up the road on the interior concourse of Durham's new park.

Durham Athletic Park originally opened in 1926 as El Toro Park. It was renamed Durham Athletic Park in 1933, then sat dormant in 1934 and 1935, when the Great Depression suspended operations of the local team. After the ballpark burned to the ground midway through the 1939 season, temporary seating was installed for the

remainder of the year; then Durham completely rebuilt the park over the following winter. At that time the steel-and-concrete structure that exists today was erected.

As for the team and players that called "the DAP" home for decades, the real Crash Davis played for the Durham Bulls in the 1940s and 1950s, when the team was a member of the Carolina League. The team was named then, as it is now, after a locally made brand of cigarettes. During the late 1960s the Bulls merged with a team from nearby Raleigh to form the Raleigh-Durham Mets, a team that played half its home games at Durham Athletic Park and half at Raleigh's Devereaux Meadow. The crowds were small at both locations, though, and in 1971 the team folded. Durham Athletic Park sat without a tenant until 1980, when the Durham Bulls rejoined the Carolina League. The old park hosted the Bulls through the 1994 season, then yielded to the strains of age and time and bid the professional game adieu. The Bulls were still a Single-A team when they moved into their new yard, and then in 1998 they joined the Triple-A International League.

As for *Bull Durham*, widely considered one of the best sports movies of all time, its effect on American film and sport cannot be overstated. After the movie was released and received rave reviews, Hollywood re-kindled its love affair with sports movies, a trend that continues to this day. Interest in minor-league baseball also skyrocketed in the wake of the movie's success, as a new generation of fans flocked to bush-league ballparks near and far. Ironically, the minor-league attendance boom of the early 1990s that was fueled by the movie led to the eventual replacement of many older minor-league stadiums, Durham Athletic Park included. But unlike the old yards in many cities, Durham's classic ballpark still stands as a monument to a simpler era.

Although the ballpark gates are supposed to be locked when the park is not in use, visitors will find them frequently open during daylight hours. Even if the gates are closed, though, the inside of the park is visible from the outfield and from the gates on the third-base side. Each fall Durham Athletic Park hosts two of Durham's most popular annual events, the Bull Durham Blues Festival and the World Beer Festival, and beginning in the spring of 2008, it will serve as the home park of the North Carolina Central University baseball team, which is scheduled to begin playing a Division I schedule at that time. There is also a proposal currently under consideration in Durham to transform part of the old park into a minor-league baseball museum. Here's hoping this comes to pass.

Durham Athletic Park

= 16 =

MICKEY MANTLE'S RESTAURANT AND SPORTS BAR

42 Central Park South | New York, New York

Once you get past the irony of naming a sports bar after Mickey Mantle, who died young, of course, as the result of liver cancer brought on by years of alcohol abuse, a trip to the ultratrendy Mickey Mantle's is sure to be enjoyable both for Yankees fans and Yankees detractors alike. "The Mick" was an American icon, after all, who transcended team and league loyalties, embodying perhaps better than any other player the romanticized image of the game and of its players that existed before the wool would be gradually removed from a nation's collective eyes as media coverage of the game became more sophisticated and beat writers more objective.

As it turned out, our boys of summer were just as fallible and human as the rest of us, and in time we would learn that Mantle was no exception. But for any fan who came of baseball age during the 1950s or 1960s, the idea of the Mick—the quintessential country kid who sought nothing more from life than to have as good a time as possible while playing the game he loved—still evokes a certain degree of magic and innocence, even if the adult mind knows better.

In the heart of Manhattan, Mickey Mantle's

Restaurant and Sports Bar does its best to rekindle the romanticism once associated with the Grand Old Game. To say the walls are lavishly decorated with memorabilia from baseball's Golden Era would be shortchanging Mantle's some, since the owners, upon running out of wall space, erected display carrels jutting off the walls to create a boutique where more artifacts can be found. The on-site memorabilia counter, manned by New York–based Gotta Have It, offers an inventory of collector items for sale.

Among the most interesting pieces is a photograph of Mantle shaking hands with another American hero, John F. Kennedy. Another favorite is the original plaque that hung at Yankee Stadium's Monument Park to honor Mantle from 1969 until 1996, when a full-size monument replaced it in the Bronx. There are also old uniforms from Mantle, Joe DiMaggio, Ted Williams, Jackie Robinson, and other players; old stadium chairs from the original Yankee Stadium; and vintage magazine covers from *Time*, *Life*, *Men*, and *Sports Illustrated*. The life-size cutout of Babe Ruth, autographed by more than 150 big leaguers, is another unique piece. In 2007 the restaurant added

Mickey Mantle's Restaurant

perhaps its most fascinating item of all, a circa 1961 replica of the original Yankee Stadium, which has been valued at $150,000. The model is 1½ feet high and covers 49 square feet. It features working light towers, a replica of the old scoreboard, and 64,000 molded pewter seats in their original lime green color.

The Mick was fifty-six years old when Mickey Mantle's Restaurant and Sports Bar opened in 1988. He visited regularly, as did fellow celebrities from the sporting world and baseball fans from around the country. Mantle finally entered an alcohol rehabilitation center in 1994 and received a liver transplant in June of 1995. But the cancer had already spread to the rest of his body, and he passed away on August 13, 1995.

More than a decade later, the restaurant that bears his name continues to thrive as a baseball landmark and Manhattan hot spot. Regular dinner guests include such luminaries as Yankees general manager Brian Cashman; retired players like Joe Pepitone and Don Mattingly; media personalities like Bob Costas, Jerry Springer, and Chris Matthews; and football legends like Dan Marino, Mike Ditka, and Jimmy Johnson. The menu features country specialties like hickory-smoked ribs, chicken-fried steak, and blackened cowboy steak, as well as a wide range of creative pasta dishes. And when the time comes for the first pitch, the twenty-eight high-definition TVs at Mantle's ensure that no matter where patrons are sitting they have a good view of the action.

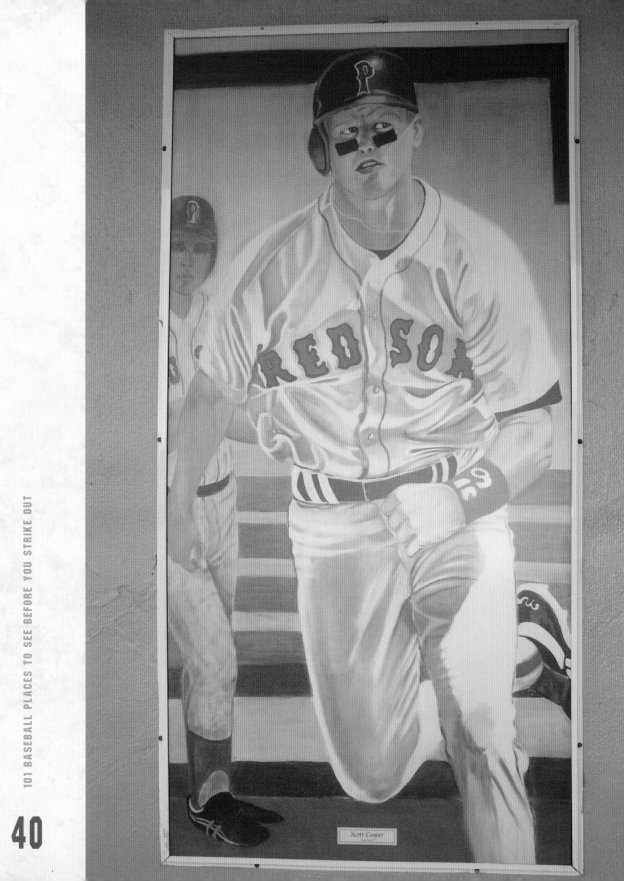

★ ★ ★

= 17 =

McCOY STADIUM

1 Ben Mondor Way | Pawtucket, Rhode Island

There are a whole bunch of reasons why fans should make a special effort to visit the home of the Pawtucket Red Sox. To begin with, McCoy Stadium is one of the few remaining minor-league parks built by FDR's Works Progress Administration, and its charming covered grandstand, which dates back to 1942, transports visitors back to an earlier era in the game's history. More than that, McCoy—which has been home to the top team in the Red Sox system since 1973—possesses a rich history, the details of which are well represented by colorful displays on the concourses that turn the ballpark into a veritable baseball museum. These exhibits celebrate the International League Triple Crown that Jim Rice won as a member of the "PawSox" in 1974, the batting title Wade Boggs claimed in 1981, the perfect games Bronson Arroyo and Tomo Ohka pitched in the early 2000s, the classic pitcher's duel between Yankees prospect Dave Righetti and New England native Mark Fidrych in 1982, and so on.

Claiming the most space of all on the concourse, though, a seemingly endless line score tells the story of the longest game in professional baseball history, a thirty-three-inning affair that took place at McCoy in 1981. On a chilly night before Easter, the PawSox and Rochester Red Wings began play at eight o'clock. The Red Wings carried a 1–0 lead into the bottom of the ninth, but then the PawSox scored a run on a wild pitch to send the game into extra innings. Twelve innings later, and well after midnight, the Red Wings took a 2–1 lead in the top of the twenty-first. But in the bottom of the inning, the PawSox knotted the game on a double by Boggs. And the innings kept coming, and going, while the fans kept shivering, nodding off, and then eventually departing. The game was finally suspended at 4:07 A.M. after thirty-two innings. A few months later, in June, the teams resumed the game, and it took just one frame to determine a winner. Pawtucket's Dave Koza knocked a single into leftfield in the bottom of the thirty-third to score Marty Barrett and give the home team a 3–2 win. Boggs went 4 for 12 in the game, while Rochester's Cal Ripken Jr. went 2 for 13. Bob Ojeda pitched one inning and got credit for the win. In all, twenty-five future big leaguers played in the marathon, which included 219 at bats, 882 pitches, and 60 strikeouts and took eight hours and twenty-five minutes to complete.

Scott Cooper mural at McCoy Stadium

As if the chance to learn more about this historic game weren't enough reason to visit McCoy, the old park also offers one of the most unusual decorative flourishes in all of the minor leagues. Adorning the concourses and entranceways, fans find dozens of 3-by-6-foot portraits of former PawSox who went on to play in the big leagues, ranging from Don Aase to Bob Zupcic. The PawSox began the tradition of honoring their former players this way back in the early 1980s, when a team employee painted the giant likenesses of notable players like Boggs, Rice, and Roger Clemens right onto the cement walls of the spiraling main entrance ramp. When a renovation in the early 1990s necessitated that these paintings be sandblasted away, the PawSox commissioned a local artist to re-create nearly fifty of them on moveable 4-by-8-foot panels.

In the early 2000s, though, another renovation that added handicap railings to the entrance ramps made these paintings too large to return to their original locations. So the PawSox donated most of them to the Pawtucket Armory Association, which auctioned them off to fans to raise money for an arts-education center. At that time the PawSox decided to take a new approach. Rather than displaying artists' renderings of notable former players, the team started using digital technology to blow up old player photos (and photos of some of the old portraits) into what appear now as oversized baseball cards. These are mounted in doorframes and hung throughout the stadium. The team has not only restored all of the old favorites—like Oil Can Boyd, Butch Hobson, Sam Horn, and Steve Lyons—to their original places on the stadium walls but has added the images of more recent Pawtucket stars as well. In 2007, for example, Arroyo, Jonathan Papelbon, Freddy Sanchez, and Kevin Youkilis all joined this sprawling wall of fame. No other minor-league team does a better job than the PawSox of honoring its legendary players, and for that reason alone McCoy Stadium is a site worth visiting.

=18=

THE BABE RUTH BIRTHPLACE AND MUSEUM

216 Emory Street | Baltimore, Maryland

George Herman Ruth entered the world on February 6, 1895, opening his eyes to the inside of a Baltimore row house that belonged to his maternal grandfather, Pius Schamberger. The Babe spent his early years learning to cuss, gamble, and smoke at his father's saloon, which stood where the right-centerfield bleachers

Babe Ruth Birthplace and Museum

are located today at Oriole Park at Camden Yards. By age seven, young George had grown so incorrigible that he was sent to St. Mary's Industrial School for Boys, a reform school on the outskirts of the city. It was there that Ruth discovered the game of baseball and there in 1914 that Jack Dunn, owner of the International League's Baltimore Orioles, discovered Ruth. Because Ruth was only nineteen when Dunn offered him a professional contract, the Orioles owner had

to accept legal guardianship of the pitcher. When Ruth reported to his first spring training a few months later, the other players teased him, calling him "Dunn's baby." The nickname eventually became "The Babe," and it stuck.

Putting aside any paternal feelings he may have felt toward Ruth, Dunn sold his contract to the Red Sox before the 1914 season was through. And so, just five months after leaving reform school, the Bambino started three big-league games for Boston and won two of them. The next year, he went 18-8 and helped the Red Sox to the first of three World Series titles he would win with them.

Today, Ruth's early days in Baltimore and his prolific major-league career as a pitcher and hitter are celebrated at the Babe Ruth Birthplace and Museum, which, as its name suggests, resides inside the very brick row house where Ruth was born. The museum opened in 1974 with help from Ruth's widow, Claire, and his two daughters, Dorothy and Julia. Over the years it grew to become not just a shrine to Ruth but a Baltimore Orioles and Baltimore Colts hall of fame, too. With the 2005 opening of Sports Legends at Camden Yards, however, the museum has reverted back to its original purpose: honoring Ruth. The Orioles and Colts exhibits have been relocated to the new museum closer to the ballpark and a $750,000 renovation that was completed in the spring of 2007 has made more space for Ruth artifacts than ever before.

Some of the most popular exhibits are the ones that tell the stories of Ruth's birth, his childhood in Baltimore, his rookie season, his glory days with the Yankees, his funeral, and his curse—the Curse of the Bambino—that supposedly haunted the Red Sox for years. The "500 Home Run Club" honors Ruth and the ever-expanding list of other major leaguers who have hit as many as 500 long balls in their careers. Two unique artifacts are a set of 1914 Baltimore Orioles baseball cards that feature Ruth when he was a minor leaguer and a bat given to Ruth by Shoeless Joe Jackson, which both sluggers used in competition.

The museum is easy to find by foot for those approaching from Oriole Park, thanks to a trail of sixty oversized baseballs painted on the sidewalks between the two landmarks. The museum is open daily, year-round, from 10:00 A.M. to 5:00 P.M. When the Orioles have a home game, it stays open until 7:30. The cost of admission is $6.00 for adults and $4.00 for children aged three through twelve.

★ ★ ★

THE HANK AARON HOME RUN WALL

Turner Field Parking Lot | Hank Aaron Drive | Atlanta, Georgia

During most of its thirty-year existence as the home of the Braves, Atlanta–Fulton County Stadium offered little to distinguish itself from the other multipurpose stadiums of its era. For a time, shortly after its opening in 1966, the stadium featured a wigwam beyond its outfield fence that provided a home to resident mascot Chief Noc-A-Homa. And the stadium was always known as a hitter's paradise, owing to its altitude of more than a thousand feet above sea level. But for the most part, it was a forgettable facility—like so many others of the cookie-cutter ilk—that would have certainly faded into the furthest reaches of fan consciousness by now if not for one glorious moment that forever redefined it as a baseball landmark of monumental importance.

On a damp night in April of 1974, with one swing of the bat, Hank Aaron consecrated Atlanta–Fulton County Stadium as hallowed ground when he staked his claim to the most prestigious record in all of American professional sports. In usurping Babe Ruth as baseball's all-time home-run king, Aaron ensured that the stadium would never be forgotten. What fan can't immediately close his eyes and conjure the image of Aaron's magical 715th homer? His swing, compact and powerful. The ball, sailing over the head of Dodgers leftfielder Bill Buckner, then landing in the Braves' bullpen. The trot around the bases, faster than usual, as the aged slugger tried to outrun a pair of over-zealous well-wishers who'd made their way onto the field. The celebration to follow at home plate. . . .

For many baseball fans this moment is still frozen in time. It was a "baseball moment," yes, but it was one that reached beyond the normal boundaries of sport to help hasten the cultural evolution of a nation. Not only had Aaron broken a record that for decades had been thought to be unbreakable, but he had done so amidst an incredibly trying social atmosphere that had discouraged his progress at every step simply because he was a black man living in white America. With number 715 Aaron silenced the bigots who had made threats on his life in the hope of ensuring that baseball's most glamorous record remained a white man's achievement. Aaron's homer sent the message that, although the bigots might continue to assail the notion that all Americans deserved equal opportunities to succeed, ultimately their rancor would prove futile in halting the wheels of progress.

Although Atlanta–Fulton County Stadium was demolished in the wake of Turner Field's opening next door in 1997, its memory—and the memory of what Aaron accomplished on its field—lives on. A stretch of the left-centerfield fence over which Aaron's record-breaking home run sailed stands today as a monument to this triumphant moment in history. The fence is located within the parking lot across the street from Turner Field. In addition to housing the fence, the lot also outlines Atlanta–Fulton County Stadium's warning track and infield dirt in red brick and offers large metal plates where the bases once laid.

Aaron ended the 1973 season with 713 homers, leaving him just one long ball shy of moving into a tie with Ruth. On Opening Day of the next season, he drew even with the Bambino when his very first swing of the year resulted in a three-run homer in Cincinnati. Four days later, on April 8, 1974, Aaron stepped into the batter's box against the Dodgers' Al Downing in the second inning of the Braves' first home game and drew a four-pitch walk. His next at bat came in the fourth inning with a runner on first and no outs. Aaron watched the first pitch bounce in the dirt for ball one, which caused the crowd of 53,775 expectant fans to groan audibly. With his next pitch Downing challenged Aaron with a high fastball, and Aaron swung. And the rest, as they say, is history.

Today a visit to the site where Aaron hit his record-breaking dinger is sure to bring goose bumps to the skin of any fan who appreciates the game's history. Even when the asphalt and brick field has begun to fill with cars, fans can step into the right-handed batter's box, take aim at the plaque atop the fence some 385 feet away that reads simply "715," and take a phantom swing. Then they can retrace Aaron's race around the brick base paths while imagining how the aging slugger must have felt in the seconds immediately after he rewrote baseball's record books.

★ ★ ★

= 20 =

ROSE PARK WIFFLE BALL COMPLEX

16th Street and South West Street | Mishawaka, Indiana

It's Game Seven of the World Series . . . the bottom of the ninth inning . . . down by three runs . . . the bases loaded . . . two outs . . . a three-two count . . . the pitcher winds . . . the batter swings. . . .

While most readers—except those with names like David Ortiz, Bill Mazeroski, and Bobby Thomson—will only dream of experiencing the adrenaline rush of standing in a batter's box at a packed stadium under such dramatic circumstances, any baseball fan worth his salt has projected himself into this role at least fifty times, probably as the shadows cast by his house or garage rendered his backyard too dark to see, obscuring the fluttering plastic ball that had provided him and his friends with an evening of enjoyable competition.

Since its invention in Shelton, Connecticut, in 1953, the Wiffle Ball has made dreamers of us all. The game was the perfect antidote for a rapidly urbanizing America that no longer outfitted every neighborhood with 5 acres of open space suitable for hardball or with eighteen like-minded individuals

Mehlo Ermeti of Redondo Beach, California, at the Wiffle-Ballin' for Kids tourney

to facilitate a game even if such a field existed. With its plastic ball perforated on one side and its 30-inch-long yellow plastic bat, Wiffle Ball introduced fans to a baseball-like game that could be played in a fraction of the space and time needed for a real game. Furthermore, it reduced the number of players required for a game to only two. And it eliminated the need for cumbersome and expensive equipment like bats, extra balls, gloves, bases, and catcher's gear.

Through the years we have made Wiffle Ball a regular part of our daily lives, bringing it along on camping expeditions, trips to the beach, company picnics, and other special occasions. While Wiffle Ball's casual players number in the millions, it has also engendered a cult following of serious players, who view it not so much as a game but as a sport. The 1980s, 1990s, and early 2000s witnessed the steady growth of regional and national tournaments devoted to

Wiffle Ball, to the point where today there are more than one hundred such tourneys held in the United States each year.

With a midsummer trip to the suburbs of South Bend, Indiana, the traveling fan can pay homage to this unique variation of the National Pastime and to the legion of athletes who choose to play it for keeps . . . as well as for fun. The oldest and largest Wiffle Ball tournament in the country also just happens to utilize the largest Wiffle Ball complex in the world. The pride of Mishawaka, Indiana, twenty-two-field Rose Park welcomes more than fifty teams to its 18-acre site over the last weekend of July each year to determine the best five-man Wiffle Ball squad in the world. The tournament attracts entrants from across the Midwest, as well as ones from such faraway states as California, Georgia, Maryland, and Montana. The entry fee is $150.00 per team, with the proceeds benefiting a local treatment center for emotionally disturbed youngsters named the Children's Campus.

The tournament was born in the summer of 1980, when teenagers Larry Grau and Jim Bottorff, childhood friends both working summer jobs for the local parks department but at different ends of the city, hatched a plan so they could spend more time hanging out together during the workweek. They unified their two youth sports camps by creating a Wiffle Ball league for the kids they counseled; then they staged a big tournament at the end of the summer. For several years the two founders kept the

tournament going as a regular late-summer event. Even after they moved away from Mishawaka, they and several of their old friends, who had also scattered to points across the country, would reunite to play Wiffle Ball once a year in their hometown. As the tournament became a national event, other Mishawakans kept it going. In 2005 ownership of the tournament, which was known as the World Wiffle Ball Championship for its first twenty-five years, was transferred to the Children's Campus and renamed the Wiffle-Ballin' for Kids Tournament.

Each July twenty-two fields are configured within the boundaries of what are otherwise three regulation-size baseball diamonds at Rose Park. The Wiffle Ball fields offer 6-foot-high outfield fences 85 feet from home plate, bases 40 feet apart, and pitchers' rubbers 30 feet from the plate. During the tourney the players run the bases, unlike many backyard Wiffle Ballers, and observe rules that allow for "pegging," so long as the runner is not struck above the neck, and count a force-out at first base as soon as the ball arrives in the pitcher's hand, no matter where he is standing. Games are six innings, but a forty-five-minute time limit and fifteen-run mercy rule sometimes end them sooner. Watching twenty-two games unfold all at once on the first day of the tournament is truly a sight to behold. There may not be a crack of the bat to hear, and the players may not "flash the leather" in the traditional sense of the term, but there are plenty of home runs to see, plenty of diving catches,

101 BASEBALL PLACES TO SEE BEFORE YOU STRIKE OUT

plenty of baffling trick pitches, and plenty of late-inning heroics as players dig into the batter's boxes with their games and seasons on the line. It's every Wiffle Baller's fantasy, and it plays out over and over again on this one special weekend each year in Indiana. The first day of the tournament pits teams against one another in pool play—each entrant is guaranteed to play at least four games—then the top half of the field advances to play on the second day, which follows a single-elimination format. Finally, when the field has been whittled down to just two teams, the finalists square off before a lively crowd of a few thousand people.

★ ★ ★

= 21 =

THE JACKIE ROBINSON CENTER

1020 North Fair Oaks Avenue | Pasadena, California

Just a few blocks from where Jackie Robinson's boyhood home once stood, baseball fans find a fitting tribute to the man who broke baseball's color barrier and helped add momentum to the civil rights movement. The Jackie Robinson Center is not a museum—although it does display artwork and photographs that pay homage to its namesake—but rather it is a multipurpose community center with a mission to enhance the lives of the "culturally, economically, and socially diverse population in the Northwest area of Pasadena."

Certainly, this is a legacy that would make Jackie Robinson proud. The 18,000-square-foot center opened its doors for the first time in 1974. It offers health screenings, educational programs, legal counseling, addiction counseling, income-tax assistance and rec-reational programs for local citizens in need of these important services. It is also the driving force behind several annual events, including Pasadena's Black History Parade and Festival, which takes place in February.

For baseball fans wishing to reflect on the role that Jackie Robinson played in transforming a nation and its National Pastime, the center displays photographs and paintings of Robinson. Many of these pieces have been provided by the Baseball Reliquary, including the center's most unusual piece, a replica of Robinson's longtime home park, Brooklyn's Ebbets Field. Confectionary artist William Robert Steele began the piece in 2001 under commission from the Baseball Reliquary. It was originally supposed to be constructed entirely out of cake frosting, but when it became apparent to Steele that

Portrait of Jackie Robinson

frosting lacked the structural integrity to support a five-story stadium facade, two decks of seating, seven light towers, a rightfield scoreboard complete with a "Hit Sign, Win Suit" billboard, and the rest of the decorative flourishes that would be necessary to create a miniature version of Ebbets that replicated the original in every possible way, the artist decided to also utilize other materials like wood, plastic, and clay.

The resulting 50-by-39-inch-long, 15-inch-high model was unveiled during a special ceremony at the Jackie Robinson Center in May of 2002. Steele was on hand for the unveiling, of course, and happily signed a baseball to be inserted into the display case that now houses his model. Hard to believe though it may be, Steele, who learned his craft at the Baking School of Technology in Belfast, Northern Ireland, said that the baseball he signed that day was the first one he had ever held in his hands.

As for the center's paintings, a canvas entitled *Jackie Robinson Icon* stands out among the others, owing to its vivid depiction of Robinson as a sort of modern-day saint. Wearing his Dodger blue, Robinson is ensconced by a foreground of brightly colored flowers. A linked-chain halo—symbolic of the chains that once restrained the African-American people—frames Robinson's head in the background, its links broken apart directly above the "B" on his Brooklyn cap.

Jackie Robinson was born in Cairo, Georgia, in 1919, but before his first birthday his mother moved her five children across the country to live with relatives at 121 Pepper Street in Pasadena. The house has since been razed, but a historic plaque on the sidewalk marks its former location. Robinson excelled in athletics at Pasadena's Washington Junior High School and at John Muir High School, then enrolled at Pasadena Junior College, where he spent two years before moving on to UCLA in 1939. While in Los Angeles, Robinson's athletic prowess brought him national fame, as he starred on the Bruins' baseball, basketball, football, and track teams. He won twenty-four varsity letters in all, then left UCLA midway through his senior year to enlist in the army for World War II. After completing his service and toiling in the Negro Leagues and minor leagues, Robinson became the first African American to play major-league baseball in more than half a century when he trotted out to first base at Ebbets Field on April 15, 1947.

Today, the Jackie Robinson Center is open Monday through Thursday from 8:00 A.M. to 9:00 P.M. and Friday from 8:00 to 5:00. At a plaza across the street from City Hall, Pasadena also honors Robinson and his older brother Mack, a star athlete in his own right, who won a silver medal in the 200 meters at the 1936 Berlin Olympics. There, on **Garfield Avenue**, two gigantic bronze sculptures depict the brothers' faces looking out at the city that was their home.

MIDWAY STADIUM

1771 Energy Park Drive | St. Paul, Minnesota

The reemergence of baseball's unaffiliated minor leagues, or independent leagues, during the 1990s, was largely fueled by the mounting disgust fans felt for the major-league game in the wake of the 1994 work stoppage. As fans turned away from the greedy players, even greedier owners, and high ticket prices that were sure to get even higher once MLB finally hashed out a new work agreement, fans turned back to the simple charm of the bush leagues. Throughout the 1990s minor-league attendance steadily climbed, and soon new leagues and new teams began sprouting up across the country, many of which operated outside the bounds of organized baseball.

No team personified the quirky ethos and devil-may-care attitude of Indy Ball quite like the St. Paul Saints. That was true in 1993, when the Saints debuted as a member of the fledgling Northern League, and it is true today, when they are the top draw in the American Association. Since the very outset, the Saints have consistently sold out their 6,000-seat Midway Stadium by making a day at the ballpark a full family experience that is as much about fun peripheral activities as about the game itself.

While other teams, both in affiliated and unaffiliated ball, have striven to emulate Saints co-owner Mike Veeck's "fun is good" approach to marketing, St. Paul still sets the bar (and then raises it once or twice a season) when it comes to crazy publicity stunts and zany ballpark characters. During games at Midway, a potbellied pig delivers fresh baseballs to the home-plate umpire, a barber cuts hair in the stands behind home plate, and an eighty-year-old Benedictine nun named Sister Rosalind Gefre offers neck massages to any fan who looks tense. Then there's Bill Murray, the famous comedian and co-owner of the Saints, who sometimes turns out at the ballpark to coach third base, heckle the umpires, and mingle with fans.

Under the direction of Veeck—whose father Bill Veeck earned a place in the Hall of Fame, thanks to his own revolutionary approach to marketing the game—the Saints have never been afraid to push the promotional envelope. They've signed washed-up big leaguers like Minnie Minoso (1993, 2003), Darryl Strawberry (1996), and Jack Morris (1996) to contracts. They've poked fun at the baseball establishment with "Bud Selig and Donald Fehr Seat Cushion Night"

Trampoline team at Midway Stadium

(one face on either side). They hosted "Bud Selig Tie Night" after the commissioner declared the big-league All-Star Game a draw in 2002. They offered "Randy Moss Hood Ornament Night" after the former Minnesota Vikings receiver bumped a police officer with his car. They staged "Two Dead Fat Guys Night" to celebrate the lives of Babe Ruth and Elvis Presley. They put mimes on top of the dugouts to provide instant replays of the game action. They sent Ila Borders to the mound to become the first female to play in a regular-season professional men's game. They've tried anything and everything to keep fans on the edge of their seats, and the strategy has worked. The Saints have finished first or second in their league in attendance every year of their existence.

As for the stadium itself, Midway's concrete seating bowl was built in 1982, primarily to serve as a high school football venue. It sits in an industrial park, alongside a set of train tracks. Scenic, it is not. But it doesn't matter. The charm of watching a game in St. Paul has less to do with the physical limitations of the ballpark than it does with the limitless imaginations of the team employees and fans who turn out to have some fun. And at least Midway Stadium offers the chance to sit outside and watch baseball, unlike the eventually-to-be-replaced dome across the river in Minneapolis.

Midway Stadium also possesses a feature that makes it worthy of a visit year-round, even when the Saints aren't in season. Outside the park a beautiful mural celebrates the Twin Cities' proud baseball history, depicting former Twins like Bert Blyleven, Rod Carew, Kent Hrbek, Paul Molitor, Tony Oliva, Kirby Puckett, Frank Viola, and Dave Winfield, as well as Negro Leagues stars like Rube Foster and Bobby Marshall of the St. Paul Gophers, and several All-American Girls Professional Baseball League stars who played for the Minneapolis Millerettes.

★ ★ ★

= 23 =

LEAGUE PARK

6601 Lexington Avenue | Cleveland, Ohio

Road-trippers who were impressed to find a respectable portion of Forbes Field still standing in Pittsburgh will be happy to discover the remains of Cleveland's League Park, which leave an even greater impression on the modern landscape. In addition to the old diamond, which still sees use today as a recreational field at the League Park Community Center, fans venturing to this part of Cleveland also find the old brick ticket office and part of the brick facade that ran along the ballpark's rightfield line.

The first major-league game on this site took place on May 1, 1891, when Cy Young pitched the National League Cleveland Spiders past the Cincinnati Reds 12–3 before a crowd of nearly 10,000 people. Like all stadiums prior to the turn of the century, League Park was a wooden structure at that time, but it would eventually be rebuilt using concrete, steel, and lots of bricks prior to the start of the 1910 season. By then the Spiders had disbanded and the American League Indians were calling the ballpark home.

League Park served the Indians through 1946, while also providing a place for the Negro League Bears to play in 1939 and 1940 and for the Negro League Buckeyes from

League Park today

1943 through 1948. From 1934 through 1946, the Indians actually split their home schedule between League Park and its eventual successor, Municipal Stadium, playing weekday games at the old yard and the better-attended Sunday and holiday affairs at the cavernous new stadium destined to one day earn the moniker "The Mistake by the Lake."

Three years after the Tribe made the permanent move to the lakeside digs, League Park was demolished. Well, mostly demolished. Fortunately for today's baseball pilgrims, not all was lost. The two-story brick building at the corner of East 66th Street and Lexington Avenue that once housed the ticket window and Indians front office was left intact. Today, the building serves as a historic, if somewhat dilapidated, youth center, and the arched brick facade that looms over the sidewalk along East 66th affords imaginative fans the chance to take a step back in time.

Just outside the main entrance on Lexington, an Ohio historical marker reads:

League Park opened on May 1, 1891, with the legendary Cy Young pitching for the Cleveland Spiders in their win over the Cincinnati Redlegs. The park remained the home of professional baseball and football teams until 1946. In 1920 the Cleveland Indians' Elmer Smith hit the first grand slam home run, and Bill Wamby executed the only unassisted triple play, in World Series history. Babe Ruth hit his 500th home run over the park's short right field wall in 1929. With the park as home field, the Cleveland Buckeyes won the Negro World Series in 1945.

Even in an era when unusual outfield configurations were the norm, League Park was known for its eccentric field dimensions. At the time of its reconstruction in 1910, several landowners beyond rightfield refused to sell their property so the field could be expanded. As a result, the distance to the rightfield foul pole measured only 290 feet, while the distance to the leftfield pole was 385. To give left-handed batters more of a challenge, the Indians erected a 45-foot-high fence in right. The lower 20 feet consisted of cement, while the upper 25 took the form of a chain-link fence supported by steel poles. For decades, fans and outfielders alike held their breath whenever a high fly ball was lofted toward rightfield. The ball could hit the lower portion of the wall and take a hard straight bounce off the cement, or it could hit the screen high above and drop gently to the warning track, or it could hit one of the support poles and careen into center field, or all the way into leftfield, or maybe into rightfield foul territory.

League Park seated about 20,000 fans throughout much of its life and was never outfitted with lights. In addition to providing a setting for Ruth's 500th dinger, it was the place where Nap Lajoie collected hit No. 3,000 in 1914, where Tris Speaker collected his 3,000th in 1925, and where Joe DiMaggio's 56-game hitting streak came to an end in 1941.

★ ★ ★

=24=
LEGENDS OF THE GAME BASEBALL MUSEUM AND LEARNING CENTER

Rangers Ballpark | 1000 Ballpark Way | Arlington, Texas

Legends of the Game is one of the finest ballpark museums in the country, if not *the finest*, thanks to its size and breadth of offerings. Occupying three floors and 24,000 square feet of exhibit space behind the rightfield home-run porch at the Rangers' stadium-to-be-renamed-yet-again-later, Legends houses the largest collection of baseball memorabilia outside Cooperstown, including more than one hundred pieces on loan from the National Baseball Hall of Fame. And lest any fan be suspicious of a museum built around the mystique of a franchise that has ranged from hapless to mediocre since its arrival in Texas in 1972, rest assured, Legends of the Game is much more than just a Rangers museum. As its name suggests, it is, first and foremost, a baseball museum.

On the first level, visitors find old jerseys, bats, gloves, trophies, and other mementos that once belonged to Hank Aaron, Ty Cobb, Roberto Clemente, Brooks Robinson, Babe Ruth, Nolan Ryan, and others. Quotes from many of the players appear along the way, amidst life-size cutouts of them frozen in their trademark batting stances, swings, or pitching deliveries. But more than honoring the legends of the major leagues, this space also pays tribute to the pioneering stars of the Negro Leagues and of the All-American Girls Professional Baseball League. In a technology-laden room nearby, electronic scoreboards display the up-to-the-minute all-time statistical leaders in all of the major batting and pitching categories, while a bank of computer monitors provides information about all the big-league ballparks, past and present. Another exhibit memorializes the grand old ballparks of baseball's yesteryear with actual stadium chairs from places like Crosley Field, Forbes Field, and the Polo Grounds.

The second floor focuses on the State of Texas's sports scene and particularly on the Lone Star State's baseball past. There are exhibits related to the arrival of the Rangers in Arlington via Washington; to one-time Rangers manager Ted Williams; to the team's original home, Arlington Stadium; and to Rangers stars like Toby Harrah, Jim Sundberg, Ivan Rodriguez, and Juan Gonzalez. Not far away, a giant map of the Southwestern United States traces the evolution of the Texas League, which was founded as an independent minor-league circuit in 1888, when it fielded teams in Austin, Dallas, Fort Worth, Galveston, Houston, New Orleans, and San Antonio. It continues to treat fans to bush-league ball to this day. Another exhibit displays the cowboy boots that Billy Martin wore when he was the manager of the Rangers in the 1970s, as well as articles of clothing that once belonged to other notable Rangers. The museum also makes room for exhibits related to the NHL's Dallas Stars and to Olympic heroes who have hailed from Texas.

On the third floor, interactive exhibits put the focus on learning. Here, youngsters find a 4-foot-in-diameter baseball that has been sawed in half so that its innards can be scrutinized; a pitch simulator that allows them to feel the force of a Nolan Ryan fastball popping into a catcher's mitt; and baseball-related learning activities in math, science, geography, and history.

During the baseball season, Legends is open Monday through Saturday from 9:00 A.M. to 4:00 P.M. and Sunday from 11:00 to 4:00. During the off-season, it is open Tuesday through Saturday from 10:00 to 4:00.

Admission costs $12.00 for adults, $10.00 for adults over the age of sixty-two and college students, and $7.00 for youngsters. The fee includes a pass for a stadium tour that takes visitors to the statue of Nolan Ryan on the centerfield plaza, down onto the field, into the Rangers' dugout, and upstairs to the press box and owner's suite.

★ ★ ★

= 25 =
THE CANADIAN BASEBALL HALL OF FAME AND MUSEUM

386 Church Street South | St. Marys, Ontario

While baseball has never enjoyed the popularity in the Great White North that it has in the Lower 48, there's no disputing that the American Game is beloved by many Canadians, even if it places second, after hockey, on their list of favorite sports. And baseball's history in Canada is a long and proud one. In fact, while Hoboken, New Jersey, and Cooperstown, New York, have carried on a friendly debate through the decades over which city was the site of the first baseball game ever played, a Canadian town also sometimes enters into the conversation. Building its case around an article that appeared in *Sporting Life* magazine in 1886, the Ontario town of Beachville asserts that it hosted the first baseball game in North America on June 4, 1838, a year before Abner Doubleday's supposed Cooperstown game and four years before Alexander Cartwright's Elysian Fields game in Hoboken.

There's only one problem with this claim. Well, actually two. The Beachville game involved five bases, not three, and it required eleven fielders per team, not nine. But even if this early contest wasn't exactly baseball as we know it, it was the beginning of a hardball heritage that has continued to grow in Canada ever since. In the early years of professional baseball, Canada supplied more players to the major leagues than any other foreign country. In 1884 twenty-nine Canadians suited up for big-league clubs, a record that has yet to be broken, although the chances would seem good that it will be soon. Following in the footsteps of legendary players like Fergie Jenkins, Larry Walker, and Reggie Cleveland, the current crop of Canadian big leaguers—which includes talented stars like Jason Bay, Erik Bedard, Eric Gagne, Rich Harden, and Justin Morneau—continues to grow. In 2006 twenty-three Canadians appeared in big-league games.

Canadian Baseball Hall of Fame

The idea for a Hall of Fame dedicated to celebrating baseball's tradition in Canada originated in 1983, when a small exhibit appeared at the Toronto Blue Jays' Exhibition Stadium. After stopovers in a couple of subsequent locations, in 1989 the Canadian Baseball Hall of Fame and Museum found a permanent home in the southwestern

Ontario town of St. Marys. The hall currently occupies a century-old stone building, while a fundraising effort takes place to allow for the construction of a larger facility to replace it next door. Plans are also in the works to build a stadium around one of the three baseball fields on the 32-acre complex, a facility that will utilize more than 2,000 seats from Exhibition Stadium.

In the meantime, the hall as currently constituted offers a wide range of exhibits related to the Beachville game; early Canadian major leaguers; the Vancouver Asahis, a minor-league team of Japanese-Canadians who were interred during World War II; Canadian minor-league teams like the ones that starred Tommy Lasorda and Jackie Robinson; the Montreal Expos and Toronto Blue Jays; the career of Jenkins; Exhibition Stadium, Jarry Park, Olympic Stadium, and other Canadian stadiums; and current Canadian players in the majors. Among the items on display are a bat and ball signed by Babe Ruth; the seat that marked the upper-deck landing spot of the longest home run in Olympic Stadium history, a blast by Willie Stargell; Jenkins's 1971 Cy Young Award; and the batting helmet that Joe Carter was wearing when he hit his walk-off homer to clinch a Blue Jays victory over the Phillies in the 1993 World Series.

The exhibit space also pays tribute, of course, to the hall's inductees, which included seventy-eight members as of early 2008. Each year on the third Saturday in June, a new crop of people is enshrined. The rules for eligibility stipulate that a player must be retired for three years and that if a person is not Canadian, he or she must have done something significant in baseball in Canada. Indeed, there are plenty of non-Canadian members of the Canadian Baseball Hall of Fame. In most cases these are players, coaches, and team executives who distinguished themselves in careers with the Expos and Blue Jays—people like Gary Carter, Joe Carter, Andre Dawson, Cito Gaston, Pat Gillick, Steve Rogers, and Dave Stieb. Robinson, who played for the International League's Montreal Royals in 1946, a year before he would break the major-league color barrier, and Lasorda, who pitched nine seasons for the Royals, from 1950 to 1955 and 1958 to 1960, are also members.

The hall is open during the warmer half of the calendar year. In May it welcomes visitors on Saturdays from 10:30 A.M. to 4:00 P.M. and on Sundays from noon to 4:00. From June through the first week of October, it is open Monday through Saturday from 10:30 A.M. to 4:00 P.M. and Sunday from noon to 4:00. Admission costs $7.50 for adults, $6.00 for senior citizens, $3.75 for children, or $15.00 for the entire family.

=26=

TED WILLIAMS MUSEUM AND HITTERS HALL OF FAME

Tropicana Field | St. Petersburg, Florida

Baseball fans received some bad news in early 2007 when it was announced that the Ted Williams Museum would be closing its doors for the final time at its diamond-shaped facility in Hernando, Florida. Unfortunately, the museum had experienced a decline in visitor attendance at its out-of-the-way location in the north-central part of the Sunshine State, where Williams spent his later days. When Williams was alive, it had attracted prominent players, past and present, and prominent Americans like Muhammad Ali, George H. W. Bush, Bob Costas, Curt Gowdy, and Bobby Orr, who brought with them crowds of baseball fans. But after Ted's passing in 2002, the project that had been so close to his heart since opening in 1994 could no longer draw the same volume of celebrities and fans needed to sustain it.

Within just a few days of announcing it would be closing, though, the museum issued another press release, this one to announce it had brokered a deal with the Tampa Bay Devil Rays to move its displays chronicling Williams's life in baseball, in the military, and as a fisherman to Tropicana Field. The Hitters Hall of Fame would also

be making the move. And so in March of 2007 the Ted Williams Museum and Hitters Hall of Fame began its second life on the Trop's outfield concourse. Although it's always sad to leave an old familiar home, this was a great move for an already excellent baseball museum that is now more convenient to visit for a great many baseball fans.

Since reopening, the museum displays all of the trademark items from its Hernando location, including Ted's first professional contract to play for the Minneapolis Millers, a 150-pound stuffed tarpon that Ted caught on fly equipment in the Florida Keys, Ted's golf clubs, Ted's rifle, pictures of Ted in his World War II flight gear, and exhibits honoring the great stars of the Negro Leagues and Ted's friend and all-time home-run king Sadaharu Oh of the Tokyo Giants.

The centerpiece of the museum, though, remains the Hitters Hall of Fame. Conceived of by Williams himself, the Hitters Hall celebrates the accomplishments of the twenty greatest hitters (other than Williams) who ever lived, as well as the achievements of more than fifty other hitters who have since been added to the exclusive group. The original twenty whom

Ted considered the best batsmen of all time are Babe Ruth, Lou Gehrig, Jimmie Foxx, Rogers Hornsby, Joe DiMaggio, Ty Cobb, Stan Musial, Joe Jackson, Hank Aaron, Willie Mays, Hank Greenberg, Mickey Mantle, Tris Speaker, Al Simmons, Johnny Mize, Mel Ott, Harry Heilmann, Frank Robinson, Mike Schmidt, and Ralph Kiner. Each is honored with a display case of memorabilia and photographs. Among the more than fifty subsequent inductees are old Red Sox friends of Williams like Dom DiMaggio, Carlton Fisk, Dwight Evans, Carl Yastrzemski, and Jim Rice, as well as Pete Rose and present-day players like Alex Rodriguez and Nomar Garciaparra.

The museum is free and accessible on game days to Tropicana Field ticket holders. It opens two hours before first pitch and remains open throughout the game.

★ ★ ★

= 27 =

BASEBALL BOULEVARD

First Street and Central Avenue | St. Petersburg, Florida

Anyone interested in learning more about Florida's history as a spring-training hotbed will enjoy a stroll along Baseball Boulevard. On the sidewalks of ten city blocks between Al Lang Field—St. Petersburg's longtime Grapefruit League ballpark—and Tropicana Field—the regular-season home of the Tampa Bay Devil Rays—home-plate-shaped markers tell the story of baseball's early days in the Sunshine State.

The walk begins with a bronze bust of Al Lang, the grandfather of the Grapefruit League, outside the waterfront ballpark that bears his name. The story of how the St. Petersburg mayor brought spring baseball to Florida dates back to the early 1900s. In those days most big-league teams trav-eled to underdeveloped southern states like Alabama, Arkansas, and Georgia in the weeks before each new season was to begin to get their players in shape. As far as the teams were concerned, the more remote a camp's location the better, as rural environments offered less temptation for the rambling players of the era. In those days the players worked second jobs in the off-season and didn't have the luxury of devoting much time to winter conditioning regiments. Thus, weight loss and extended sobriety were the two main springtime goals for most teams, rather than skill refinement and player evaluation. Teams trained in isolation, and spring exhibitions between different big-league teams were rare.

But then Lang imagined that spring training could be something more. He envisioned a centralized location in South Florida where teams would scrimmage one another before audiences of paying fans. Hoping to not only revolutionize the spring game but also transform St. Petersburg from a small fishing village into a resort town, Lang traveled to St. Louis in December of 1913 to meet with St. Louis Browns president Robert Hedges and Browns manager Branch Rickey. Lang enchanted the two men, filling their minds with images of a spring filled with trophy fishing, sunshine, and baseball. He also made sure to mention that St. Petersburg was a dry town. Lang offered the Browns a 20-acre lot rent free for one year. Hedges and Rickey took the bait.

In February of 1914 the Browns arrived in St. Petersburg, and several other teams followed their lead, traveling farther south than they ever had before to play exhibitions. On February 27, 1914, the Browns lost to the Cubs 3–2 at a field near St. Petersburg's Coffee Pot Bayou in the first professional baseball game ever played in Florida. More than 4,000 spectators turned out for the game, many arriving by boat at a special dock installed for the occasion.

Due to a financial dispute between Lang and the Browns, the team did not return in 1915. But Lang was undeterred in his quest to make St. Petersburg a spring-training hub. In 1922 Waterfront Park opened as the spring home of the Boston Braves, who would make their spring camp in the city through 1937. In 1925 the Yankees also came to town, leaving their previous camp in New Orleans after heavy-drinking slugger Babe Ruth wore out his welcome on the bayou. Almost immediately, Ruth was in trouble again, this time with an alligator that chased him off the outfield grass of St. Petersburg's Crescent Lake Park. In between games and 'gator racing, Ruth danced at the Coliseum and entertained guests on the tuba at the Jungle Country Club. By 1929 ten of the sixteen major-league teams were training in Florida.

There have been glorious moments in St. Petersburg baseball, like the time the Yankees and Cardinals met in the 1942 World Series after they had shared the same spring-training ballpark; sad moments, like the time Lou Gehrig collapsed during a 1939 exhibition game, foreshadowing the end of his streak of 2,130 consecutive games played and the onset of his terrible illness; zany moments, like the time a trainer parboiled Joe DiMaggio's ankle during a spring treatment in 1936, causing the Yankee Clipper to miss the first month of the season; and even zanier moments, like the day in 1940 when fans turned out at Waterfront Park to watch Donkey Baseball—grown men playing the Grand Old Game while riding donkeys. All these moments and more are captured on the monuments along Baseball Boulevard. And there are even a few hot-dog stands along the way, too, for fans who have a hankering for that time-honored ballpark treat while they learn more about the game's past.

THIS STADIUM DEDICATED MARCH 12, 1977
IN HONOR OF

ALBERT FIELDING LANG
1870 — 1960

FLORIDA'S SUNSHINE AMBASSADOR
TO MAJOR LEAGUE BASEBALL

IT WAS THROUGH HIS DEDICATION,
VISION AND LOVE OF THE GAME THE
BIG LEAGUES DISCOVERED FLORIDA'S
EXCELLENCE AS A CONDITIONING SITE
AND ST. PETERSBURG BECAME BASEBALL'S
SPRING TRAINING CAPITAL.THE STADIUM
IS BUILT ON THE SITE OF AL LANG FIELD,
ERECTED IN 1947

Al Lang plaque along Baseball Boulevard

★ ★ ★

= 28 =

BATCOLUMN

600 West Madison Street | Chicago, Illinois

Baseball's blue highways lead to a wide range of sculptures related to the Grand Old Game. To begin, there are the life-size statues of the local franchise's favorite players to be found in nearly every major-league city. Ted Williams stands outside the rightfield gates of Fenway Park in Boston, Stan Musial outside Busch Stadium in St. Louis, Babe Ruth outside Oriole Park in Baltimore, Willie Mays in San Francisco, Roberto Clemente in Pittsburgh, Bob Feller in Cleveland, and so on. Some cities and teams, meanwhile, go to even greater lengths to fuse the baseball world and art world, moving beyond realistic tribute pieces into the realm of more abstract works that, though they may border on the absurd, make their own statements about the special place the game holds in the minds and hearts of local residents.

Outside Safeco Field in Seattle, for example, fans will find a giant bronze baseball mitt with a hole in the middle to symbolize the ball. Outside Coors Field in Denver, fans find an ornate arched entryway decorated with colorful sculptures that trace the evolution of the ball in all of its many forms, from tetherballs to meatballs, to crystal balls, to moth balls, to Christmas-tree balls, to dozens of different sports balls, including, of course, baseballs. Outside Turner Field in Atlanta, fans find massive multicolored baseballs reflecting the histories of all thirty big-league teams. Outside Jacobs Field in Cleveland, fans find colorful guitars that honor favorite Indians players. And anyone who's watched *Baseball Tonight* is no doubt aware of the giant baseball glove beyond the leftfield fence in San Francisco and the massive Coca-Cola bottle made of baseball gear high above the field in Atlanta.

To visit the granddaddy of all baseball sculptures, though, fans must travel to the City of Broad Shoulders, where there stands a 100-foot-tall, 20-ton, shiny metal baseball bat. The massive monument stands in neither of the city's two famous baseball neighborhoods, but rather almost exactly midway between them, in front of the Harold Washington Social Security Administration building. The piece, known as *Batcolumn*, was commissioned jointly by the Art in Architecture Program of the United States General Services Administration and the National Endowment for the Arts and created by Swedish pop artist Claes Oldenburg.

Oldenburg, who spent part of his childhood in Chicago in the 1950s when his father was stationed in the city as a Swedish diplomat, began the sculpture in 1975 and completed it in 1977. His other works, which can be found in cities around the world, include an oversize hot dog, a giant clothespin, a big lipstick tube, a jumbo-size toothbrush, and an enormous ashtray, to name just a few of the mundane objects he has transformed into massive pieces of pop art.

But there's nothing mundane about a baseball bat, at least not to the game's legion of followers, and Oldenburg did well to create in *Batcolumn* a work that captures the essence and power of the slugger's best friend. Even when viewed from blocks away, there's no doubting that this tapered metal column that grows ever higher and ever wider in a web of intricate silver scaffolding is in fact a baseball bat. Although *Batcolumn* must be viewed through a more abstract lens than the ones through which baseball travelers might observe the more lifelike, bigger bats in Louisville, where a 120-foot-high Louisville Slugger breaks the skyline, and in the Bronx, where a 138-foot-tall exhaust pipe outside Yankee Stadium has been painted to resemble the bat Babe Ruth once swung, Chicago's big bat seems all the more striking due to its shimmering incandescent quality.

A plaque on *Batcolumn*'s concrete base reads:

For his commission to create a public sculpture for the Social Security Administration building, Claes Oldenburg selected the baseball bat as an emblem of Chicago's ambition and vigor. The sculpture's verticality echoes the city's dramatic skyline, while its form and scale cleverly allude to more traditional civic monuments, such as obelisks and memorial columns. The pattern of the sculpture's crisscrossing structural latticework forms an elegant silhouette against the open sky. Claes Oldenburg emerged in the early 1960s as one of the leading figures of American Pop Art, a movement that took its inspiration from popular culture, such as comic strips, advertisements, and mass-produced consumer goods. Oldenburg's art transforms these everyday objects through dramatic shifts in scale and materials. His art embraces the complexity of modern society and is intended to bring art into direct contact with daily life.

Whether or not baseball road-trippers will, in fact, find themselves embracing the "complexity of modern society" upon visiting *Batcolumn* is a matter that's subject to debate. But here's guessing that any traveling fan who also happens to be a weekend softball slugger will never again look at his 34-inch, 30-ounce Mizuno quite the same way after visiting it.

McKechnie Field

★ ★ ★

=29=

McKECHNIE FIELD

1611 Ninth Street West | Bradenton, Florida

During March fans seeking the quintessential Grapefruit League experience need look no further than McKechnie Field in the Gulf Coast town of Bradenton. While spring training has blossomed into a big business in recent years and has reinvented itself, thanks in part to the construction of an impressive, though less than quaint and cozy, array of new ballparks in Florida and Arizona, McKechnie stays true to the idyllic small-time roots of spring baseball's yesteryear.

One of the first things visitors notice upon arriving at the ballpark is that there are no light towers at McKechnie. Every game is played beneath the warm Florida sun, the way the forefathers of the Grapefruit League intended. Likewise, there is no "seating bowl." Instead there are three freestanding grandstands—one behind home plate, one along the first-base line, and one along the third-base line. These covered stands mimic the wooden boxes that stood at ballparks across the country before the concrete-and-steel stadium-construction era dawned in the 1910s.

In Bradenton all of the fans sit close enough to the field to hear the home-plate umpire's ball and strike calls, and to see

for themselves which players are chewing tobacco, which ones are spitting sunflower seeds, and which ones are blowing Bazooka bubbles. You can't say that about too many of today's other spring parks.

Want history? McKechnie has it aplenty. Grapefruit League baseball has been played on this field since 1923, when the St. Louis Cardinals arrived, beginning a spring tradition that would bring to town such legends of the game as Babe Ruth, Hank Aaron, Jimmie Foxx, and Eddie Mathews. During the 1930s the Cardinals took to dispatching Dizzy Dean to Bradenton a few weeks ahead of his teammates, since the fun-loving hurler had a tendency to get himself into trouble when he wintered over in swinging St. Louis. To everyone's surprise Ole Diz fell in love with sleepy little Bradenton, so much so that he bought a service station on the Tamiami Trail and spent his every waking hour away from the ballpark pumping gas. And you probably thought the Red Bird teams of the era earned their "Gashouse Gang" nickname due to some overly stinky train rides the beat reporters endured as they rode the rails with the team from St. Louis to points elsewhere in the baseball universe!

McKechnie Field is named after Hall of

Fame manager Bill McKechnie, who distinguished himself during a career that spanned the years 1922 through 1946, while he piloted the National League clubs in Pittsburgh, Boston, and Cincinnati. Upon his retirement, McKechnie headed for Bradenton and proceeded to make himself a springtime fixture at the tiny ballpark on the corner of Ninth Street and 17th Avenue, until his passing in 1965.

The stadium, which has been rebuilt several times through the decades, underwent its most recent renovation prior to the 1993 spring season. In addition to serving as the spring home of the Pirates, McKechnie hosts a handful of Gulf Coast League games each summer, although the rookie-league Pirates play most of their schedule a few miles away at **Pirate City** (1701 Roberto Clemente Memorial Way).

★ ★ ★

= 30 =

PITTSBURGH NEGRO LEAGUES FIELDS

Multiple Locations | Pittsburgh, Pennsylvania

During the heyday of the Negro Leagues, Pittsburgh stood above all other American cities as the undisputed hub of the "black baseball" universe. The Steel City was home to not one but two of the finest Negro Leagues teams in the land—the Homestead Grays and the Pittsburgh Crawfords. Both clubs offered fans the chance to witness the daily heroics of some of the best ballplayers—of any era, creed, or color—to ever lace up a pair of spikes. Today, all these decades later, the memories of both teams are kept alive at various sites in and around Pittsburgh where historic markers and relics of an era long gone by pay homage to their greatness.

The Grays were founded in 1910 by a man named Cumberland Posey, who played for, managed, and owned the team. Originally, the Grays played at West Field in the suburb of Munhall, but as they grew more popular, they often played their weekend games at Forbes Field. Later they began "hosting" some of their games at Griffith Stadium in Washington, D.C., while playing their Pittsburgh schedule at Greenlee Field in the city's Hill District. Greenlee doubled as the home of the Crawfords, who originally played at Ammon Field but switched to Greenlee after legendary Pittsburgh club owner Gus Greenlee bought the team and footed the cost of the $100,000 stadium. That park opened in 1932 and quickly drew praise as the finest black-owned ballpark in the land (at the time it was common for Negro Leagues teams to simply use the

71

home stadium of the nearest big-league or minor-league club).

Throughout most of their days, the Negro Leagues comprised a loosely organized and ever-changing assortment of black teams that played against one another while also playing barnstorming games against semi-pro teams across the country; thus, definitive team records and individual-player statistics related to the Negro Leagues are hard to quantify. This much is certain though: the brightest of Pittsburgh's many stars was a barrel-chested catcher known universally in his day as "the black Babe Ruth." Josh Gibson began his career with the Grays in 1929, switched to the Crawfords in 1930, and proceeded to belt seventy-five home runs in 1931. After being part of what many historians consider the best black club ever—the early 1930s Crawfords, which featured four other future Hall of Famers in Satchel Paige, Cool Papa Bell, Oscar Charleston, and Judy Johnson—Gibson rejoined the Grays in 1937 and paired with another future Cooperstown inductee, Buck Leonard, to lead the Grays to nine consecutive Negro National League titles. Although it is uncertain exactly how many home runs Gibson hit between 1929 and 1946, most debates concerning his long-ball prowess begin around the 800 mark and escalate from there. Tragically, Gibson's career, and life, ended abruptly in January of 1947, just a few short months before Jackie Robinson would break Major League Baseball's color barrier. The great slugger, who had suffered from a brain tumor and battled substance-abuse problems, was felled by a brain hemorrhage at age thirty-five.

Baseball pilgrims today can visit several of Gibson's and his contemporaries' old stomping grounds. Only fragments of a glorious past remain, but if you look hard enough, you will find them. A plaque at 2217 Bedford Avenue marks the former site of **Ammon Field** and recalls some of Gibson's accomplishments. Amateur baseball is still played near the site at what is now called Ammon Park. A similar marker stands outside the **Crawford Grill** (2141 Wylie Avenue), recognizing the club that Gus Greenlee once owned for the role it played in black social life in the 1920s, 1930s, and 1940s. Inside, old photographs pay tribute to the jazz legends and ballplayers who passed through the Crawford's doors. Still another marker, on **Amity Street** near the Fifth Avenue ramp, remembers the Grays and their era of dominance.

More than any other old Negro Leagues park in greater Pittsburgh, **West Field** (Main Street, Munhall) still retains much of its original shape, existing as a dilapidated monument around a field that is today the home of the Munhall–West Homestead Baseball Association's Colt League. The seventy-year-old bleachers, dugouts, and locker rooms still remain. And as of mid-2007, a proposal championed by Josh Gibson's great-grandson, Sean Gibson, and Pittsburgh Steelers backup quarterback Charlie Batch was slowly clipping its way through a web of bureaucratic red tape spun by the borough of Munhall. If funded and carried out, the proposal would restore parts of West Field while also transforming it into a new multimillion-dollar, 350-acre, youth sports complex for children in Homestead, West Homestead, and Munhall. Here's hoping that the project not only succeeds but also incorporates some sort of museum or historic exhibit honoring the great Josh Gibson.

★ ★ ★

= 31 =

MONUMENT PARK

Legends Field | One Steinbrenner Drive | Tampa, Florida

Outside Legends Field—the Yankees' spring-training home—fans find a palm tree–adorned miniature version of Yankee Stadium's famed Monument Park. Tampa's Monument Park consists of sixteen pinstriped baseball-shaped plaques, each of which displays the uniform number of a Yankees' hero whose number has been retired by the team. Beneath the numbers, blue placards offer quotations from the players themselves, summaries of their accomplishments, and general words of praise about them.

Lou Gehrig's plaque reads, LOU WAS ONE OF THE MOST PROLIFIC YANKEE HITTERS OF ALL TIME. FROM 1923–1939. HIS SKILLS AND INNER STRENGTH WERE THINGS OF BEAUTY ON THE BALL FIELD AND EARNED HIM THE NICKNAME, "THE IRON HORSE."

Babe Ruth's reads, FROM 1920–1934. SINGLE-HANDEDLY LIFTED BASEBALL TO NEW HEIGHTS WITH HIS UNLIMITED TALENT AND UNBRIDLED LOVE FOR THE GAME. HIS ENORMOUS CONTRIBUTIONS TO BASEBALL AND THE YANKEES MADE HIM THE MOST CELEBRATED ATHLETE WHO EVER LIVED.

Joe DiMaggio's reads, I WANT TO THANK THE GOOD LORD FOR MAKING ME A YANKEE.

This well-landscaped attraction debuted in 1996, when the City of Tampa opened Legends Field on a 31-acre plot across the street from Raymond James Stadium, home of the NFL's Tampa Bay Buccaneers. The baseball complex was built by Tampa at a cost of $30 million to lure the Grapefruit League Yankees away from their longtime spring haunt in Fort Lauderdale to the city where George Steinbrenner keeps his year-round home.

The Legends Field design reflects many similarities to Yankee Stadium's, appealing at once to the region's many transplanted New Yorkers longing for a taste of home and to native Floridians who may never have the opportunity to visit the hallowed ballpark in the Bronx but can sample the Yankee magic right in their own backyard.

BABE RUTH

NY

UNIFORM NUMBER RETIRED: 1948

FROM 1920-1934, BABE
SINGLEHANDEDLY LIFTED BASEBALL TO NEW
HEIGHTS WITH HIS UNLIMITED TALENT AND
UNBRIDLED LOVE FOR THE GAME
HIS ENORMOUS CONTRIBUTIONS TO
BASEBALL AND THE YANKEES
MADE HIM THE MOST CELEBRATED
ATHLETE WHO EVER LIVED

Babe Ruth monument at Tampa's version of Monument Park

The seats are all Yankee Stadium Blue, and the field dimensions are the same as at Yankee Stadium. The home-run porch in right-field is just 314 feet from home plate, the fence in straightaway center measures 408 feet, "Death Valley" in left-center measures 399 feet, and the leftfield foul pole is 318 feet from home plate. Beyond the outfield fence in left, a massive (by Grapefruit League standards) scoreboard features an 18-by-24-foot diamond-vision video board supported by cement pillars, further evoking the configuration of Yankee Stadium. Decorative white arches and filigree extend high above the

Legends Field stands on the face of the roof, mimicking the facade that spans the outfield in New York. And lest anyone forget who the home team is, giant blue windscreens above the top row of seats bear one letter apiece, combining to spell Y A N K E E S.

During the summer months Legends Field doubles as the home of the Florida State League Tampa Yankees. But even on days when neither the springtime nor summertime Yankees are playing at Legends, the Yankee complex is well worth a visit for any fan looking to experience a bit of the Yankee mystique in South Florida.

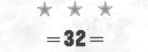

=32=

GROWDEN MEMORIAL PARK

Second Street | Fairbanks, Alaska

In keeping with a tradition that has continued for more than a century, Fairbanks, Alaska, ushers in the start of each summer by playing a baseball game in the middle of the night. On the date of the summer solstice, the sun dips below the northern horizon for less than two hours in this city located just south of the Arctic Circle, and even when the sun is out of sight, it provides enough indirect light for baseball to be played and observed without stadium lights.

After utilizing several different local fields during its first half-century, the "Midnight Sun Game" has been played at Growden Memorial Park since 1963. The cozy stadium is the home of the Alaska Goldpanners and is a pleasure to visit on any day of the thirty-five-game Alaska Summer League season. The experience is extra special, however, on the one day a year when the home team doesn't take the field until 10:30 P.M. for a game that begins at sunset in the spring and finishes after sunrise in the summer. On this night without darkness, the jovial fans don visors and sunglasses, drink beer, and eat hot dogs, and when the clock strikes midnight, the game

Growden Park

stops so they can sing the "Alaska Flag Song." It is surreal enough simply to be sitting outside in broad daylight at midnight; add a baseball game to the equation, and the experience becomes nothing short of mind-blowing.

The Goldpanners are one of six teams in this popular collegiate league that attracts players from all over the country. While they have played in every Midnight Sun Game since 1960, their opponent changes every year. In recent decades, instead of playing one of their usual Alaskan rivals, the Goldpanners have invited a travel team from the Lower 48 to play in the game. This not only ensures that the home crowd will be firmly behind them, but it also all but guarantees that they will pre-

vail. Facing jetlagged and usually less-talented competition, the Goldpanners have not lost a Midnight Sun Game since 1987, when a club from California beat them.

Interestingly, the Growden Park grandstand contains some of the stadium chairs and benches that once appeared at Sick's Stadium, the home of the Pacific Coast League Seattle Rainiers and American League Seattle Pilots. The seating capacity is listed at 3,500, but crowds have been known to exceed 5,000 on the date of the Midnight Sun Game. The only knock on this park is that it features an artificial turf infield (the outfield grass is real), but this is forgivable, considering how quickly winter turns to summer in Alaska.

The first Midnight Sun Game was played in 1906 between two local bars, the California Bar and the Eagles Club, whose players nicknamed themselves the "Drinks" and the "Smokes," respectively. The two teams played nine innings at an amateur field in Fairbanks as June 21 turned to June 22, and when were finished both the players and 1,500 spectators agreed that the game should become an annual rite of spring , . . and summer. The event featured bar teams and military teams during its first several decades, utilizing several different fields. Since beginning their affiliation with the game in 1960, the Goldpanners have given future major leaguers like Tom Seaver, Dave Winfield, Harold Reynolds, and Terry Francona the chance to showcase their skills in one of the most unusual baseball spectacles on the planet.

Another Alaska Baseball League venue that warrants a look-see during any fan's trip to the Forty-Ninth State is **Herman Brothers Field** (Glenn Highway, Palmer). Located on the Alaska State Fairgrounds, the home park of the Mat-Su Miners offers a view of the snowcapped Chugach Mountains from its small wooden grandstand.

The Alaska Baseball League begins play in the second week of June and continues through the final week of July. The league champion travels to Wichita, Kansas, to participate in the National Baseball Congress World Series, which hosts its own series of midnight games during its "Baseball Around the Clock" extravaganza. Of course, the folks in Wichita have to turn on the ballpark lights at Lawrence-Dumont Stadium when they play *their* late games.

★ ★ ★

= 33 =

THE BILLY GOAT TAVERN

430 North Michigan Avenue | Chicago, Illinois

When the Boston Red Sox won the 2004 World Series and finally silenced talk that Babe Ruth had placed a hex on his old team, Boston passed the mantle of baseball's most infamous and longest-running curse to Chicago, where the "Curse of the Billy Goat" lives on. According to Billy Goat mythology, the Cubs' fortunes took a turn for the worse when legendary Chicago barkeep Billy "Billy Goat" Sianis bought two tickets to Game Four of the 1945 World Series and arrived at the turnstiles with his lucky goat Murphy in tow. Sianis, who had adopted the animal a few years earlier, after it had jumped off a passing truck outside his downtown saloon, assumed he'd be allowed to bring old Murphy into the Wrigley Field stands with him.

After being politely told that no animals were allowed inside Wrigley, Sianis appealed to none other than P. K. Wrigley himself. But the Cubs owner only reiterated the ballpark's *Homo sapiens*–only policy, offering Sianis a terse "No." When Sianis asked "Why not?" Mr. Wrigley reportedly said, "Because the goat stinks." It was then that Sianis, a Greek immigrant well versed in the ancient art of the stink-eye, proclaimed, "The Cubs will never win a World Series so long as the goat is not allowed in Wrigley Field."

Never mind winning a World Series, the Cubs have only won one World Series *game* since that turning point in franchise history. They lost three out of the final four contests against the Tigers to drop the 1945 World Series and haven't returned to the October Classic in more than six decades since. This, from a team that prior to the incident had won ten National League pennants and the World Series in 1907 and 1908. Hmm, think Cubs fans were a bit hasty in riding Steve Bartman out of town after that National League Championship Series meltdown against the Marlins in 2003? It would seem that greater forces than a souvenir-crazed twenty-six-year-old may have conspired to do in the Cubs after all.

Today, those interested in learning more about the Curse of the Billy Goat can visit any of the several Billy Goat Tavern locations across Chicago, where old newspaper articles and photographs related to the curse, as well as to Chicago sports history, decorate the walls. The original Billy Goat Tavern, set below street level on North Michigan Avenue, is a Chicago landmark that has welcomed into its cozy dining room such prominent Americans as George H. W. Bush, George W. Bush, Bill and Hillary Clinton, Al Gore, Jay Leno, Bill Murray, Harrison Ford, John Cusack, Charlton Heston, Frank Sinatra, Ronnie Woo Woo, and John Belushi, who based his famous "Cheeseborger, Cheeseborger" skit on *Saturday Night Live* on the antics of an overzealous Billy Goat employee.

Although, the curse has helped keep the Billy Goat in the public eye and prospering all these years, the Sianis family and the loveable losers of the National League have long since made their peace. On Opening Day of the 1984 season, Sam Sianis, the nephew of Bill and owner of today's Billy Goat establishments, was invited by the Cubs to walk on the Wrigley Field lawn with a goat believed to be a direct descendent of Murphy. After Sam said that all was forgiven, the Cubs won the National League East crown and then the first two games of the best-of-five National League Championship Series against the Padres. But the Cubs lost the final three games and missed out, once again, on a chance to play in their first World Series since the goatless 1945 affair. Apparently the Opening Day gesture, while heartfelt and nice, was not enough to satisfy the ghost of old Billy Goat Sianis after all.

So, as long as the Cubs keep playing and

keep losing, fans and pundits alike will continue to point to the curse as one explanation for their failure. And hungry customers who have an appreciation for baseball myth and an appetite for juicy burgers will continue to frequent the Billy Goat Tavern.

=34=

JACKIE ROBINSON'S GRAVE

Cypress Hills Cemetery | 833 Jamaica Avenue | Brooklyn, New York

Although he was born in Georgia and grew up in Southern California, Jackie Robinson is buried, fittingly, in Brooklyn, where in 1947 he broke baseball's color barrier. Robinson's ten-year Hall of Fame career began on April 15 of that year, when he started at first base for the Dodgers as a twenty-eight-year-old rookie. He went hitless in three at-bats against the Boston Braves, but the erosion of more than half a century of discrimination in the game had finally begun. In June Larry Doby would become the first African American to play in the American League, taking the field with the Cleveland Indians. In October, Robinson—who batted .297, scored 125 runs, and collected a National League–best 29 stolen bases—would be named baseball's first "Rookie of the Year."

The story of how Jackie Robinson helped transform the game and more importantly the nation of its followers began in California, where he starred as a high school and collegiate player, and continued to Kansas City,

Montreal, Daytona Beach, and other towns and cities along the way, where he refined his skills. But the story culminated in Brooklyn, where Robinson proved what so many forward-thinking individuals had contended for years—that a black man could hold his own in the major leagues. And more than that, he proved that a black player could be one of the very *best* players on the diamond. In 1949, two years after breaking into the Majors, Robinson won the National League's Most Valuable Player award, when he batted a league-best .342 with 112 runs scored, 203 hits, 16 home runs, 124 runs batted in, and 37 steals, while playing in all 156 Dodgers games at second base. This in an era, mind you, when middle infielders were typically light-hitting defensive specialists.

Robinson won his only World Series title in 1955, when the Dodgers downed the Yankees in seven games. By then his skills had begun to diminish. After a second mediocre season in 1956, the Dodgers sold his contract to the New York Giants, but rather than exchange his beloved Dodger blue for the uniform of his cross-town rivals, Robinson opted to retire. He finished with 1,518 hits, 137 home runs, a .311 batting average, and 197 stolen bases, numbers that certainly would have been higher had he broken into the big leagues at a younger age.

After finding that no team would hire him as a big-league coach or manager, Robinson pursued several private business interests that included owning a clothing store in New York and a restaurant chain. He also became a vocal civil rights activist, campaigning for several politicians and serving on the board of the NAACP and as a special assistant to New York governor Nelson Rockefeller. As physically gifted as he had been as a young man, by the time Robinson was inducted into the National Baseball Hall of Fame in 1962, his body had begun to fail him. He suffered from diabetes and heart problems and passed away in 1972 at the age of 53 in Stamford, Connecticut.

Robinson's headstone is understated when compared to some of the other famous baseball graves across America, but there is elegance and grace in its simplicity. The stone's epitaph, which was written by Robinson himself, reads: A LIFE IS NOT IMPORTANT EXCEPT IN THE IMPACT IT HAS ON OTHER LIVES. Beneath these words, Robinson's signature is etched in granite. A visit to this quiet cemetery and a few moments spent reflecting on these words by which Robinson lived his life do much to remind traveling fans of the contributions this brave and selfless individual made to our country.

Within the next few years, there may be an additional Robinson landmark to visit in New York as well. Upon breaking ground on their new stadium, the New York Mets announced a partnership with the Jackie Robinson Foundation to establish the Jackie Robinson Museum and Learning Center, which is scheduled to open at a site to be determined in Lower Manhattan in 2009.

=35=

THE LOUISVILLE SLUGGER MUSEUM & FACTORY

800 West Main Street | Louisville, Kentucky

A trip to Louisville offers baseball wanderers the chance to marvel at the biggest baseball bat in the world. The 120-foot-tall, 68,000-pound whopper standing outside the most famous baseball-bat company in the land is made of steel, but painted to resemble the wood grain of a real bat. It rises quite a bit higher than the five-story brick building it leans against, serving as a beacon for those in search of the Louisville Slugger Museum & Factory.

Inside the museum, exhibits trace the evolution of the bat, offering examples of the sticks that famous sluggers like Ty Cobb, Babe Ruth, and Ted Williams wielded, as well as models that modern-day players like Derek Jeter, Ken Griffey Jr., and David Ortiz swing. Another popular attraction is a 12-foot long baseball glove made of 450-year-old Kentucky limestone, in which children can sit and play. The glove weighs 17 tons and could only be installed after the museum's front doors were removed to allow for its entry.

The twenty-minute tour of the Hillerich & Bradsby Company factory demonstrates how planks of white ash and maple harvested from the company's 6,500 acres of forest in Pennsylvania and New York are lathed into the best baseball bats in the business. Hillerich & Bradsby sells more than one million bats per year, thanks largely to the more than 60 percent of current major leaguers who swing its popular Louisville Slugger. The typical big leaguer goes through about one hundred bats per season, custom ordering hardwood to account for the weight, length, barrel, and handle dimensions that best suit his style.

The woodworking shop that grew to become the most prolific bat maker in the industry was founded in Louisville in 1856 by German immigrant Fred Hillerich. In those early days the shop made balusters, bedposts, bowling pins, and butter churns, not baseball bats. Then in 1880 young Bud Hillerich began working as an apprentice in his father's shop. When old Fred wasn't looking, his son made baseball bats for himself and his friends to use. One day Bud made a special bat to help his favorite player out of a horrific slump. Pete "The Old Gladiator" Browning was the star of the American Association's Louisville Eclipse, but he was really struggling at the plate in the early part of the 1884 season. He couldn't buy a hit and was willing to try anything to change his luck. So on a warm spring day he stepped into the batter's box with one of Bud's handmade models on his shoulder.

Before long Browning was knocking balls all over the yard. He went on to bat .336 that season and never swung another type of bat until his retirement ten years later. By then word had spread, and many other major leaguers were swinging Louisville Sluggers, too, including Pittsburgh Pirates star Honus Wagner, who helped cement Hillerich & Bradsby's place in the game when he signed an endorsement deal with the company in 1905. Ty Cobb signed a similar contract in 1908.

Today the museum that tells the story of this unique American enterprise is open Monday through Saturday from 9:00 A.M. to 5:00 P.M. and Sunday from noon to 5:00. Admission costs $9.00 for adults and $4.00 for children. Factory tours run every day but Sunday, and every fan who takes the tour receives a miniature souvenir bat.

Louisville Slugger Museum

= 36 =

SHOELESS JOE JACKSON MEMORIAL BALLPARK

406 West Avenue | Greenville, South Carolina

Even if he couldn't say it "wasn't so" when asked on the steps of a Chicago courthouse to refute allegations that he and seven of his White Sox teammates had conspired to fix the 1919 World Series, Joe Jackson was one of the greatest hitters ever to play the game. And his hometown of Greenville, South Carolina, chooses to remember him more for his grace on the field, where he accumulated the third-highest lifetime batting average of all time, than for the circumstances surrounding his premature departure from the game. Although Jackson was never convicted of a crime, baseball commissioner Kenesaw Mountain Landis toed a hard line with the so-called "Black Sox," banning them from baseball in 1921. Jackson was thirty-one years old at the time and the owner of a .356 average over thirteen seasons. He would play semipro ball under a number of fake names over the next several years before returning to his boyhood home of Greenville in 1929. He opened a liquor store in town and could be found behind its counter until he suffered a heart attack and passed away in 1951.

A tour of the Jackson landmarks in Greenville begins with a visit to Shoeless Joe Jackson Memorial Ballpark, where the slugger honed his legendary swing and first wielded the 48-ounce bat that he famously called "Black Betsy." Jackson was just thirteen years old when he played his first semipro game on the field that now bears his name. In those days the field was called the Brandon Mill Ballpark, and it was there, just a few years later, that Jackson was discovered and signed to his first professional contract by Connie Mack. A plaque marking the historic significance of the location is inscribed with the words:

As a thirteen-year-old, Joe Jackson earned a position on the Brandon Mill Team. He possessed a talent so uncommon that legends grew from his deeds. His home runs were known as "Saturday Specials," his line drives "blue darters." His glove "a place where triples die." Shoeless Joe was the greatest natural hitter ever to grace the diamond, and was such an inspiration that Babe Ruth chose to copy his swing. He was banished from baseball for his complicity in the 1919 Black Sox scandal, yet his memory still moves across the conscience of America.

Joe Jackson statue at Greenville's West End Market

Not far from the field, at **West End Market** a bronze statue depicts Jackson finishing one of his prodigious left-handed swings. His tiny fielding glove is tucked neatly into one of his back pants pockets. The statue, which incorporates bricks from Comiskey Park in its base, was sculpted by Doug Young, who made it in the lobby of the Greenville City Hall in 2002, while members of the public observed his work.

After visiting the hallowed grounds where Jackson's baseball career took flight amidst so much hope and glory and this rendering of Jackson in his prime, tourists can follow Pendleton Street to the place where Jackson sought refuge after he was banned: the site of his **liquor store** (1262 Pendleton). According to Ken Burns' documentary *Baseball*, Ty Cobb once stopped into the store to buy a pint of whiskey while passing through Greenville and was saddened to find a broken-down Jackson behind the counter. "Don't you know me?" Cobb asked his old rival, and Jackson replied, "Sure, I know you. But I wasn't sure you wanted to know me. A lot of them don't."

Other points of interest along Greenville's Joe Jackson tour include the site of the **Jackson home** (119 East Wilburn Avenue), where Jackson lived with his wife Katie from 1933 until his death; the actual redbrick Jackson house, which has been moved to a new location near **West End Field** (945 South Main Street), the home of the South Atlantic League's Greenville Drive; and the Jackson grave at **Woodlawn Memorial Park** (Wade Hampton Boulevard). Jackson's tombstone is nothing fancy, but it is easy to find thanks to the baseballs, bats, white socks, and other memorabilia that pilgrims leave behind. The inscription on the stone does not refer to Jackson as "Shoeless Joe," a nickname he earned early in his career after removing a pair of tight-fitting spikes and batting barefoot, but as "Joseph W. Jackson."

Together these Greenville landmarks memorialize a great player and by all accounts a decent human being, who unfortunately got involved with the wrong crowd and out of greed or ignorance, or both, made a decision he would regret for the rest of his life. The game has known no figure more tragic than Joe Jackson, who had all the talent in the world but no place left where he could exhibit it, and a visit to Greenville does much to remind fans of the temptations we all must face in life and of the price we may pay if we make poor choices.

★ ★ ★

= 37 =
JOE ENGEL STADIUM
1130 East Third Street | Chattanooga, Tennessee

Although it lost its place in minor-league baseball when the Southern League Chattanooga Lookouts moved to a new downtown ballpark at the start of the 2000 season, historic Joe Engel Stadium still sees use as a high school and college field and is a site that anyone who appreciates the game's old-time yards should visit. Possessing a history as rich as any still-standing bush-league park and a cozy covered grandstand that transports fans instantly back to a simpler time, this park is one of the truly underappreciated gems on baseball's landscape.

The story of how Engel Stadium carved out its unique place in the game begins in the 1920s, when Washington Senators owner Clark W. Griffith sent former big-league pitcher and vaudeville entertainer Joe Engel to Chattanooga to construct a new ballpark for one of Washington's minor-league clubs. Engel coordinated the ballpark construction and then decided he liked Chattanooga so

Joe Engel Stadium

much he wanted to stay there to run the team. The park opened in 1930, and Engel immediately began applying the lessons he'd learned in his postbaseball career as an entertainer to his management of the Lookouts. Among his many publicity stunts were a raffle that awarded a $10,000 house to a lucky fan; a trade in which Engel sent a Lookouts shortstop packing in exchange for a turkey; a pregame elephant hunt that took place on the outfield lawn; a midgame ostrich race in the outfield; and the installation of a barber's chair behind home plate.

The most famous Engel gimmick of all, though, and the one that put Chattanooga on the national baseball map, occurred in 1931. That spring Engel signed a seventeen-year-old woman named Jackie Mitchell to a contract in advance of a New York Yankees visit for an exhibition game. When the big leaguers arrived, Engel sent Mitchell to the mound. All the young lady did was strike out the first two batters she faced, Babe Ruth and Lou Gehrig. Within a matter of days, grainy black-and-white footage of this extraordinary feat was showing at movie houses across the country, and fans in faraway cities were debating whether the at bats had been staged or legitimate. Forward thinking as always, to stifle talk of the teenager whose wicked sidearm sinker had humbled two of baseball's brightest stars, Commissioner Kenesaw Mountain Landis declared there was no place for women in baseball and voided Mitchell's contract. So much for progress. Chattanoogans still talk about the historic moment, though, as each generation of local fans passes down the story to the next.

The ballpark that was Engel's playground for years today offers a classic redbrick facade and a cozy grandstand full of wooden seats tucked beneath a roof supported by exposed steel girders. Beneath the stands fans find their way lit by antique iron lamps that were added during an early 1990s renovation that restored the ballpark to its 1930s glory. For several decades the field's most distinguishing feature was its sheer size. Throughout its days as a minor-league venue, Engel Stadium's centerfield fence measured a distant 471 feet from home plate. Recently though, an intermediary fence less than 400 feet from the plate was installed to make the field more appropriate for amateur play. The effect is similar to that at Yankee Stadium, where the original leftfield fence still stands at the back of Monument Park, while a shorter, nearer fence cuts in front of it.

Engel Stadium's principal occupant these days is Tennessee's Temple University baseball team. The Crusaders, who play a National Association of Intercollegiate Athletics (NAIA) schedule, use the field for their home games and practices. Beginning in early February and continuing through April, the field offers a busy slate of weekday doubleheaders that typically start at 1:00 P.M. At least once per season, the Engel Stadium lights are turned on and the Crusaders square off against their crosstown rivals, the Covenant College Scots, to see who will claim the Mayor's Cup.

★ ★ ★

=38=

CROSLEY FIELD REPLICA

Blue Ash Sports Center | 11540 Grooms Road | Blue Ash, Ohio

Fans who seek out the location of Cincinnati's fabled Crosley Field at the corner of Findlay Street and Western Avenue will be disappointed to find only a small plaque and a few old stadium chairs marking the site at what is now an industrial park. However, just twelve miles northeast of Cincinnati in the town of Blue Ash, fans can explore a classy tribute to the park that served as the hub of Cincinnati's hardball heroics from 1912 until the middle of the 1970 season.

Crosley Field scoreboard

The Crosley Field replica in Blue Ash, which was built in 1988, mirrors the old park's field dimensions right down to the famous 4-foot-high incline that gently rises between medium-depth leftfield and the home-run fence. It also features a five-story-high reconstruction of the old park's scoreboard above the fence in left. Except for the line score, which is left blank so that the board can serve a useful purpose when the field hosts amateur games, the scoreboard is frozen in time, bearing the same appearance as it did when the last big-league pitch was thrown at Crosley in June of 1970. The uniform numbers and fielding positions of the home team and visiting San Francisco Giants appear in the order of each team's lineup that day, while the out-of-town scores of the day are also displayed. There is also a square-faced Longines clock mounted atop the scoreboard, just like the one that existed for so many years at Crosley. To complete the old-time effect, some of the original ticket booths and more than 400 stadium chairs from the original Crosley Field are set around the infield. No, the old stadium facade and grandstands have not been reproduced. This is a community rec field, mind you, not a big-league facility.

In addition to this fine Crosley Field replica, the 37-acre Blue Ash Sports Center includes swimming pools, an amphitheater, soccer fields, tennis and basketball courts, and ten other baseball fields, including one that replicates the cookie-cutter field dimensions of Crosley's successor, Riverfront Stadium.

Clearly, though, the Crosley Field replica is the main attraction in Blue Ash. While the field sees its most regular use as the home park of the Moeller High School baseball team, it also hosts occasional Reds old-timers' games. Autographed plaques hang behind the home dugout honoring such Cincinnati legends as Johnny Bench, Dave Concepcion, George Foster, Dave Parker, and Pete Rose who have stopped by Blue Ash to take their old positions at Crosley one last time. A larger plaque remembers the original Crosley Field, reading, IN THE HEART OF THE WEST END, NESTLED AMONGST THE HILLS THAT SURROUND CINCINNATI WAS A PLACE WHERE FOR YEARS PEOPLE YOUNG AND OLD PERIODICALLY CONGREGATED BY THE THOUSANDS . . . CROSLEY FIELD.

Indeed, Crosley Field struck an iconic presence in the Queen City during its long reign. Baseball had been played at the corner of Findlay and Western dating back to 1884, when the stadium was known as League Park. After a fire in 1902 destroyed the facility, it was rebuilt and renamed the Palace of the Fans. After another fire, ten years later, the stadium was rebuilt using concrete and steel. Cincinnati opened its new park the same month Boston unveiled Fenway Park and Detroit inaugurated Tiger Stadium. Of the three additions to the big-league landscape, Crosley, which would be called Redland Field until being renamed in honor of Reds owner Powel Crosley in 1933, was the smallest, offering just 20,000 seats in its cozy double-decked grandstand.

While Crosley provided a backdrop for many historic moments—including eight no-hitters, two All-Star games, four of the games played during the controversial 1919 World Series, and parts of three other World Series—it is best remembered as the place where night baseball made its major-league debut on May 24, 1935. Seeking to increase attendance in the midst of the Great Depression, the Reds installed light towers and invited President Franklin Delano Roosevelt to throw the ceremonial "first switch" to light up the Cincinnati sky. After the lights flickered on, the Reds posted a 2–1 win over the Philadelphia Phillies.

★ ★ ★

= 39 =

OZZIE'S RESTAURANT AND SPORTS BAR

645 Westport Plaza | St. Louis, Missouri

St. Louis's reputation as one of the best baseball towns in the country is certainly well deserved. The Cardinals have notched more World Series trophies than any team in the nonpinstriped division and through the generations have featured some of the game's most iconic stars. The Gateway City's baseball reputation involves something more than the local team's ten World Series trophies and fifteen player plaques at the Hall of Fame, though. It also involves the fans. The men and women who transformed the old Busch Stadium's stands into a sea of red on a nightly basis for four decades and who now similarly color the seats at the new Busch Stadium are a special breed of baseball aficionado. Unlike the equally renowned hardball fanatics in East Coast cities like Boston, New York, and Philadelphia, whose passion often takes the form of booing and jeering when the home team doesn't perform as expected, Cardinals fans are regaled for their undying support of their team. Through good times and bad, these friendly folks are always behind their boys of summer. That doesn't mean they're not as passionate as their fickle baseball

brethren on the Atlantic Coast. They're just more philosophical about the inevitable ups and downs presented by any long baseball season.

Given the nature of the relationship between the Red Birds and their fans, it should come as little surprise that there are three restaurants in town that are associated with former Cardinals players. These joints—affiliated with Al Hrabosky, Mike Shannon, and Ozzie Smith—all offer their own collections of Cardinals memorabilia and their own ways for fans to connect to the home team. They are all excellent at what they do, but when it comes time to watch the big game, Ozzie's Restaurant and Sports Bar is the venue of choice among rank-and-file Cardinals fans. Indeed, on the day the Cards clinched the 2006 World Series against the Tigers, baseball luminaries like Willie McGee, Whitey Herzog, and Reggie Jackson were on hand to watch the game with the restaurant's namesake and a throng of fans, many of whom waited in a long line outside to get in.

Ozzie's has more than fifty TVs; an expansive pub menu that includes that St. Louis favorite, toasted raviolis; and walls lavished

Bat standings at Ozzie's Restaurant

with Cardinals jerseys and photos. A whole wall displays images from Ozzie's Hall of Fame induction day at Cooperstown, while another chronicles Mark McGwire's seventy-homer season in 1998. Baseball bats on another wall reflect the standings in all six of baseball's divisions. Most impressively of all, though, fans will find all thirteen of Ozzie Smith's Gold Glove awards arranged in a vertical display case.

Fans looking for a meal on the pricier end of the dining-out spectrum should visit **Mike Shannon's Steaks and Seafood** (620 Market Street). Shannon was the starting right-fielder for the Cardinals when they won the World Series in 1964 and the starting third baseman when they won the World Series in 1967. After retiring in 1971, he moved into the Cardinals broadcast booth, where he has been a mainstay ever since. Besides working for the Cardinals radio network, Shannon owns this trendy restaurant, which features a trademark "tower of baseballs" in its main dining room. The four-sided floor-to-ceiling display showcases autographed balls from just about every notable Cardinals player over the past four decades. Meanwhile, autographed bats flank the fireplace, and Cardinals photos adorn the walls. There are also three separate function rooms, each of which is named after, and decorated with memorabilia depicting, a famous Cardinals player: the Stan Musial Room, the Bob Gibson Room, and the Albert Pujols Room. Prominent members of the Cardinals organization like manager Tony La Russa and general manager Walt Jockety are regular dinner guests, and Shannon himself stops by after Friday-night home games to broadcast a postgame show from the restaurant.

Finally, for some fun on the wild side, Cardinals fans head to **Al Hrabosky's Ballpark Saloon** (800 Cerre Street). The "Mad Hungarian" spent eight of his thirteen big-league seasons in a Cardinals uniform, none finer than the 1975 campaign when he went 13-3 with a National League–leading 22 saves for the eventual world champs. Since 1985 Hrabosky has worked as the color commentator on Cardinals television broadcasts, and since 2004 he and his wife have owned this lively club near Busch Stadium.

★ ★ ★

= **40** =

CENTENNIAL FIELD

University of Vermont campus | Colchester Avenue | Burlington, Vermont

Depending upon whom they ask, inquiring fans are apt to get a number of different answers to the question, which is America's oldest minor-league ballpark? The topic inevitably leads to debates concerning what qualifications should apply to make a park eligible for consideration. How extensive a renovation can a stadium undergo before it becomes a "new" stadium? Does a stadium's "life" date back to its first minor-league game or to its first use as a baseball field at any level? Is it enough for an old-time yard to host just one game a year, while the local nine plays the rest of its schedule elsewhere? And so on.

It is not this author's intent to weigh in on which minor-league stadium has the right to call itself the nation's oldest. So I will simply say that Burlington's Centennial Field offers as charming an old-time environment as fans will find anywhere, one that seems better suited for what the quintessential minor-league experience must have been in the 1930s than what it is today. The narrow wooden seats pack fannies tightly together in four grandstand sections behind home plate. Steel pillars rise up intermittently to support a low roof. A press box barely big enough to hold the public-address announcer and the local radio broadcaster sits

Centennial Field scoreboard

behind the last row in back of home plate. On either side of the grandstand, two sections of concrete bleachers provide excellent views to cushion-bearing fans. A small scoreboard appears on the back of the adjacent football field's bleachers in left, while the rest of the outfield view showcases lush green trees. On a summer night a refreshing breeze blows through the park off nearby Lake Champlain. The environment is pristine, the crack of the bat is always audible,

and the focus is on the game, where it belongs. This is bush-league baseball the way it surely was meant to be.

Centennial Field opened as a college field on April 17, 1906, when the University of Vermont beat the University of Maine 10–4. The field was named at that time in honor of the one hundredth anniversary of UVM's first graduating class. Seven years later the wooden grandstand burned to the ground, prompting the installation of "temporary" wooden bleachers that stood for more than a decade. Finally, in 1922 UVM constructed a new concrete-and-steel grandstand. Today this structure appears almost exactly as it did then.

According to UVM, Centennial Field is "currently honored with the distinction of being the oldest complete grandstand structure in use in minor-league baseball." The university's promotional materials dutifully point out, however, that Centennial Field's history as a *minor-league* venue is relatively brief compared to the histories that many other bush-league stadiums can boast. During its first three decades, Centennial Field was used almost exclusively as a college field, excepting the occasional exhibitions that brought to town big leaguers like Smokey Joe Wood, Harry Hooper, Tris Speaker, Larry Gardner, and Ray Collins. From 1936 through 1950, the ballpark hosted a semipro Northern League team. In 1955 Burlington joined the affiliated minor leagues for the first time when the Kansas City A's sent their Class C prospects to Burlington to play in the Provincial League. When that circuit went out of business after just one season, Burlington returned to being solely a college-baseball town; and Centennial Field lost that distinction too when UVM discontinued its varsity baseball program in the 1960s.

Baseball bounced back in Burlington, though, and today it thrives. UVM reinstated baseball in the 1970s; then in 1984 minor-league baseball returned to the Green Mountain State when a Cincinnati Reds' Double-A team brought the Eastern League to Burlington. The local franchise switched to an affiliation with the Seattle Mariners in 1988, just in time to welcome Ken Griffey Jr. and Omar Vizquel to Centennial Field. The eighteen-year-old Griffey batted .279 with 2 HR and 10 RBI in seventeen games for Vermont, while the twenty-one-year-old Vizquel wowed fans with flashy defense and stole 30 bases.

The Mariners affiliation lasted just that one season, though, and from 1989 through 1993 the city was left without a minor-league team again. But Burlington's fortunes turned in 1994, when the short-season New York–Penn League dispatched a Montreal Expos affiliate to Centennial Field. The city's membership in the league and its player-development relationship with the franchise that would become the Washington Nationals continue to this day. The Vermont Lake Monsters attract more than 3,000 fans a game to 4,400-seat Centennial Field, more than enough to ensure that minor-league ball will remain in Burlington.

The Lake Monsters' season begins in mid-June and continues through the first week of September. And in March, April, and May the UVM Catamounts, who play about fifteen home games a year, offer fans another reason to visit Burlington. Both older fans who remember what the minor leagues used to be like and younger fans who have no such memories but would like to find out should make a point to visit Burlington to experience the pastoral beauty of Centennial Field.

=41=

CHAPPELL'S RESTAURANT & SPORTS MUSEUM

323 Armour Road | North Kansas City, Missouri

Just a short ride from Kaufman Stadium, fans can find the largest collection of sports memorabilia housed in any bar or restaurant in the United States. Since opening in 1986, Chappell's Restaurant & Sports Museum has steadily expanded its physical dimensions and its sports collection to the point where it now includes more than 10,000 items. Clearly, the place is a labor of love for owner Jim Chappell, a long-time friend of former Kansas City and Oakland A's owner Charlie O. Finley, who delights in leading first-time visitors from wall to wall, while providing background information on his collection's most interesting pieces.

Some of the articles on display date back to Mr. Chappell's boyhood days, when he first started collecting. Others have been purchased since the restaurant opened. There's the pair of boxing gloves that Muhammad Ali autographed; the three helmets that Joe Montana donated—one each from his days with Notre Dame, the San Francisco 49ers, and the Kansas City Chiefs; Olympic torches from two different Olympic Games; the trunks worn by Sylvester Stallone in *Rocky*; Super Bowl rings; team pennants; antique athletic equipment; scores of autographed jerseys; and more.

For traveling baseball fans, Chappell's most interesting item is the 1974 World Series trophy, a keepsake from Finley, who apparently had trophies to spare after his rough-and-tumble A's won their third title in a row, beating the Dodgers. Also noteworthy are baseballs autographed by diamond kings like Babe Ruth, Ty Cobb, Dizzy Dean, and dozens of others; vintage baseball uniforms; a beautiful LeRoy Neiman painting of George Brett that is autographed by both the artist and the subject; Chesterfield cigarette posters featuring Ted Williams and Stan Musial—and that's just the tip of the iceberg. The best bet is for patrons to arrive early, order a cold drink, and amble around for a while before settling down at a table or barstool. That's one of the nice things about Chappell's: it is laid out in a way that leaves room for visitors to wander without getting in the way of the staff or dinner guests.

Chappell's, which was recently named one of the best sports bars in the country by no less an authority than *Sports Illustrated*, attracts visitors from around the country. In addition to serving as a restaurant, sports bar, and museum, it also functions as a college classroom when students and faculty members from Northwest Missouri State stop by for their weekly Sports Memorabilia class. Chappell's is open Monday through Thursday from 11:00 A.M. to 10:00 P.M. and on Friday and Saturday from 11:00 to 11:00. There is no admission charge for those wishing to check out the sports artifacts, but hungry road-trippers will likely find it hard to leave without dropping a few dollars after getting a glimpse (and whiff) of such trademark menu items as the half-pound hamburgers, filet mignons wrapped in bacon, and delicious Kansas City strip steaks.

★ ★ ★

=42=

THE IVAN ALLEN JR. BRAVES MUSEUM

Turner Field | Hank Aaron Drive | Atlanta, Georgia

As baseball's popularity has boomed in recent years, many big-league teams have sought to capitalize on the seemingly endless reserve of fan interest in the game by reinventing their stadiums as year-round attractions. Rather than welcoming fans through their gates on only eighty-one special dates per season, these facilities today offer visitors a bevy of baseball experiences to enjoy even when the home team is on a road trip or in the middle of its off-season. The stadium that does the best at engaging and entertaining fans when there's no baseball to be played is Turner Field. In fact, a game-day visit to the ballpark in Atlanta allows fans scarcely enough time to take in all of the peripheral attractions that Turner has to offer. To get the full Turner Field experience, it is almost necessary to spend one day at the park when the Braves *are* playing and one when they *aren't*.

After passing through Monument Grove—an exterior plaza laden with monuments, plaques, and sculptures that celebrate legendary Braves like Eddie Mathews, Warren Spahn, Hank Aaron, Phil Niekro, and Dale Murphy—fans arrive at the Ivan Allen Jr. Braves Museum, which, like the plaza before it, pays tribute to all three distinct eras of Braves history: Boston (1871–1952), Milwaukee (1953–1965), and Atlanta (1966–present). The Boston section is highlighted by a beautiful mural of the South End Grounds, which from 1871 through 1915 served as the home field of the franchise that would eventually come to be known as the Braves. In those earliest days of National League baseball, the Boston club went by a variety of names, including the Beaneaters,

Championship lockers at the Braves Museum

Bees, Doves, Red Stockings, and Rustlers, as illustrated by the museum's "What's in a Name?" exhibit. This part of the museum also includes photographs and artifacts related to the Braves' involvement in the 1914 and 1948 World Series, which they won and lost, respectively.

Another exhibit from the early years details Babe Ruth's final twenty-eight major-league games, which he spent with the Braves in 1935. Another exhibit honors Braves players who served in the military, displaying, among other items, the Purple Heart that Spahn was awarded after suffering a foot injury in Germany during World War II.

As for the Milwaukee section, the highlight is a 26-foot-long section of an original B&O railroad car, just like the ones the big leaguers rode between cities in the 1950s. Visitors can walk through the car to get a better sense of what a player's life was like before the advent of the luxury charter and stretch limo. Another exhibit in this section of the museum celebrates the Braves' 1957 World Series win with photographs of key team members like Lew Burdette, Spahn, Aaron, and others.

The Atlanta section displays a dugout bench from Atlanta–Fulton County Stadium, the ball that Hank Aaron smacked over the leftfield fence at that park to surpass Ruth on the all-time home-run ledger, Murphy's 1982 and 1983 National League MVP trophies, the Braves' 1995 World Series trophy, and a locker of mementos related to each of the seasons—between 1991 and 2005—during

which the Braves won a record fourteen straight division titles.

The museum also houses the Braves Hall of Fame, which honors the expected cast of famous players, as well as former Braves owner Ted Turner and popular television commentator Skip Caray. Nearby, the Braves Leader Board—a giant scoreboard that tracks the team's all-time leaders in a variety of hitting and pitching categories—receives continual updates.

After perusing the museum's many interesting exhibits, visitors can take the hour-long Turner Field Tour. One stop that is unlike any place fans will encounter at the other big-league ballparks is Scouts Alley. The interactive attraction offers computer kiosks that fans use to recall the old scouting reports related to nearly two hundred current and former Braves. Did the scouts have future Atlanta stars like Murphy and Greg Maddux pegged for greatness back when they were still in the minor leagues? Why did the Atlanta brain trust so aggressively pursue pitchers like Mike Hampton and Paul Byrd? Did a young Andruw Jones project to be a member of baseball's fifty-homer club someday? A visit to Scouts Alley answers these questions and countless others.

Another bright spot along the tour is found upstairs on the third deck, where the Coca-Cola Sky Field offers a base path where fans can test their speed running from home to first and where they can marvel at a 38-foot-tall Coke bottle made entirely of baseball bats, gloves, balls, cleats, catcher's gear, pitching rubbers, and other pieces of baseball equipment. The tour also takes fans into the press box and broadcast booth, into a luxury box, and down to the clubhouses and dugouts.

During games, the museum is open to ticket holders only at a cost of $2.00. For those visiting on off days during the season or before a night game, it is open from 9:00 A.M. to 3:00 P.M., and visitors pay $5.00 to visit the museum or $10.00 to visit the museum and take the tour. During the off-season, the museum is open Monday through Saturday from 10:00 A.M. to 2:00 P.M., and the tours start every hour.

★ ★ ★

= 43 =

MAVERICKS STADIUM

12000 Stadium Way | Adelanto, California

Given the recent proliferation of new stadium-construction projects across the country, it is difficult for today's traveling fan to pass through the turnstiles of a previously unvisited ballpark and not be, in some way, reminded of a previous visit to some other park. Observant bush-league travelers have surely noted the recurrence of familiar ballpark designs, such as the old-time model with its covered-grandstand; the more modern, sunken-field walk-around-concourse approach, with its unobstructed sightlines and easy access to concessions; and the double-decked miniature big-league-stadium concept, with its cement-centric design.

At the same time, fans have surely noticed similarities in the types of neighborhoods where communities have chosen to build their hardball havens. For years the just-outside-the-city stadium was in vogue, with its pastoral wall of green trees running above the outfield fences, while more recently communities have begun building their baseball parks downtown again, perhaps in the hope of sparking an urban renewal in their city, or on the waterfront, to showcase the local river or bay and, whenever possible, a scenic bridge or two as well.

Indeed, it is next to impossible for the well-traveled fan to happen upon a minor-league venue that provides a game-day setting completely unlike some other one he has encountered previously. But 75 miles northeast of Los Angeles, in the southern part of the Mohave Desert, there is just such a place. Here, the High Desert Mavericks and their California League opponents take to the field in an environment that is derivative and reminiscent of none other in the professional baseball

Mavericks Stadium

universe. Mavericks Stadium shines like an oasis of green grass and red clay amidst an otherworldly panorama of sand dunes, tumbleweed, desert sage, and scraggly Joshua trees. This stark landscape, known for its brilliant sunsets and majestic mountain views, provides a backdrop for a game that is as beautiful as it is unique. Beyond the fence in left, the massive support stanchions of some nearby power lines loom prominently over the field, while in center and right, distant buttes rise above the miles of uninterrupted desert between them and the ballpark.

In the thin desert air, which often reaches temperatures greater than 100 degrees Fahrenheit during the summer, solidly struck baseballs, and even those not so solidly hit, travel great distances. Adelanto's altitude, at more than half a mile above sea level, conspires with the heat to turn normally routine fly balls into home runs and to make a hitter's paradise of Mavericks Stadium. Thus, hearty fans able to weather the afternoon heat and swarms of scurrying reptiles in the stadium parking lot enjoy high-scoring games at this enchantingly alien baseball location. As the sun sinks below the horizon, the ballpark further asserts its originality. Not only does the temperature drop precipitously, often falling into the 60s, but the ballpark becomes engulfed in a darker, quieter sort of night than at any other minor-league stadium, owing to its remote location.

As for the facility itself, Mavericks Stadium is cozy, with a seating capacity of just 3,800, but certainly large enough to support the 2,000 or so spectators who turn out to root for the local California League team. The seats run between the corner bases, sunken neatly below the concourse. Above the concourse, a peaked awning provides much-needed shade for the folks at ground level,

and the slim pillars that support the awning create less wind resistance than a traditional stadium facade would. This allows for free and easy airflow during the twilight hours, when a breeze sweeps across the desert, bringing relief to fans.

The stadium was built by Adelanto for $6.5 million and opened just in time to welcome the Riverside Red Wave to town in 1991. Although former Kansas City Royals star George Brett owns the Mavericks along with two of his brothers, High Desert ended its affiliation with the Kansas City organization in 2007 to begin a new player development contract with the Seattle Mariners.

=44=

THE TY COBB MUSEUM

The Joe A. Adams Professional Building | 461 Cook Street | Royston, Georgia

Although fans and fellow players viewed him as a misanthrope throughout his twenty-four-year big-league career, in his retirement Ty Cobb distinguished himself as one of baseball's first great philanthropists. He donated hundreds of thousands of dollars to a scholarship fund for students from his home state of Georgia, and he contributed more than $100,000 to build a hospital in his hometown of Royston. Since opening as a twenty-four-bed facility in 1950, Cobb Memorial Hospital has grown

to become the Ty Cobb Healthcare System, which today includes multiple hospitals, convalescent homes, and clinics throughout northeastern Georgia. Fittingly, the original Cobb medical campus includes a museum that honors the life and times of the "Georgia Peach."

Cobb never earned more than $40,000 in any season as a ballplayer, but he was a savvy businessman who had made himself into a multimillionaire by the time he retired in 1928 at the age of 41. His shrewdest move

Sign welcoming visitors to Ty Cobb's hometown of Royston

was investing in Georgia-based beverage company Coca-Cola. After serving as a Coca-Cola spokesman for a few years early in his career, Cobb took out a loan against his future earnings as a player and bought his first one thousand shares of company stock in 1918. Later, his wealth would allow him to buy three of the company's bottling plants, and by the time of his death in 1961 his estate would be worth nearly $12 million.

The Ty Cobb Museum opened on July 17, 1998, on the thirty-seventh anniversary of Cobb's death. Its mission is "to foster education and understanding to the broadest possible audience of the greatest baseball hitter of all time, Tyrus Raymond Cobb." In other words, it endeavors to introduce fans to a kinder, gentler Cobb than the overly aggressive, racist bully he is often portrayed as in contemporary films, literature, and history books. The museum succeeds in this regard, as well as in honoring the on-field accomplishments of a man who led the American League in batting twelve times, collected 4,191 lifetime hits, and posted a career batting average of .366—better than anyone else who has ever played.

Some of the museum's most interesting artifacts include a set of Cobb's dentures, his Shriner's fez, one of his fielding gloves, his childhood Bible, one of his hunting rifles, and the medallion he was awarded in 1907 for winning the first of what would be nine consecutive batting titles. There is also a display of more than one hundred bats that collectively honor the members of the museum's "Century Club," those who have donated at least $100 apiece to support its efforts.

An exhibit entitled "The Cobb Style of Baseball" pays tribute to Cobb's all-out approach to the game, offering several large cutouts of him in action. One of these captures Cobb chopping at a ball with his unorthodox choked-up hands-apart swing; another catches him squaring around to lay down a bunt; another, sliding past a catcher's tag to steal home— something he did thirty-five times. Also popular is the museum's theater, which presents a thoughtful video tribute to Cobb that combines archival video footage and photos with commentary from baseball luminaries like Peter Gammons and Chipper Jones.

The museum is open Monday through Friday from 9:00 A.M. to 4:00 P.M. and Saturday from 10:00 to 4:00. Admission costs $5.00 for adults, $4.00 for senior citizens, and $3.00 for students. Other points of interest in Royston include the Cobb family mausoleum at **Rosehill Cemetery** (Route 17 South) and the Cobb statue at **Royston City Hall** (634 Franklin Springs Street).

While it would be historically naïve to adopt an image of Cobb as an entirely benevolent hero of the game's early years, it would also be inaccurate, as this fine museum in Royston points out, to write him off as a one-dimensional figure without any redeeming qualities. A trip to Royston does much to enhance fans' understanding of this complex character, who in his day was considered an even bigger star than Babe Ruth.

★ ★ ★

=45=
JOE DiMAGGIO'S ITALIAN CHOPHOUSE

601 Union Street | San Francisco, California

Although Martinez, California, gets to bill itself as the "birthplace" of Joe DiMaggio, the truth is that the little future Yankee Clipper spent only his first year in Martinez before moving with his family to San Francisco's North Beach neighborhood. Today an upscale restaurant in North Beach

not only bears DiMaggio's name but also reflects the class and meticulous attention to detail with which he always carried himself. Joe DiMaggio's Italian Chophouse opened in 2006, featuring a dark wooden interior, elegant chandeliers, an upscale menu, and an extensive wine list that includes more

Booth with Marilyn Monroe photo at Joe DiMaggio's Restaurant

than 225 selections. And most importantly of all, as far as baseball fans are concerned, the Chophouse offers a wealth of DiMaggio memorabilia on its walls. There are photographs of Joe posing with his Yankee teammates; with his celebrity friends like Toots Shor and Frank Sinatra; and with his wife, Marilyn Monroe.

DiMaggio's is owned and operated by Dundum Sports & Entertainment, which specializes in celebrity-themed restaurants like Bing Crosby's (Walnut Creek), Willie McCovey's (Walnut Creek), and Center Court with Chris Webber (Sacramento). Joltin' Joe's joint is the most upscale of DSE's restaurants and features the best collection of old photographs. Some feature Joe in fancy clothes with the aforementioned fellow celebrities, while others are old game shots, and still others are family photos.

As for the menu, it offers many nods to DiMaggio's Italian heritage and to his life story. A fisherman's son, Joe would no doubt approve of the Sicilian Fisherman's Stew, which combines lobster, mussels, clams, shrimp, and chunks of white fish in a buttery base. It's hard to say what Joe would think of the tiramisu, which comes topped by a piece of chocolate shaped in the familiar silhouette of Marilyn. Other specialties include an assortment of thick-cut aged Midwestern steaks, homemade sausages, and rabbit three ways.

As the story goes, Joe dropped out of high school at the age of sixteen to play semipro baseball. By 1933 he was starting in the out-field for the Pacific Coast League San Francisco Seals. After hitting in 61 straight games that year and then struggling through an injury-plagued 1934 campaign, he batted a staggering .398 in 1935, clubbing 34 home runs, collecting 154 RBIs, and leading the Seals to the league title. For his efforts, he earned circuit MVP honors and a shot at the big leagues. The Seals sold his contract to the Yankees, and the next season Joe played in 138 games, batting .323 with 29 homers and 125 RBIs. And his Hall of Fame career was under way.

Today diners in the Bay Area reconnect with this American hero as they gaze at the images of him on the walls and eat their meals. Regular visitors to DiMaggio's include current Giants owner Peter McGowan, fellow icon Willie Mays, and actor Bill Murray.

★ ★ ★

= 46 =

CARDINAL GIBBONS SCHOOL

3225 Wilkens Avenue | Baltimore, Maryland

From the top row of Section 355 at Oriole Park, the eagle-eyed fan can spot the smokestack of the Cardinal Gibbons School—better known to baseball fans as St. Mary's Industrial School for Boys, as it was called when Babe Ruth spent his childhood and teenage years on campus. If this distant glimpse, coupled perhaps with a visit before or after the game to the Babe Ruth Birthplace and Museum, piques your interest in all things Bambino, the school is just a 3-mile drive west of Camden Yards.

The institution might well be called "The

School that Ruth Built," owing to a fundraising drive the Sultan of Swat championed in the 1930s to rebuild it after it had been ravaged by fire. Ruth and friends mustered more than $100,000 to outfit St. Mary's with the stone building visitors find on its grounds today. In Ruth's day St. Mary's was an orphanage and reform school for unruly boys whose parents couldn't control them. Today Cardinal Gibbons is a highly respected Catholic middle school and high school for local boys.

Although Ruth's life and career after St. Mary's would be characterized by his immense appetite for pleasures of many kinds and by his unapologetic disregard for many of society's mores, there is no doubt that his twelve years at the school turned his life around. When the Baby Babe entered St. Mary's at age seven, he was an incorrigible lad who seemed destined, even at that young age, to live a life of corruption. When he left the school at nineteen, he was a young man who had found a father figure and role model in Brother Matthias, who refused to give up on Ruth and who shared with him his love of baseball—and the young Ruth had a clear idea of what he wanted to do with his life: he wanted to be a ballplayer. Many historians have pointed to the time that Ruth spent at St. Mary's as the origin of the great affection for children he demonstrated throughout his later life. Each time Ruth would make time to visit a sick or neglected child, according to this school of thought, he saw a bit of his former self in the youngster and hoped that a bit of the Brother Matthias in him would shine through to the child.

During the 1950s St. Mary's closed its doors for a while, before it reopened in the early 1960s as Cardinal Gibbons. It continues to be run by the Christian Brothers, who provide local boys in grades six through twelve with a top-notch education. Baseball, of course, is still a big part of the school's extracurricular activities. The varsity and junior varsity squads play on the very grounds where Ruth honed his skills as a catcher and pitcher. Interestingly, during his days as a backstop, Ruth would catch and throw the ball with his right hand, because the school didn't own a left-handed catcher's mitt. Today the Cardinal Gibbons Crusaders, who have plenty of equipment for both their right-handed and left-handed players, begin play at Babe Ruth Field during the first week of March and conclude in mid-May, with weekday games typically beginning at 3:30 P.M. As part of their schedule, the Crusaders host an annual four-team tournament known as the "Babe Ruth Classic." While the field may be the very one on which Ruth played, it is worth noting that the orientation of home plate has changed. In Ruth's day the location of home plate was out in what is now centerfield.

= 47 =

THE ST. LOUIS CARDINALS HALL OF FAME MUSEUM

Seventh Street and Walnut Street | St. Louis, Missouri

An already excellent baseball attraction promises to become even better when the St. Louis Cardinals Hall of Fame Museum moves from its present location within the International Bowling Hall of Fame to new digs being built especially for it at the St. Louis Ballpark Village. The $650 million mixed-use residential and commercial neighborhood will occupy the six city blocks where the old Busch Stadium stood. Though the village won't be entirely finished until 2011, entertainment venues like the Cardinals museum, a new aquarium, and several baseball-themed restaurants should be ready by mid-2009, when the Cardinals are scheduled to host the All-Star Game.

Among the exhibits that will surely make the move from the museum's current 5,000 square feet of space to the facility more than two times that size awaiting it are ones commemorating each of the Cardinals' National League–record seventeen pennants; the nine players whose numbers have been retired by the team—Ozzie Smith, Red Schoendienst, Stan Musial, Enos Slaughter, Ken Boyer, Dizzy Dean, Lou Brock, Bruce Sutter, Bob Gibson, and Rogers Hornsby, who played in an era before uniform numbers

were worn but is still honored; the American League St. Louis Browns, who played in St. Louis from 1902 through 1953; the Negro League St. Louis Stars, who played in the city in the 1920s and 1930s; Browns Hall of Famer George Sisler; the 1944 Streetcar Series between the Cardinals and Browns; and the Gashouse Gang Cards of the 1930s.

Some of the most interesting artifacts are models of Sportsman's Park and the old Busch Stadium, as well as stadium chairs and lockers from the two old yards; the Cardinals' World Championship trophies from 1967, 1982, and 2006; a silk handkerchief that was among the ones given to female fans of the American Association St. Louis Browns (a precursor of the Cardinals) on Opening Day of the 1887 season; the red 1962 Corvette the Cardinals presented to Mark McGwire after he hit his sixty-second home run of the 1998 season; a bench made entirely of McGwire's old bats; Bob Gibson's shower sandals; the dirty hat reliever Steve Kline wore in 2001 when he set a team record by pitching in eighty-nine games; the shin guards Yadier Molina wore during the 2004 season; the batting helmet Albert Pujols wore in 2006; and scores of

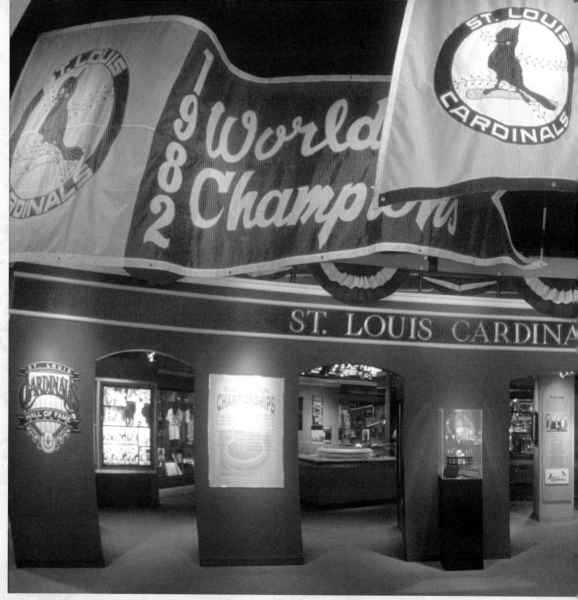

St. Louis Cardinals Hall of Fame

old photographs, game programs, baseball cards, pennants, posters, trophies, and other trinkets.

When completed, the 12-acre Ballpark Village will include 450,000 square feet of retail and restaurant space, 300,000 square feet of office space, 1,200 luxury condos, and 2,000 parking spaces, in addition to the aquarium and the Cardinals museum. The city within a city will sit adjacent to the new Busch Stadium, which opened in 2006. In the meantime, traveling fans will continue to enjoy an odd two-fer, as a single admission charge covers entry into both the baseball and bowling wings of the present museum. Laugh if you'd like, but there's no denying

that bowling is one of the world's most popular sports, if not to watch, then to play. The bowling wing traces the history of the sport back 5,000 years to a game played by the ancient Egyptians, up through the modern era, when more than ninety-five million people enjoy bowling each year in more than ninety countries.

From October through March, the museum is open Tuesday through Saturday, from 11:00 A.M. to 4:00 P.M. During the baseball season, it is open seven days a week, from 9:00 to 5:00, and it stays open until 6:30 on days when the Cardinals have a home game. Admission costs $7.50 for adults and $6.00 for children.

THE RIPKEN CENTER

Long Drive | Aberdeen, Maryland

Along Interstate 95, in the hometown of Hall of Famer Cal Ripken Jr., baseball fans will find a hardball tourist attraction that has a little bit of everything. To begin, there's a minor-league ballpark, Ripken Stadium, which serves as the home of the New York–Penn League Aberdeen Ironbirds. The short-season affiliate of— you guessed it—the Baltimore Orioles, the Ironbirds are owned by baseball's most durable iron man, who spent his entire twenty-one-year career with the O's. In addition to this state-of-the-art bush-league ballpark, the 110-acre Ripken Center also features four replica parks on its grounds, each modeled to look like a different scaled-down version of a favorite major-league stadium. Collectively, these fields serve the Ripken Youth Baseball Academy, which hosts camps and clinics from March through November and welcomes teams from across the country and around the world to the Cal Ripken World Series each August.

The Ironbirds have sold out every one of their home games since 2002, when they made their New York–Penn League debut and opened 6,300-seat **Ripken Stadium**. In fact, rather than waning as the team's novelty has worn off, the waiting list for season tickets in Aberdeen has grown, to the point where it today includes nearly 2,000 members. Ripken Stadium, widely praised for its distinctive redbrick facade and delicious blue shell crabs, is the current home of the **Ripken Museum**, located on its Club level. Eventually, the plan is to move the museum to a separate multimillion-dollar facility that will be built elsewhere on the complex, but more fundraising has to take place first. In the meantime, the museum is open to Club-level ticket holders during games and is open to the general public during business hours otherwise. The exhibits recall the career of Cal Ripken Sr., complete with Dad's old glove and catcher's gear, as well as the careers of Cal Jr. and his brother and one-time double-play partner Billy. Endeavoring to be a teaching tool for children, the museum showcases large banners that display facts about the Negro Leagues, baseball's place in American culture, and the history of baseball in Maryland.

Across the street from Ripken Stadium, the Youth Academy is also open to the public during daytime hours. The main attraction is **Cal Sr.'s Yard**, a scaled-down replica of

Cal Sr.'s Yard at the Ripken Center

Oriole Park at Camden Yards. In addition to copying the brick facade of Oriole Park and the outfield flag court, Cal Sr.'s Yard has its very own B&O Warehouse looming behind the rightfield fence. The privately owned building beyond the ballpark is a Marriott Courtyard Hotel, which is full each August when the twelve-year-old-and-under division of Babe Ruth League Baseball plays its two-week championship tournament at the Ripken complex. More than 700,000 children play on nearly 70,000 teams worldwide in this level of the Babe Ruth League annually, but only the top fifteen teams—ten from the United States and five from overseas—earn

tickets to Aberdeen to compete in the World Series. While the tournament has yet to reach the stature of the Little League World Series, it has grown quite a bit since its inception in 1999 and is beginning to attract the type of media and television coverage more commonly associated with the Williamsport classic.

In addition to Cal Sr.'s Yard, the Youth Academy offers fields that mimic Baltimore's Memorial Stadium, the converted football field that was the home of the Orioles from 1954 to 1991; Fenway Park, with a miniature Green Monster in leftfield; and Wrigley Field, with ivy on the outfield walls.

= 49 =

THE YOGI BERRA MUSEUM AND LEARNING CENTER

Montclair State University | 8 Quarry Road | Little Falls, New Jersey

When the topic of baseball's most colorful characters comes up, most fans agree that Yogi Berra's name belongs at the top of the list. And that's saying something. After all, we're talking about a game that has given rise to such legendary oddballs as Dizzy Dean, who once bought a service station in Bradenton, Florida, on a whim and spent an entire spring training pumping gas; Jimmy Piersall, who once ran around the bases backwards after hitting a home run; Mark Fidrych, who carried on

detailed conversations with baseballs before throwing them; Bill Lee, who spent an entire season characterizing his manager, Don Zimmer, as a "gerbil" to Boston sports reporters; Steve Lyons, who once dropped his trousers in front of 33,000 fans so he could shake the dirt out of his underwear after diving into a base; and scores of other eccentrics.

As for the former Yankees catcher whose goofy persona inspired Hanna-Barbera to create a cartoon bear in his likeness in the 1950s and who more recently has costarred

Yogi Berra at his museum

in commercials with celebs like Yao Ming and the AFLAC duck, Berra has built his reputation not so much by what he's *done* as by what he's *said*. The man oft referred to as the "master of the malapropism" is credited with coining such familiar phrases as "It ain't over till it's over"; "It's déjà vu all over again"; "Ninety percent of the game is half mental"; "You can observe a lot by watching"; "When you come to a fork in the road, take it"; "The future ain't what it used to be"; and "Nobody goes there anymore; it's too crowded."

More than just being a comedic and surprisingly insightful observer of human nature, Berra was, of course, also a stellar ballplayer.

He earned his pinstripes and plaque in Cooperstown by slugging 358 home runs and batting .285 over an eighteen-year career that included a record fourteen World Series appearances. Much like the man himself, there is more to the Yogi Berra Museum and Learning Center than the casual observer might initially assume. Yes, the museum includes the expected exhibit detailing Yogi's impact on American culture and the English language, providing the backstories related to some of his more famous and outrageous quotations. And yes, it features plenty of memorabilia from Berra's career—including all ten of his World Series champion rings and the mitt he used to catch Don Larsen's perfect game in the 1956 World Series. And yes, it offers the requisite nods to the Yankees mystique—including a video history of baseball with a very heavy focus on the Yanks' role therein. But the museum also provides interesting exhibits related to the way the game used to be played back in the 1800s and early 1900s; a tribute to the All-Century Team that was named in 1999; a collection of dolls modeled after famous players like Willie Mays, Jackie Robinson, and Babe Ruth; an ever-changing assortment of artifacts borrowed from the National Baseball Hall of Fame; and educational programs designed to foster sportsmanship and good citizenship in youngsters.

For a Yankees fan, or any fan of the game, the museum is well worth the $6.00 cost of admission for adults or $4.00 for children. It is open Wednesday through Saturday from noon to 5:00 P.M., and Mr. Berra can sometimes be found on the premises. The old catcher, who was awarded an honorary doctorate from Montclair State University in 1996, has lived in Montclair since his playing days. He originally uttered his "fork in the road" saying when giving a dinner guest directions to his house. As it turned out, either branch of the fork led to his home, so Yogi's directions, like most of the things he has said through the years, kind of made sense after all.

As an added bonus, fans hoping to catch a ballgame during their venture into the Garden State needn't look any farther than a ballpark right next door to the museum. **Yogi Berra Stadium** is home to the Division III Montclair State Red Hawks during the spring and to the independent Can-Am League's New Jersey Jackals during the summer. The 3,400-seat facility opened in 1998, the same year as the museum. On days when the Jackals have a home game, the museum stays open until 7:00 P.M.

★ ★ ★

=50=
THE SPORTS LEGENDS MUSEUM AT CAMDEN YARDS

301 West Camden Street | Baltimore, Maryland

Located within historic Camden Station at the gateway of Eutaw Street, the Sports Legends Museum at Camden Yards is a veritable treasure trove of baseball memorabilia. The museum offers exhibits related to the two incarnations of the Baltimore Orioles, Babe Ruth, Cal Ripken Jr., and the two Negro Leagues teams that once played in Baltimore. Other sports are also represented in exhibits dedicated to

Sports Legends Museum at Camden Yards

the Baltimore Colts and Ravens of the NFL, the University of Maryland, the Preakness Stakes, and the evolution of duckpin bowling. The life of Johnny Unitas receives especially heavy treatment, thanks to the former Colt's generous donations to the museum.

But the museum's highlight is its extensive collection of baseball artifacts. Many of these were originally displayed at the Babe Ruth Birthplace and Museum, just two blocks away, until 2005, when the same nonprofit group that runs the Ruth Museum opened Sports Legends. To facilitate the

move, Camden Station, which dates back to 1855, was restored to its former glory. The building had been uninhabited since 1971, before undergoing a $16 million renovation that was funded by the state of Maryland, the city of Baltimore, and the Orioles. Now, the sprawling sports emporium occupies 22,000 square feet on the first two stories of the old station, while Geppi's Entertainment Museum occupies the third floor.

Baseball fans will enjoy learning about the original Baltimore Orioles, a National League team that departed the city in 1903 to become the New York Highlanders, who later became the Yankees. There are also artifacts related to the minor-league Orioles, who played in the International League until the St. Louis Browns moved to Baltimore in 1954. Babe Ruth made his pro debut for these early Birds back in 1914. The "Babe Ruth, American Icon" exhibit traces the cultural impact that Ruth had on the United States and on the world outside the U.S. as well. Visitors learn about Ruth's depiction in theater and film and about his sojourns to foreign lands. One of the museum's most interesting artifacts is a kimono that Ruth wore during a barnstorming tour of Japan in 1934.

"Nine Innings of Orioles Baseball" tells the story of the current Orioles franchise, beginning in 1954 and continuing to the present. The team's three world championships and Ripken's amazing consecutive-games-played streak highlight the exhibit, as does the Orioles Hall of Fame.

The Black Sox and Elite Giants of the Negro Leagues are also remembered, most notably by a replica of a bus modeled after the vehicles that the Negro Leagues teams of the 1940s used to travel from city to city. Another interesting exhibit is a faux hotel room designed to look like the one that Jackie Robinson and his roommate, Sam Lacy, a Baltimore sports reporter, lived in during Robinson's rookie year in Brooklyn.

During the baseball season the Sports Legends Museum is open seven days a week from 10:00 A.M. to 6:00 P.M., except on game days, when it stays open until 7:30. During the off-season, it is open Tuesday through Sunday from 10:00 A.M. to 5:00 P.M. Admission costs $10.00 for adults, $8.00 for senior citizens, and $6.50 for children aged three through twelve.

★ ★ ★

=51=

THE DOUBLE PLAY RESTAURANT

2401 16th Street | San Francisco, California

Baseball pilgrims won't find any part of the San Francisco Giants' original home, Seals Stadium, still standing to mark the site of the first big-league game ever played in California. Today a shopping center smothers the hallowed grounds where San Franciscans enjoyed nearly three decades of minor-league games and then celebrated the arrival of the newly migrated Giants on April 15, 1958. The home team defeated the Los Angeles Dodgers 8–0 that day to officially begin the era of West Coast baseball. The Giants would use the former minor-league park for two seasons, then open Candlestick Park in 1960.

Though Seals Stadium may be gone, it has not been entirely forgotten in its old neighborhood. At the Double Play Restaurant, which is located across the street from where the ballpark once stood, fans find a shrine to the old yard. The Double Play's wealth of relics and memorabilia related to the stadium and its three resident teams—the Pacific Coast League Seals (1931–1958), the Missions (1931–1937), and the National League Giants (1958–1959)—makes it a site that anyone interested in the history of West Coast baseball will certainly enjoy, and its beautiful wraparound mural in the back banquet room makes it a spot any fan of old-time ballparks will relish. The mural portrays Seals Stadium during a game between the Seals and the Oakland Oaks, leaving the modern viewer to feel as though he has suddenly stepped back in time and landed in the 1930s.

The oddest piece of memorabilia at this veritable baseball museum is a copy of a letter that Giants owner Horace Stoneman sent to Giants season ticket holders prior to the start of the 1960 season, trumpeting the arrival of Seals Stadium's successor, Candlestick Park. It reads, "The new stadium is a beautiful structure. I believe it is the finest sports arena anywhere. . . . All San Franciscans have reason to be proud of it as one more expression of civic enterprise and progress. . . ." Other items on display are ballpark photographs, baseball mitts, old-time jerseys and caps, a few seats from Seals Stadium, and the rounded top of the flagpole that once rose high above the centerfield fence.

A favorite local hangout since 1909, the Double Play was certainly well positioned to chronicle the rise and fall of baseball in San Francisco's Mission district. Its patrons watched with anticipation as Seals Stadium was constructed in the early 1930s; then they helped fill its 23,000 seats when the Seals and Missions arrived in the spring of 1931. In 1933 the local fans watched in amazement as an eighteen-year-old San Franciscan named Joe DiMaggio hit safely in sixty-one straight games to establish a professional record that still stands.

In other cherished moments in time, Seals fans watched the home team post a remarkable 115–68 record in 1946, en route to a fourth-straight Pacific Coast League championship, and in 1957 the fans watched the Seals bid the Pacific Coast League adieu by claiming their fourteenth and final title. During those halcyon days of Seals baseball, the team's players could often be spotted bellying up to the bar at the Double Play before, after, and sometimes even *during* games across the street. According to Double Play lore, it was not uncommon for a starting pitcher to wander across the street for a drink after he'd been removed from the game.

In 1958 and 1959, the Double Play became a major-league hangout, as the Giants and their big-league opponents attracted 2.7 million fans to the neighborhood. The euphoria in the Mission was short-lived though, because San Francisco opened Candlestick in 1960, rendering Seals Stadium obsolete. The old ballpark was promptly demolished but not before Double Play patrons raised one last pint to the old yard and not before the restaurant scarfed up as much memorabilia from the park as it could, memorabilia that today keeps the memory of Seals Stadium alive for a whole new generation of fans to enjoy.

The Double Play serves breakfast and lunch Monday through Friday, from 7:00 A.M. to 2:30 P.M. It is closed on weekends.

★ ★ ★

=52=
THE HUNTINGTON AVENUE GROUNDS

Northeastern University Campus | 400 Huntington Avenue | Boston, Massachusetts

Just a mile from Fenway Park, baseball pilgrims find a bronze statue of Cy Young that depicts the great hurler on the mound, staring in to read a sign from an imaginary catcher as he readies to deliver a pitch. The statue is located on the spot where the pitcher's mound once rose in the middle of the diamond at the Huntington Avenue Grounds, an early home of the Boston Pilgrims, who would eventually become the Red Sox. The site is significant for several reasons but most notably for being the spot where in 1903 the first game of the very first World Series was played.

While it is true that previous postseason series, such as ones that pitted the National League's regular-season champion against its runner-up and ones that saw the National League's champ play the American Association's champ, had at times been referred to by the sporting public as the "World Series," the 1903 tilt between the Pilgrims and Pittsburgh Pirates represented the first post-season clash between the regular-season winners from the National League and the fledgling American League. And more than that, the series took place at a time when several of the rules that historians would later point to as markers of the beginning of baseball's "modern era" had just been established. In 1903, for example, the three-year-old American League accepted a rule that the National League had adopted earlier and began counting foul balls as strikes. Nonetheless, it would still be years before the arrival of such modern baseball staples as the lively ball, uniform numbers, webbed gloves, dugouts, and relief pitchers.

The first World Series was not without its controversy. After Young and his Pilgrims

Cy Young statue at the Huntington Avenue Grounds

lost three of the first four games—including the very first, in which Young was defeated 7–3—Boston rebounded to win the best-of-nine series in eight games. But the finale, played in Boston on October 13, was witnessed by the smallest crowd of the series. While gatherings of 16,000 to 18,000 had turned out at the Huntington Avenue Grounds for the first three games in Boston, only 7,455 spectators filed into the ballpark stands for Game Eight. This because Boston's "Royal Rooters" decided to boycott the game after they arrived home from the away games in Pittsburgh only to discover that Pilgrims management had sold their usual block of seats to ticket scalpers. Nonetheless, Boston prevailed 3–0 behind the pitching of Bill Dinneen, a hard-throwing right-hander who won three of his four starts in the series while posting a 2.06 ERA.

It is Young's likeness, though, and not Dinneen's, that has stood in a courtyard at Northeastern University since its unveiling on October 1, 1993—the ninetieth anniversary of the first World Series game. And fittingly so. The immortal Young, who went 2-1 with a 1.85 ERA in his only World Series, won 511 games during his twenty-two-year career. Dinneen won 170 and lost 177 over his twelve seasons. Young also authored the first perfect game in American League history from the Huntington Avenue Grounds mound, blanking the Philadelphia A's 3–0 on May 5, 1904.

The statue is located outside Churchill Hall along a footpath named World Series Way. It shows Young with his socks pulled up high, with the collar of his Boston jersey neatly laced together below his neck, and with his five-fingered glove resting on his left thigh. At its base an inscription reads, AT THIS SITE IN OCTOBER 1903 BASEBALL'S WINNINGEST PITCHER LED BOSTON TO VICTORY IN THE FIRST WORLD SERIES. Sixty feet, six inches from where Young toes the rubber, a bronze home plate is laid in the grass.

Not far from where this shiny version of Young stands, a plaque on the exterior of Northeastern's Cabot Center reads, HUNTINGTON AVENUE AMERICAN LEAGUE BASEBALL GROUNDS, ON WHICH IN 1903 FOUR GAMES OF THE FIRST WORLD SERIES WERE PLAYED. THE BOSTON AMERICANS DEFEATED THE PITTSBURGH NATIONALS FIVE GAMES TO THREE. THIS PLAQUE IS LOCATED APPROXIMATELY ON WHAT WAS THEN THE LEFT FIELD FOUL LINE. ERECTED MAY 16, 1956. Inside the building, a display case on the second floor offers a small collection of old photos and wool jerseys from those earliest days of Boston baseball.

While the much larger Fenway Park replaced the Huntington Avenue Grounds as the home of Boston's American League nine in 1912, the World Series has enjoyed greater staying power. During the more than a century since that first Fall Classic, the World Series has endured times of poverty, illness, war, and civil strife while chiseling out its own special identity in the national consciousness. Only two autumns have passed without a World Series since 1903: After the Pilgrims won the American League title for a second consecutive season in 1904, John McGraw, the cantankerous manager of the National League champion New York Giants, refused to play them. Then in 1994 acting commissioner Bud Selig canceled the World Series due to the labor dispute between the owners and players.

★ ★ ★

= 53 =

FRANK NAVIN'S GRAVE

Holy Sepulchre Cemetery | 10 Mile Road | Southland, Michigan

If the first pages you turn to whenever the latest issue of *Baseball America* arrives in your mailbox are the ones toward the back devoted to baseball necrology, then there's a place fifteen miles north of Detroit that you'll surely want to visit during your baseball odyssey. Holy Sepulchre Cemetery offers the chance to not only see one of the most unusual baseball-related tombs in the land—the one in which former Tigers owner Frank Navin rests—but also the graves of several other former big leaguers, including Hall of Famers Charlie Gehringer and Harry Heilmann, as well as Dick Radatz and Billy Rogell. All five individuals toiled for the Tigers, although Radatz is better remembered for his days with the Red Sox.

Navin ascended to a place of prominence in the baseball world during the earliest era of the American League, serving as the president and owner of the Tigers from 1903 until his untimely death in 1935. Famous for squabbling with Ty Cobb during contract negotiations and for building Tiger Stadium—called "Navin Field" from 1912 through 1934—Navin watched his team beat the Chicago Cubs in the 1935 World Series, then fell off a horse a month later and died.

Although he loved riding and wagering on the ponies, Navin's gravesite pays homage to an animal of another kind. Life-size Tigers flank his tomb, the two bronze beasts striking regal if slightly tarnished poses, as if to ward off evil spirits . . . or White Sox fans.

As for Heilmann, he was a .342 lifetime hitter who spent his first fifteen seasons on Navin's payroll, then played his final two years with the Reds. Gehringer batted .320 over nineteen seasons—1924 through 1942—all spent at second base for the Tigers. While the resting places of these hardball gods are less ornate than their old boss's, the granite slabs that remember their lives are just short walks from Navin's tomb and certainly worth seeking out. (As experienced crypt crawlers know, hunting for a tombstone is at least half the fun, so plot numbers have purposely been omitted here.)

Rogell, a defensive whiz who played shortstop in 150 of the Tigers' 152 regular-season games in 1935 and in all six of their World Series games, batted .267 over a fourteen-year career that began with the Red Sox in 1925, spanned ten years with the Tigers from 1930 through 1939, and concluded with the Cubs in 1940. Radatz, whose hulking figure earned him the nickname

FRANK NAVIN'S GRAVE

123

"the Monster," was one of baseball's first great closers. His brilliance was short-lived, though. After starring at Michigan State on the baseball diamond and basketball court, Radatz broke in with the Red Sox in an era when three- or even four-inning saves were the norm. As a rookie in 1962, he led the American League with 62 relief appearances, posting a 9–6 record with 24 saves and 144 strikeouts in 124 innings. The next season, he went 15–6 with 25 saves and 162 strikeouts in 132 innings; then in 1964 he went 16–9 with 29 saves and 181 strikeouts in 157 innings. Has there been a more dominant reliever over a three-year period at any other time in baseball history? To go with his impressive win and save totals, Radatz's aggregate earned run average over those first three seasons was 2.17. But such heavy use caught up with him, and his right arm began to falter. By midseason 1966

he'd been traded from Boston to Cleveland, and by the end of the 1969 season, which he split between Montreal and Detroit, it was time for him to retire.

There are hundreds of cemeteries across the United States that lay claim to at least one former major leaguer and scores that offer repose to Hall of Famers. To visit all of these would not only be impractical but would push the baseball traveler over that fine line separating the devoted baseball pilgrim from the borderline-scary baseball neurotic. For any fan who would like to do a bit of headstone hunting, without invoking comparisons to that crazy lady who has been stalking Bob Uecker for the last ten years, think of Holy Sepulchre Cemetery as a one-stop shopping spot where you can experience the baseball-tombstone scene on several levels and then return to an exploration of less morbid pursuits.

★　★　★

=54=
THE ESPN ZONE/BABE RUTH PHOTOMOSAIC

1472 Broadway | New York, New York

Although those purists among the nation's legion of sports-bar devotees may bristle at the Walmartization of American watering holes, there's no denying that the eight ESPN Zones spread across the country have created a viewing, dining, and recreating experience that the neighborhood

Babe Ruth Photomosaic, ESPNZone

125

saloon just can't provide. These trendy full-family fun centers cater to the hardcore sports buffs who enjoy every minute of every game, thanks to their walls and bathrooms laden with television screens, while also meeting the needs of the kids—who find hours of entertainment shooting hoops, playing air hockey, or playing video games, and nonfans—who find plenty of tasty offerings and a wide range of beers and other drinks to choose from on the menu.

Every ESPN Zone offers its own unique array of local sports memorabilia and art. The most impressive of these exhibits is found at the ESPN Zone in Times Square, where a photomosaic image of Babe Ruth overlooks an interior stairwell. The 10-foot-by-12-foot image of the Bambino's face is composed of 1,392 different New York Yankees baseball cards. It was crafted by Robert Silvers, the inventor of this new-age type of art. Silvers was a graduate student at the Massachusetts Institute of Technology's Media Lab when he created his first photomosaic in 1996. A few years later he was commissioned to render Ruth. He has since been commissioned to produce portraits of former vice president Al Gore, Microsoft chairman Bill Gates, King Hussein of Jordan, and Jesus Christ (whom he chose to depict using more than 600 images of the Dead Sea Scrolls). Silvers' work has appeared on the covers of *Life*, *Newsweek*, and *Playboy*, among other periodicals.

With regard to his Ruth piece, Silvers recalled, "The Babe Ruth was particularly difficult because we used real baseball cards, and we had to lay them in an order I determined. My process is a combination of handwork and computer work, which compared the shapes and colors within each card to see where to place each to look like Babe Ruth. The process wouldn't place a card somewhere if it would look better in another location. The Ruth is one of my finest pieces because it is made from such a great collection of images and because the great subject allowed me to do such a good job."

It is truly a wonder to observe how Ruth's face seems to slowly fade away as you walk closer and closer to the wall of baseball cards. Then, after you've had your fill of studying the tiny photos of Yankees like Bob Shirley, Al Downing, Jose Rijo, Billy Martin, Wade Boggs, Duke Sims, Pat Dobson, Bobby Richardson, Roy White, Andy Stankiewicz, Sparky Lyle, Danny Cater, Mickey Rivers, Ron Guidry, Bobby Murcer, Chris Chambliss, and Oscar Gamble, you can step back and watch one of the most famous faces in history retake its shape right before your eyes. Just be careful not to fall down the stairs while stepping slowly away from the wall in a Yankee-induced stupor!

★ ★ ★

=55=

THE HEROES OF BASEBALL WAX MUSEUM

99 Main Street | Cooperstown, New York

Occupying the same brick building that once housed a Mickey
Mantle museum, the Heroes of Baseball
Wax Museum treats the more than two hundred people who file through its doors on
busy summer days to an experience unlike
any other the American baseball road has
to offer. With a sly wit and astute attention
to detail, the museum renders in life-size
wax statues the likenesses of more than
thirty-five favorite baseball icons set against
period-specific backdrops.

Some of the exhibits offer straightforward
historical depictions. There's Ted Williams
captured in the follow-through of what was
surely a monstrous home-run swing. There's
Mantle leaping to make a catch against the
461-foot sign in centerfield at Yankee Stadium, Lou Gehrig bowing his head to speak
somberly into a microphone as he delivers
his famous luckiest-man-on-earth farewell
speech, and Wade Boggs riding a victory lap
around the Bronx atop a New York City Police Department horse. Other legends like
Ty Cobb, Jackie Robinson, and Babe Ruth
get their just due as well.

Some of the funnier exhibits blend together multiple historic events or baseball

personas from different eras—like the exhibit
that depicts the tallest player in major-league
history, the 6-foot, 10-inch Randy Johnson,
standing beside the shortest player ever, the
3-foot, 7-inch Eddie Gaedel, who pinch-hit
for Bill Veeck's St. Louis Browns in 1951 and
drew a walk. Still other exhibits toy with historic fact—like the one that portrays a young
Pete Rose, clad in his Reds uniform, standing
behind a microphone beneath a banner that
reads, NATIONAL BASEBALL HALL OF FAME INDUCTION
CEREMONY. There are also nods to baseball's
presence in pop culture, including an exhibit that depicts *Seinfeld* character George
Costanza standing at the desk of Yankees
owner George Steinbrenner; as was always
the case on the show, only the back of the
Boss's head is visible to viewers.

These wax statues are created by a pair
of artists in England, who update the displays every few years after consulting with
museum ownership. In addition to these
lifelike figures, the Heroes of Baseball Wax
Museum also features a virtually real batting cage where visitors can take their hacks
against their favorite big-league pitchers and
a theater where baseball bloopers play all
day long on a continuous reel. The museum

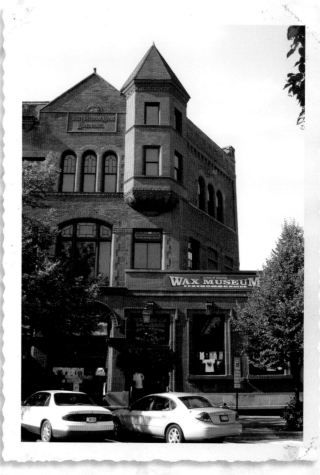

Heroes of Baseball Wax Museum

keeps regular hours during the spring, summer, and fall months and then opens sporadically during the winter, usually during school vacations and holidays. During the busy seasons, the museum is open seven days a week from 9:00 A.M. to 5:00 P.M. Admission costs $9.95 for adults and $7.95 for children and senior citizens.

Other favorite peripheral attractions in Cooperstown include the batting cages at **Cooperstown Fun Park** (4850 State Highway 28) and **Doubleday Batting Range** (2

Doubleday Court), the **Cooperstown Bat Company** (118 Main Street), where visitors can purchase personalized souvenir bats, and the **Seventh Inning Stretch** (137 Main Street) memorabilia store.

A bit farther away, fans enjoy an old-time minor-league experience at **Damaschke Field** (Neawah Park, Oneonta), a ballpark that opened in 1906, that currently serves as the home of the New York–Penn League Oneonta Tigers. The Tigers begin play in mid-June and finish in early September.

=56=
McCOVEY COVE

Pier 38/The Embarcadero | San Francisco, California

Wrigley Field has its rooftop bleachers across the street on Waveland Avenue. Fenway Park has its Green Monster seats perched atop the tallest outfield fence in baseball. Miller Park has its Uecker Seats suspended above the rightfield corner about 600 feet from home plate. But any debate concerning which major-league stadium offers a one-of-a-kind vantage point from which fans might enjoy a game must invariably arrive at AT&T Park in San Francisco. Although the sightlines are obstructed, to say the least, by the backside of the rightfield bleachers, every fan should experience a game on the waters of the China Basin Channel—or "McCovey Cove"—at least once.

Not traveling the country with your kayak? Don't despair. **City Kayak** on the Embarcadero, right near the ballpark, offers kayak rentals year-round. During day games, anyone can rent a kayak and paddle to McCovey Cove, which is just five minutes away from the marina. The rental charge is $15.00 per hour or $10.00 per hour for those who make arrangements ahead of time. During evening games, City Kayak offers an escorted trip to and from McCovey Cove. The only items traveling fans should bring are a small

radio to listen to the game, a telescoping fisherman's net in case a long ball should splash down nearby, some sunscreen, some peanuts and Cracker Jacks, and perhaps a change of clothes—just in case. From these calm waters fans can see the arched retaining wall that separates the ballpark from the sea, the backs of the rightfield foul pole and light banks, and the people seated in the upper deck around the infield. And every time a high fly ball or popup leaves a hitter's bat, kayakers are treated to a fleeting glimpse of the baseball.

The shortest distance a fair ball must travel to splash down in McCovey Cove is 352 feet—307 to reach the foul pole and another 45 to clear the strip of land between the ballpark and the water. This may not seem very far, but as of early in the 2007 season the Giants and their opponents had combined for only fifty-four splashdowns in AT&T Park's first seven years. This can be attributed to the fact that the distance a ball must carry to reach the cove increases quickly as the outfield fence slants away from the foul pole to create as expansive a rightfield as there is in baseball. In right center, a ball must carry 421 feet just to leave the yard, then another 50 feet to reach the water.

McCovey Cove outside AT&T Park

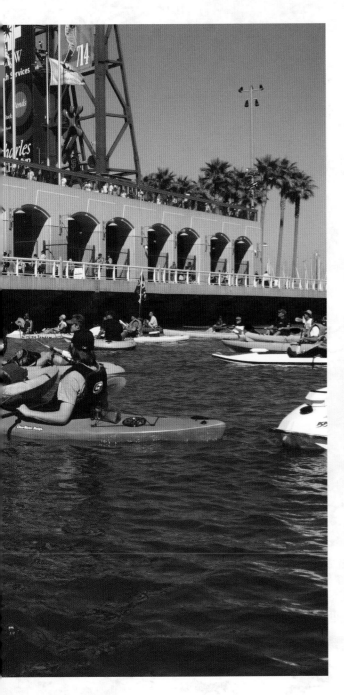

Of the first forty-one Giants' homers to land in the salty water, Barry Bonds hit thirty-three of them. The oversized slugger chalked up his first splash landing on May 1, 2000, when he took the Mets' Rich Rodriguez deep; then Bonds hit eight more wet ones before Felipe Crespo became the second Giant to reach the cove against Arizona's Bret Prinz on May 28, 2001. Two years would pass before a Giants player not named Bonds or Crespo made a splash, as J. T. Snow finally added his name to the short list of soggy sluggers in an interleague game against Minnesota's Kyle Lohse on June 3, 2003.

Despite the fact that balls really don't reach the water all that often, cove floating really is a popular pastime for many Giants fans. The number of floating folks varies widely from game to game, though, depending on the weather and water conditions. But any fan of the game who finds him- or herself in San Francisco—during the baseball season or even out of season—will enjoy spending an hour or two paddling around McCovey Cove and taking in the wonders of this unique ballpark "neighborhood."

Also worth visiting during a trip to the ballpark neighborhood is **McCovey Point at China Basin Park**. This public green space behind the left- and centerfield fence offers sweeping views of McCovey Cove and of the ballpark, a statue of Willie McCovey, a self-guided Giants History Walk, and plenty of room for a game of catch.

★ ★ ★

=57=

FORBES FIELD SITE

The University of Pittsburgh Campus |
230 South Bouquet Street | Pittsburgh, Pennsylvania

While fans can find historic markers and plaques in cities across the country acknowledging the one-time presence of fabled ballparks from baseball's early days, Pittsburgh does the memory of its old yard one better, providing a considerable stretch of Forbes Field's original outfield wall to visit, as well as the old park's home plate, which still lies in its original position . . . even if a building has been constructed around it.

A visit to the University of Pittsburgh grounds allows baseball travelers to pay homage to a stretch of the 12-foot-high red brick wall that once spanned the outfield at Forbes. Today the wall grows a healthy crop of ivy in the summer months, while still displaying the same old distance-from-home-plate-markings—457 to the deepest point in left-center and 436 to center—as when the Pirates played their last game at Forbes in 1970. The flagpole, which stood in fair territory deep in the outfield from the park's opening in 1909 through its final game, is also still in place. After the wall ends, a path of brick laid in the sidewalk and street continues to trace the wall's old

course, leading to a plaque in "left field" that marks the spot where Bill Mazeroski's walk-off home run left the yard to propel the home team past the Yankees in Game Seven of the 1960 World Series. Meanwhile, across the "Forbes Quad" in the lobby of the Joseph M. Katz Graduate School of Business, home plate lies beneath a protective layer of Plexiglas.

At the time of its opening, Forbes was considered one of the most ornate ballparks yet built. And before long its concrete and steel design became standard issue in ballpark-construction projects across the country. Pirates owner Barney Dreyfuss was initially chastised by fans for building Forbes in a bustling downtown section of Pittsburgh, but those same fans were all smiles when the Pirates won their first World Series later that year, beating the Detroit Tigers four games to three. Over the ensuing decades Forbes would witness many memorable moments. On the final day of the 1920 season, the Pirates hosted the Cincinnati Reds for the only tripleheader in major-league history. Cincinnati won two out of three to clinch third place in the National League, while

Forbes Field flagpole and fence

Pittsburgh dropped to fourth. On August 5, 1921, the first major-league game broadcast over radio was played at Forbes between the Pirates and the Philadelphia Phillies; the Pirates won 8–5 as listeners tuned in to Pittsburgh's KDKA. On May 25, 1935, Babe Ruth slugged the final three home runs of his career at Forbes as a member of the Boston Braves. In 1951 the movie *Angels in the Outfield* was shot at Forbes.

But the most memorable moment of all occurred in the final game of the 1960 October Classic. Although the heavily favored Yankees outscored the up-and-comers from the National League by a margin of 55 to 27 in the seven-game series, the Pirates prevailed, thanks to Mazeroski, who broke a 9–9 tie in the final inning with a homer off Ralph Terry. The ball sailed over the head of helpless Yankees rightfielder Yogi Berra—who was splitting catching duties with Elston Howard by that point in his career—and crashed through the tree branches above the leftfield fence. Before "Maz" could reach home plate, a throng of fans had spilled onto the field, and a raucous celebration was under way. Pittsburgh had won its first World Series in thirty-five years. Today Pirates fans young and old still gather at the Forbes Field site on October 13 each year to listen to the radio broadcast of the famous shot.

BIG LEAGUE DREAMS
REPLICA FIELDS

Several locations throughout California

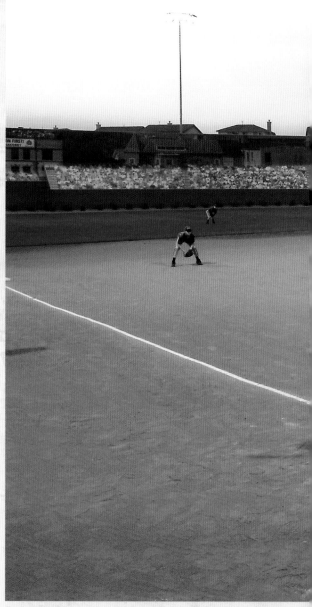

Big League Dreams Wrigley Field replica

Given the surge in popularity that youth soccer has enjoyed in recent years; and the growing passion that today's children and teens have for sports like lacrosse and skateboarding, which were once viewed as fringe pastimes but are becoming part of the mainstream; and the stranglehold basketball still has on the inner-city sports scene; and the amount of time modern children spend playing video games, IM-ing their friends, and downloading tunes onto their iPods; it's no wonder that old-timers can often be heard lamenting that "kids just don't play baseball anymore." The truth is, we adults don't either. While half a century ago Americans from all walks of life turned out at their village or neighborhood common to play and watch the game, today our busy lives afford scarcely enough time to hit the gym for a 30-minute workout on the way home from work, let alone to play nine innings.

Well, as the 1990s drew to a close, one group of forward-thinking entrepreneurs wasn't ready to give up on the idea that baseball could still be the National Game. With a *Field of Dreams*–like faith, a company called

Big League Dreams, USA, thought that if it built the right kind of baseball fields, players would materialize to use them. The company's diamonds, like the one Ray Kinsella chiseled into his Iowa cornfield, would have to be magical. And so the company decided to create replicas of the most famous major league parks in the hope that people would turn out just to see what it would feel like to step to the plate on one of the hallowed lawns of their childhood dreams.

The company launched an aggressive campaign to broker development agreements with towns and cities across California. And before long, these curious new sports complexes began taking shape where previously there had been abandoned shopping centers or brambly hillsides beside interstates. Each Big League Dreams site offers anywhere from three to six replica stadiums modeled after nostalgic American ballparks like Fenway Park, Wrigley Field, Forbes Field, Crosley Field, Ebbets Field, Yankee Stadium, Tiger Stadium, and the Polo Grounds. The fields are laid out in cloverleaf patterns, built to three-quarters scale, and lighted, and they feature stadium seating behind home plate.

The model of Yankee Stadium features decorative white arches and filigree across the outfield, just like the original in the Bronx. The scoreboard reflects the line score from Don Larsen's perfect game in the 1956 World Series. The bleachers in straightaway center are left empty, to serve as a batter's eye for hitters, while a crowd of New Yorkers is painted into the bleachers above the fence in left and right. Fenway Park features a copy of the Green Monster in left, of course, with its black-slate scoreboard frozen in time at the moment when Carlton Fisk hit his dramatic walk-off home run in Game Six of the 1975 World Series. At Wrigley Field the brick outfield wall is covered in ivy, the bleachers are packed with fans, the manual scoreboard rises in center, and the rooftops of a faux Waveland Avenue hover over the field, providing views to cutouts of beer-drinking Chicagoans.

All the fields do well to capture the aesthetic flair that made the parks they mimic special. Owing in part to the fine attention to detail with which the parks were crafted, and in part to the fact that we Americans really do love baseball—and not just watching it but playing it, too, even if we need to be reminded of this from time to time—the Big League Dreams parks have been hugely successful. When the Northern California city of Redding opened a complex featuring replicas of Wrigley, Fenway, and Yankee Stadiums in 2004, for example, it did so with the hope of attracting 125,000 players in its first year. In fact, the first twelve months lured more than 350,000 ballplayers to the complex.

Youth, adult, and senior baseball and softball leagues account for most of the action at the Big League Dreams sites, while regional tournaments sometimes draw as many as seventy teams at a time. During normal daylight hours, whichever fields are not in use are open to road-tripping fans, who, for a $2.00 fee, can enter the complex and have a game of catch or have lunch at the Stadium Club, a family-style sports restaurant that overlooks the fields.

Big League Dreams complexes can be found in **Cathedral City** (33700 Date Palm Drive); **Chino Hills** (16333 Fairfield Ranch), where the championship game scenes for the movie *The Benchwarmers* were filmed; **Manteca** (1077 Milo Candini); **Mira Loma** (10550 Cantu-Galeano Ranch Road); and **Redding** (20155 Viking Way). The company is currently working to establish complexes in Texas.

* * *

=59=

THE REDS HALL OF FAME AND MUSEUM

Great American Ballpark | Main Street | Cincinnati, Ohio

On the west side of Cincinnati's Great American Ballpark, fans find an excellent baseball museum. Although the Reds have been inducting retired stars into their team Hall of Fame since 1958, when Ernie Lombardi, Johnny Vander Meer, Paul Derringer, Bucky Walters, and Frank McCormick composed the first class, the expansive team museum is a new addition to the Cincinnati landscape that was made possible by the opening of Great American in 2003. Decades earlier at Crosley Field plaques commemorating the team's Hall of Famers had been displayed on beams above the concession concourse, but during the team's tenure at Riverfront Stadium, they were tucked away in a closet, and the Reds even stopped inducting players into their hall for a while.

But now that the Reds are at Great American the plaques have found a home, and the team is inducting worthy players once again. As of 2007, bronze busts honored sixty-three former Reds players, three former managers, and two former front-office executives. Yes, the Reds honor more of their former members than any other franchise but rightfully so. After all, they are the game's oldest team, and they've sure had their share of standouts through the years.

The plaque gallery in Cincinnati is reminiscent of the one at the National Baseball Hall of Fame at Cooperstown. And no, Pete Rose doesn't have a plaque here either, but an exhibit honoring Rose was unveiled at the museum in 2007, and a rose garden visible from the museum windows marks the spot where Rose's record-breaking 4,192nd hit landed in left-centerfield at Riverfront in 1985. As for the players who *are* enshrined, familiar names like Bench, Foster, Griffey, Perez, and Seaver top the list, while other honorees

Pete Rose Exhibit at the Cincinnati Reds Hall of Fame

include less-acclaimed Reds like Tom Browning, Eric Davis, Don Gullet, and Jose Rijo.

Other highlights of the museum include the Palace of the Fans Theatre, where visitors sit in an old-style grandstand and watch footage from Rose's career on a screen modeled to look like the old scoreboard at Crosley; a 50-foot-high wall made of 4,256 baseballs; an 1869 display that remembers the earliest days of the Reds with life-size statues of brothers Harry and George Wright; an exhibit detailing the controversial 1919 World Series in which the Reds beat the Chicago "Black Sox"; an interactive area where fans can step into a batter's box and watch in fear as a 95-mile-per-hour fastball whizzes past; a gallery dedicated to the Reds' five

World Series–winning teams; and an interactive radio broadcast booth where fans can call their own games.

From March through September the museum is open on nongame days Monday through Saturday from 10:00 A.M. to 5:00 P.M. and Sunday from noon to 5:00. On game days it is open to the public from 10:00 until the ballpark gates open, at which time it becomes accessible to ticket holders to the current game only. During the off-season, it is open Tuesday through Saturday from 10:00 to 5:00. On nongame days admission costs $8.00 for adults, $6.00 for senior citizens, and $5.00 for youths. On game days, admission is $5.00 for visitors with a same-day ticket stub.

= 60 =

BOBBY VALENTINE'S SPORTS GALLERY CAFÉ

225 Main Street | Stamford, Connecticut

While baseball lore provides abundant examples of players and coaches who have made profound contributions to the sport's evolution, only a select few baseball personalities have transcended the bounds of the playing field to make further-reaching cultural contributions to our nation. And Bobby Valentine is one such individual. A former utility man who toiled for five teams during a forgettable ten-year big-league career and then managed the Texas Rangers and New York Mets, Valentine currently serves as manager of the Chiba Lotte Marines in the Japanese Pacific League. Since returning to Japan in 2003 for a second managerial stint in the Far East (he'd spent the 1995 season with the Marines between his big-league skipper gigs), Valentine has reinvented himself as the most successful foreigner ever to guide a Japanese club. His success and widespread popularity in the baseball-crazed Land of the Rising Sun has helped bridge the gap between Major League Baseball and the Japanese leagues, making it easier than ever for players and coaches to migrate across the Pacific in either direction in pursuit of expanded hardball opportunities. It has also landed Valentine's smiling mug on a wide range of

"Bubby"-endorsed products in Japan, including beer bottles, packs of chewing gum, and lunch boxes.

But Valentine's contributions to U.S. and Japanese baseball relations may not be the most significant achievements his life's work has yielded to big-bellied baseball fans. For that, fans must look to Stamford, Connecticut, where in 1979, shortly after retiring as a player, Valentine opened a baseball-themed restaurant in his hometown. There, in his first year as a restaurateur, Valentine had a culinary stroke of genius that would transform a nation . . . or at the very least the lunch menus at a nation's sandwich shops.

Just before closing time one night, a hungry traveler wandered into Valentine's restaurant and ordered a sandwich. Valentine suddenly flushed. Only a few minutes earlier he had used the last sub roll he had on hand. But his restaurant had just opened, and Bobby didn't want to turn away a paying customer. So he thought fast and improvised. He cut a pita pocket in half the flat way, laid some meat and cheese on it and added some condiments, then rolled it up so that it was approximately the length and width of a sub. Bobby Valentine had just invented the sandwich wrap, an offering that over the next three decades would become standard lunchtime fare at restaurants across the United States.

Today, Bobby Valentine's Sports Gallery Café keeps plenty of rolls in stock just in case and also an ample supply of the flat breads with which it makes its trademark wraps. The wrap menu includes six selections: Cajun chicken, beer-battered fish, Thai noodle, chicken Caesar salad, buffalo chicken, and Cobb salad. Also popular at Bobby V's are baseball-named munchies like the Rollie (chicken) Fingers, DiMaggio (mozzarella) Stixx, and Gold Glove Quesadillas. Bobby V's also serves juicy half-pound burgers, named and topped in honor of the six teams for which Valentine suited up as a player, coach, and manager. The unique one of these is the Padres Burger, which comes topped with a heaping serving of Bobby V's buffalo-style onions and blue cheese dressing.

A popular hangout for Stamford sports fans whenever the Mets or New York Rangers are playing, Bobby V's features plenty of baseball memorabilia on its walls and around its rectangular bar. On display are old baseball cards, autographed photos, *Sports Illustrated* covers, game-worn uniforms, and other items that Valentine has collected through the years. Bobby V's is open Monday through Friday from 11:30 A.M. to 1:00 A.M. and Saturday and Sunday from noon to 1:00 A.M. Baseball fans will also find another Valentine-owned eatery right next door, the **Victory Deli** (235 Main Street), which is open Monday through Friday from 8:00 A.M. to 5:00 P.M.

Also nearby and worth visiting in Stamford is the **Jackie Robinson Park of Fame** (West Main Street), where fans find a life-size statue of Robinson. The baseball icon moved to Stamford in 1955 while still a member of the Brooklyn Dodgers and spent his final two decades in the city before passing away in Stamford in 1972 at the age of fifty-three. The statue, which was unveiled in 1999, is emblazoned with the words COURAGE, CONFIDENCE, AND PERSEVERANCE.

★ ★ ★

= 61 =

JACKIE ROBINSON BALLPARK

105 East Orange Avenue | Daytona Beach, Florida

A year before he broke the major-league color barrier and became the first African American to play in a regular-season big-league game since Moses Fleetwood Walker was released by the Toledo Blue Stockings in 1884, Jackie Robinson

Jackie Robinson Ballpark in Daytona Beach

reported for his first spring-training camp in March of 1946. He reported to Daytona Beach, Florida, a town that had been hand-picked by Branch Rickey to serve as the site of the Dodgers' integration due to its pro-gressive attitude toward race relations. At a time when blacks were treated like second-class citizens throughout the Deep South, Daytona matriarch Mary McLeod Bethune had fought to ensure civil rights and edu-cational opportunities for the blacks in her community, and by 1946 there was a thriv-ing black middle class in Daytona Beach.

Unfortunately, Daytona Beach was an island of tolerance amidst a sea of hatred Robinson would face that first spring in Florida. At points elsewhere in the state, Robinson was prevented from taking the field by racist threats and by laws prohib-iting blacks from participating in sporting events with whites. In Sanford, for example, a police chief threatened to stop a game if Robinson didn't leave the field. In Jack-sonville a stadium was padlocked an hour before game time. But at Daytona Beach's City Island Ballpark, Robinson was made to feel welcome. His first game as a member of the Dodgers' International League affiliate, the Montreal Royals, occurred on March 17, 1946, when he trotted out to second base for a Sunday afternoon exhibition against Brooklyn's big leaguers. More than 4,000 people were on hand to witness the occa-sion, including about a thousand members of Daytona's African-American community,

who were required to sit, it must be noted, in a segregated area along the rightfield foul line. Robinson went 0-for-3 but reached on a fielder's choice, stole a base, and scored a run. Most importantly, though, he was cheered by the crowd, white and black, every time he came to the plate.

More than a year later, after he had won the 1946 International League Most Valuable Player award and the 1947 Major League Rookie of the Year award, Robinson ac-knowledged the importance of that first game at Daytona Beach, saying, "When I got home, I felt as though I had won some kind of victory. I had a new opinion of the people in the town. I knew, of course, that everyone wasn't pulling for me to make good, but I was sure that the whole world wasn't lined up against me. When I went to sleep, the applause was still ringing in my ears."

City Island Ballpark was renamed Jackie Robinson Ballpark in 1990, and entered into the National Register of Historic Places in 1998. Today it is home to the Daytona Cubs, the top-drawing team in the Florida State League. Outside the ballpark, visitors find a scenic river walk that traces the banks of the intracoastal waterway and an impres-sive bronze statue of Robinson standing with two young children. The statue depicts Robinson in his Montreal uniform. Inside, a small museum offers mementos and in-formation related to Robinson's first spring game in Daytona.

★ ★ ★

= 62 =

THE YANKEE TAVERN

72 East 161st Street | Bronx, New York

After vacating the Polo Grounds—where they had spent ten seasons paying rent to the New York Giants—and moving into brand-new Yankee Stadium in 1923, the Yankees didn't waste much time before cementing their own unique franchise identity, one that from the very start was tied to the regal blue colossus in the South Bronx. In the first game ever played at Yankee Stadium, emerging icon Babe Ruth swatted a three-run homer to lead the home team to victory over the rival Boston Red Sox. Ninety-eight regular-season and four postseason wins later, the Yankees capped Yankee Stadium's inaugural season by celebrating their first World Series championship, which they won, for good measure, against their old landlord, the Giants. Today the Yankees can trace all of their subsequent titles back to the tradition of excellence that began that special first year.

Another tradition was born during that magical 1923 season, too, one that Yankees fans have happily honored for generations. Before the Yankees' first summer in the Bronx came to a close, the Bastone family opened a new dining and drinking establishment on the corner of Gerard Avenue and 161st Street that quickly became a popular watering hole for not only Yankees fans but also for players like Ruth and Lou Gehrig. Following Yankees' victories, an effervescent Ruth would often pop into the friendly neighborhood saloon to tip back a couple of frosty pints and buy a round for the other patrons.

Today, more than eight decades later, the Yankee Tavern is still a family-owned establishment—it's currently operated by Joe Bastone, a grandson of its original barkeep—and it's still *the* gathering place of choice for serious Yankees fans. While the neophytes, yuppies, and college kids may prefer the drink-'em-quick watering holes closer to the stadium on River Avenue, hardcore fans don't mind walking the extra steps to the same venerable bar where their fathers and grandfathers used to sit. Once there, they sip their pregame beverages of choice amidst the glorious backdrop of murals that honor Ruth, Gehrig, Mickey Mantle, and other famous Pinstripes. The walls are absolutely plastered with Yankees photographs and memorabilia. Fans find a bat that once belonged to Yogi Berra, photos of Jason Giambi and Derek Jeter, and scores of other artifacts representing all of their favorite Yankees in between. There are also six flat-screen TVs, usually tuned in to the YES Network.

The Yankee Tavern is more than simply a sports bar and baseball museum, though. It's also an excellent place to eat. The menu features classic New York deli sandwiches, fried seafood, Italian dishes, homemade soups, and combo meals like the Triple Play (hamburger, hot dog, and French fries) and Batting Fourth (hamburger, hot dog, buffalo wings, and French fries). The tavern is open for lunch and dinner seven days a week. On game days it stays open late to accommodate the postgame crowd.

★ ★ ★

= 63 =

THE HOUSE OF DAVID MUSEUM

2251 Riverside Road | Benton Harbor, Michigan

Back in the days before television and mass transportation, Americans depended on live entertainment to fill their leisure hours. Usually, rather than having to travel great distances to be entertained, they were able to sit back and wait for the entertainment to come to them. The theater and vaudeville circuits both channeled steady streams of talent into small-town America in the first few decades of the last century, and baseball, above all other sports, did its part, too. While the big cities fielded major-league teams, the mid-size cities boasted minor-league and Negro Leagues teams, and the smaller cities rallied around semipro teams. Barnstorming baseball was also popular in this era, as touring groups of major leaguers, former major leaguers, or Negro Leaguers would attract overflow crowds at small fields across the country, where they would showcase their skills against the best local nine each community could muster. The most popular of these barnstorming outfits was the House of David Baseball Team.

Today, the House of David Museum does well in preserving the memory of this odd bunch of ballplayers that transcended the normal bounds of sport, religion, and culture to chisel out a special place in American society from the 1920s to the 1950s.

The House of David was a Christian commune formed in Benton Harbor, Michigan, in the early 1900s under the auspices of uniting the twelve lost tribes of Israel. Members of the colony agreed to refrain from sex, smoking,

Members of the barnstorming House of David baseball team

drinking, meat eating, cutting their hair, and shaving, while they awaited the Millennium. Though they may have been a bit fanatical in their beliefs, that didn't diminish their shared love of baseball. With the blessing of leader Benjamin Purnell, the House of David formed its first baseball team in 1913. By the early 1920s, the commune's popular travel team had become its chief means of spreading the word about its faith and raising money. Team members were known for their long beards, unruly hairdos, thick wool uniforms, fun-loving attitude, and considerable baseball acuity. While they entertained fans in each new town with an amalgam of baseball and vaudeville, team members distributed promotional brochures espousing

their beliefs and afterward sent the gate receipts home to Michigan to keep the commune afloat.

Before long, the House of David was fielding several teams and employing mercenary players who would wear fake beards and long wigs while they waited for their own hair to grow in. These shaggy globetrotters were an inclusive bunch that often barnstormed with travel partners from the Negro Leagues. They were particularly fond of the Kansas City Monarchs, and as they became nationally known, they used their popularity as leverage to ensure that their Negro Leagues friends could eat in the same restaurants and sleep in the same hotels as they did when they visited each new town. The

House of David is also credited with inventing the now ubiquitous baseball-practice game of "Pepper," which a group of its players would perform at midfield midway through games, and with being an innovator of night baseball in the 1930s when House teams traveled the country with trucks outfitted with lighting scaffolds that could be quickly erected at each venue along the way.

Today, visitors to the House of David Museum find a wealth of artifacts related to the House's old baseball teams. Among the many hilarious photos of hairy-headed hardballers are ones of Babe Ruth, Grover Cleveland Alexander, and Satchel Paige, who all donned fake beards to play in exhibitions with the House of David. According to legend, pitcher Percy Walker once struck out the great Ruth in consecutive at bats. Also on display are old uniforms, promotional posters, and early lighting equipment from the team. More than just being a baseball landmark, the museum tells the whole story of the commune's history, which also included running a popular amusement park and zoo, sponsoring nationally regaled musical and vaudeville acts, and various other entertainment ventures.

The House of David Museum, which was founded in 1997, resides within a 4,000-square-foot building in Benton Harbor. It is open Monday through Friday from 9:00 A.M. to 5:00 P.M. and Saturday from 9:00 to 4:00. Admission is free.

★ ★ ★

= 64 =

THE NOLAN RYAN CENTER

Alvin Community College | 2925 South Bypass 35 | Alvin, Texas

Those wishing to learn more about the life and extraordinary career of the Southwest's greatest living baseball legend should venture to Alvin, Texas, where tributes to Nolan Ryan abound. Ryan, whose family moved to Alvin when he was a babe in arms, grew up in a house on Dezso Drive. He played Little League baseball in town and made the local All-Star team as an eleven-year-old. He worked as a delivery boy for the *Houston Post* and dreamed of a career as a veterinarian. After a standout career at Alvin High School, though, it became apparent to just about everyone who'd seen him pitch that Ryan was ticketed for a career in the big leagues, not the animal hospital.

Decades later, Alvin is obviously quite proud of its local hero. Whether fans approach the city on the Nolan Ryan Expressway (State Highway 288) or just about any

101 BASEBALL PLACES TO SEE BEFORE YOU STRIKE OUT

other route leading into town, they are sure to notice plenty of signage trumpeting Alvin as the "Home of Nolan Ryan." Some of these display the number 34, which Ryan wore while playing for the Houston Astros and Texas Rangers, and oversize renderings of the Hall of Famer's autograph.

Upon arriving in Alvin, Ryan pilgrims should make their first stop the Nolan Ryan Exhibit, located within the Nolan Ryan Center on the campus of Alvin Community College. About one-third of the floor space within the Center is dedicated to honoring baseball's all-time strikeout king, while the rest of the space serves the college's Continuing Education Department. The $1.2 million facility, which opened in 1996, was funded by the Nolan Ryan Foundation, which donated it to the college. In turn, the college leases the area used for the Nolan Ryan Exhibit back to the foundation. This may sound a bit complicated, but the bottom line is that Alvin is home to a nice little museum that traces Ryan's exploits from his humble beginnings as a pitcher for the Alvin High School Yellow Jackets in the early 1960s, through his three years in the minor leagues, through his epic twenty-seven-year big league adventure.

The exhibit has an interactive area where visitors can feel the smack of a Ryan fastball popping into a catcher's mitt, a feature reminiscent of the similar exhibit at the Legends of the Game Museum at the Rangers Ballpark in Arlington. There are also photos, videos, and audio broadcasts related to each of Ryan's record seven no-hitters. The hard-throwing right-hander tossed his first no-no at age twenty-six, when he led the California Angels past the Kansas City Royals 3–0 on May 15, 1973, and tossed his last at age forty-four, when he pitched the Rangers past the Toronto Blue Jays 3–0 on May 1, 1991.

The exhibit also offers user-friendly computer kiosks loaded with statistics pertaining to every one of Ryan's 807 big-league games. Want to see the box scores from each of Ryan's 324 wins or from any one of his record 215 ten-strikeout games? No problem. Meanwhile, a display of baseballs offers a ball for every one of Ryan's record 5,714 strikeouts. A Ryan timeline provides all kinds of photos, pieces of equipment, and other mementos from Ryan's years with the Mets, the Angels, the Astros, and the Rangers. Fans with deep pockets can even purchase authentic Ryan-used game balls at a cost of $299 apiece. The Nolan Ryan Exhibit is open Monday through Saturday from 9:00 A.M. to 4:00 P.M. Admission costs $5.00 for adults and $2.50 for children and senior citizens.

Other Ryan landmarks in Alvin include a statue of Ryan rearing back to deliver one of his trademark heaters outside **Alvin City Hall** (216 West Sealy Street); Ryan's favorite local eatery, **Joe's Barbeque** (1400 East Highway 6), where the walls display Ryan memorabilia; and **Nolan Ryan Field** (802 South Johnson Street), where Ryan's old high school jersey is on display in a weatherproof case.

★ ★ ★

= 65 =
THE MALL OF AMERICA/
METROPOLITAN STADIUM SITE

Killebrew Drive | Bloomington, Minnesota

In twenty-one seasons as a Major League Baseball park, Metropolitan Stadium attracted twenty-two million fans to its suburban plot between Minneapolis and St. Paul. Today, the Mall of America, which sits on the old ballpark site, draws more than forty million visitors per year. Most shoppers don't take the time to seek out the mall's subtle nods to Minnesota's baseball past, but informed fans will surely want to do just that.

Metropolitan Stadium opened in 1956 to serve as the home of the brand-new American Association Minneapolis Millers. Although the stadium was built in Bloomington, the City of Minneapolis picked up the $8.5 million construction tab. From the very outset, Minneapolis was thinking big, as in *big leagues*. The Met was built to major-league specifications and was promptly proclaimed the finest bush-league yard in the land when it opened. With a triple-deck grandstand that could seat nearly 20,000 fans and massive light banks, it was almost too impressive, some said, to languish in the minors. Indeed, it didn't languish for long. After the 1960 season, Minnesota struck a

deal with the woebegone Washington Senators, and a stadium-expansion project began soon thereafter to increase the Met's seating capacity to more than 30,000.

The hapless Washington club headed for the Land of Ten Thousand Lakes after its seventh straight losing season. It would still be five years before the franchise broke its losing skein, but when it did, it broke it in a big way, as the Twins took home the 1965 American League pennant with a 102–60 record. The Twins fell to the Dodgers in a tightly contested seven-game World Series, but the magical season had succeeded in putting Minnesota on the national baseball map, and led by the face of the franchise, Harmon Killebrew, the Twins were perennial contenders throughout the next decade.

Killebrew, who is widely considered one of the game's all-time great sluggers, belted 573 home runs in a career that began in 1954, when he got his first cup of coffee in the big leagues with Washington, and lasted until 1975, when he hit fourteen homers for the Kansas City Royals in the only season he spent outside the Senators/Twins organization. Today, the Mall of America offers a fit-

Mall of America, former site of Metropolitan Stadium

ting tribute to the man known to teammates as "Killer." Fans will find this unique baseball attraction within the mall's sprawling indoor amusement park. There, high above the rocky terrain of a log-chute ride, a red stadium chair from Metropolitan Stadium is bolted to the wall. While the seat may not sound like such an impressive baseball memento in its own right, when viewed in its proper context, it is.

The seat was the landing spot of a 534-foot home run that Killebrew smacked into the Met's left-centerfield upper deck against the Angels in 1967. The shot was the longest dinger of Killebrew's career and the longest in stadium history. To appreciate the magnitude of this epic long ball, today's fans can stand beside a bronze home plate, laid into the amusement park floor 534 feet away, and squint to make out the distant chair. The chair certainly looks like it would be reachable with a five-iron and a Maxfli, but with a Louisville Slugger and a hardball . . . well, not so much.

The Mall of America opened in 1992, eleven years after the Twins left Metropolitan Stadium to begin playing arena baseball at the Metrodome and seven years after the old stadium's demolition. Aside from offering a unique baseball attraction, the mall also features a fourteen-screen movie theater, an underwater aquarium, a wedding chapel, a dinosaur museum, and enough shopping space to make it the second-largest retail facility in the United States.

★ ★ ★

=66=
SAMFORD STADIUM–HITCHCOCK FIELD AT PLAINSMAN PARK

Auburn University | 351 South Donahue Drive | Auburn, Alabama

When it comes to enjoying the finest ballpark settings in the collegiate ranks, traveling fans would be wise to set their compasses for the South and for the Southeast in particular. True, many college programs from smaller conferences in colder climes have significantly upgraded their facilities in recent years, in many cases thanks to partnerships they've forged with independent league clubs, and there are also many excellent college parks spread across the Southwest, Midwest, and West, but to experience the very best atmospheres in college baseball, a roadie to the yards of the Southeastern Conference, Atlantic Coast Conference, and Conference USA is in order. Only here, in the South, will fans find such a high concentration of top-notch NCAA parks in such close proximity to one another.

Worthy of consideration in any discussion of the "best" college baseball environments in this hotbed of hardball activity are the diamonds at the University of Arkansas, Clemson University, Louisiana State University, the University of Miami, Florida State University, the University of Georgia, Mississippi State University, and Tulane University. But when it comes to picking the single place where the quality of the stadium combines with the enthusiasm of the local fans to make for the quintessential college-baseball experience, this author's pick is Auburn's Samford Stadium–Hitchcock Field at Plainsman Park.

Sure, the stadium's name is a mouthful, but any fan who thanks his lucky stars each night for the retro construction wave that transformed the big-league and minor-league parks in the 1990s will surely

101 BASEBALL PLACES TO SEE BEFORE YOU STRIKE OUT

Samford Stadium–Hitchcock Field at Plainsman Park

appreciate this special park as well. Following in the footsteps of seminal throwbacks like Oriole Park at Camden Yards and Jacobs Field, Plainsman Park fuses the best of the old with the best of the new. Among the many decorative flourishes are nods to the classic big-league stadiums. Red brick plays prominently in the exterior and interior designs, offering an arched main entranceway, a Wrigleyesque retaining wall between the seats and the field, and tall pillars that support a line-score scoreboard above the fence in left-center. The face clock above the scoreboard recalls the old-time clocks that once ticked away lazy summer afternoons at Ebbets Field and Crosley Field. Meanwhile, in straightaway left, a 30-foot-high "Green Monster" begins its ascent just 315 feet from home plate, just as at Fenway Park.

The seating bowl offers room for a smidge over 4,000 fans. The box seats extend from foul pole to foul pole, and the scant foul territory ensures that all of the spectators are right on top of the action. In the small covered grandstand between the bases fans find the same comfortable plastic seats as in the boxes, while out on the terraced lawn above the boxes in leftfield, fans hoping to catch some sunrays (and maybe a foul ball) spread out on the grass. The average crowd is about 2,500 Tigers rooters strong, but crowds swell toward the 4,000 mark when Auburn's SEC rivals begin coming to town in mid-March. While there are certainly larger college-baseball stadiums and ones that attract more fans—Arkansas, LSU, and Mississippi State all average in the neighborhood of 7,000 fans per game—Plainsman Park succeeds better than the rest at providing a cozy, old-time setting for a game, along with the comforts of modernity and terrific sight lines. For these reasons it belongs at the top of any fan's list of college ballparks to visit.

The quality of play is high as well. Although Auburn is still seeking its first College World Series title, the Tigers are perennial contenders for the SEC crown and for a place in college baseball's Top 25. Over the years the program has graduated such future big leaguers as Frank Thomas (.403 average, 49 homers, 205 RBI in 178 career games), Bo Jackson (.401, 17 HR, 43 RBI for the Tigers in 1985 before beginning his minor-league career in the Kansas City Royals system), and Tim Hudson (.379, 21 homers, 102 RBI in 103 games as a hitter/20–5 with a 2.94 ERA as a pitcher).

As for the ballpark's history, it dates to an opening as simply Plainsman Park in 1950. Several subsequent renovations and rededications have accounted for its current appearance and name. Jimmy Samford was an Auburn trustee and vocal supporter of a 1999 renovation. Brothers Jimmy and Billy Hitchcock were standout players for Auburn in the 1930s and later played in the big leagues.

★ ★ ★

= 67 =

McCOVEY'S RESTAURANT

1444 North California Boulevard | Walnut Creek, California

After a day spent at San Francisco's ballpark by the bay or, better yet, bobbing in a kayak on the bay, fans can retire to McCovey's Restaurant for a postgame dinner that comes complete with an impressive side order of memorabilia. The restaurant, which opened in 2003, honors former San Francisco Giants star and member of baseball's 500-home-run club Willie McCovey. A frequent dinner guest, Mr. McCovey usually eats in the private McCovey Room but makes time to say hello to patrons on his way in and out.

This casual family restaurant is shaped like a baseball diamond, and every nook and cranny is filled with old uniforms, baseball

Third base display at McCovey's Restaurant

equipment, and photographs. Some of the most impressive items include a ball signed by Satchel Paige, the trophy that McCovey was awarded for winning the National League home-run title in 1963, the trophy that McCovey received for winning the National League Most Valuable Player Award in 1969, and an autographed photo of McCovey posing alongside Johnny Carson. There are also displays that show how Louisville Slugger bats are made and how Rawlings makes the official major-league baseball. Overhead, in the middle of the "infield," a circular display traces Willie's remarkable career with an illustrated timeline.

The menu offers some ballpark treats as well as more imaginative entrées. The highlights include the signature "521 Burger," which consists of 44 ounces of ground Angus beef and is big enough to feed a family of four; the pulled-pork sandwich, which consists of slow-roasted pork shoulder on a French roll with coleslaw and crispy onions piled right on top of the meat; and the southern-style fried chicken with garlic mashed potatoes and gravy.

The man known as "Stretch" burst onto the big-league scene as a twenty-one-year-old in 1959, when he went four-for-four against future Hall of Famer Robin Roberts in his debut game. McCovey went on to bat .354 over that first season and to hit 521 home runs over a twenty-two-year career. He played his first fifteen years and his final four in San Francisco. He played the 1974 and 1975 seasons in San Diego after a widely unpopular trade and then split the 1976 season between San Diego and Oakland, but those are years most McCovey fans choose not to talk about. Today, Mr. McCovey is back home in the suburbs of the city where he amassed his Hall of Fame credentials, and his restaurant offers a wonderful tribute to the game he played for so many years and still loves.

★ ★ ★

= 68 =

TIGER STADIUM

2121 Trumbull Avenue | Detroit, Michigan

Usually, when a big-league city builds a new ballpark for its team, at the same time it also demolishes its old park. This is especially true with cities that have older stadiums in downtown locations that equate to prime space for redevelopment. Well, in Motown the wheels of change have turned a bit more slowly than in most places. The Tigers played their final game at the corner of Michigan and

Tiger Stadium

Trumbull on September 27, 1999, but Detroit is just now getting around to redeveloping the old ballpark site.

After Ernie Harwell said his final farewell to the Tiger Stadium press box; and Bobby Higginson, Tony Clark, Dean Palmer, and the rest of the players cleaned out their lockers; and the ground crew mowed the infield one last time for old time's sake, the Tigers slapped some padlocks on the stadium gates and headed northeast to Comerica Park. The new $300 million ballpark was built at one thousand times the $300,000 it cost to construct Tiger Stadium in 1912. The next season fans flooded into Detroit's festive Foxtown entertainment district to marvel at Comerica, while a mile and a half away Tiger Stadium sat dormant, facing its first idle summer in nearly nine decades.

A year passed, and then another. And still the old ballpark sat, slowly deteriorating along with the neighborhood around it. With time, many of the bars and restaurants that had depended on the baseball crowd as their lifeblood went out of business. As Detroit's famous "Corner" deteriorated, Tiger Stadium became a less and less attractive site for developers. The city of Detroit, which owned the stadium, hoped to transform the once-glorious baseball playground into an attractive retail and residential center, but the major stumbling block in any potential development deal always seemed to revolve around who would pay the hefty price of razing the old stadium. Finally, in the summer of 2006, nearly seven years after the Tigers played their last game at the Corner, Detroit mayor Kwame Kilpatrick announced the city would embark upon a plan to demolish Tiger Stadium and build a new mixed-use complex on the 8.5-acre site. The complex will include one hundred fifty condos, more than forty shops and restaurants, and—best of all as far as baseball fans are concerned—a scaled-down baseball diamond on the footprint of the original infield that will be used to host Little League games. The entrance to Tiger Stadium will also be preserved. The city plans to offset the estimated $2 to $5 million cost of razing the stadium by auctioning off stadium chairs, pieces of the foul poles, pieces of the 125-foot flagpole that stood in center field, bathroom urinals, and any other items that might have sentimental value to Tigers fans.

The "Corktown" project was just beginning in the summer of 2007 and should take a few years to complete. So visitors shouldn't be surprised if Tiger Stadium is still a work in progress when they visit Detroit. In the meantime, **Nemo's Bar and Grill** (1384 Michigan Avenue), a classic Corner haunt that has survived and prospered despite the baseball migration, provides a nice place for the weary traveler to enjoy a frosty beverage and cheeseburger while talking baseball with the locals. Maybe it's the framed front pages of old newspapers hanging on the walls that remember great Tigers moments, like Kirk Gibson celebrating the 1984 World Series win, or Cecil Fielder rounding the bases after hitting his 50th homer in 1990, or maybe it's just tradition, but Nemo's has actually seen its business improve since the Tigers moved to Comerica. On game days the popular saloon actually uses a fleet of converted school buses to ferry fans back and forth between its neighborhood and Comerica Park's.

* ★ ★ ★

= 69 =

CARROLL B. LAND STADIUM

Point Loma Nazarene University | 3900 Lomaland Drive | San Diego, California

For many fans of the Grand Old Game, shortly after they flip their kitchen calendars from December to January and officially begin to emerge from the chaos of the winter holiday season, they turn their attention to baseball once again.

Of course, the icy chill of winter still prevails throughout much of the country, and even where it doesn't Major League Baseball's spring training is still nearly two months away. But nonetheless, fans begin to dream of the games to come. During baseball's

Carroll B. Land Stadium

so-called hot-stove season, fans dissect and analyze their favorite teams' prospects for the upcoming year and then dissect and analyze them some more. Some fans congregate with other like-minded individuals to draft fantasy teams. Others tune in to the Caribbean World Series. Anything to bridge the gap to the new season.

The best cure for the winter baseball blues, however, may be found in those warmer climes where locals and tourists alike enjoy access to any number of excellent college baseball fields. Although NCAA Division I baseball teams are prohibited from practicing before February 1 and therefore don't begin playing games until late February, lower-level programs, such as the more than 200 that belong to the National

Association of Intercollegiate Athletics (NAIA), often begin their seasons much earlier.

And that brings us to Carroll B. Land Stadium, where, beginning in the final week of January, fans fortunate enough to find themselves in sunny Southern California have the opportunity to take in college baseball games at not merely one of the finer ballparks in the college baseball ranks but at any level of play. Nestled in the seaside cliffs that overlook the Pacific Ocean, the stadium treats fans to stunning views of sparkling blue ocean waves just beyond its outfield walls. It's easy to see why the palm tree–adorned park, which is home to the Point Loma Nazarene University Sea Lions, has been tabbed the country's "Most Scenic Ballpark" by *Baseball America*.

The field was originally part of the Cal–Western University campus, until Pasadena College relocated to San Diego in 1973 and took it over along with the rest of Cal–Western's facilities. Pasadena College baseball coach Carroll B. Land made the move along with the team he'd been guiding since 1961, and Mr. Land played a leading role over the next three decades in renovation efforts that would install dugouts, improve the outfield walls, expand the seating areas, and add concession stands and restrooms to "Crusader Field." Land would serve the Pasadena College/Point Loma Nazarene University baseball program for thirty-nine years before retiring from the head coaching post in 1998 to accept full-time responsibilities as Point Loma Nazarene's athletic director. At that time the university decided to rename the baseball field in his honor.

Whether fans find themselves in Southern California during the months of January through May, when the Sea Lions, who belong to the Golden State Athletic Conference, play more than thirty home games—most beginning at 2:30 in the afternoon—or during the summer months, breathtaking Carroll B. Land Stadium warrants a visit. After checking out the view from the infield seats and from the grassy knoll down the rightfield line, visitors can head to the observation deck atop the nearby athletic training facility to better enjoy the juxtaposition of the field's green grass and the ocean's blue waves. It is truly a sight to behold.

★ ★ ★

=70=

THE ORIGINAL BASEBALL HALL OF FAME MUSEUM

Dome Souvenirs Plus | 901 South Third Street | Minneapolis, Minnesota

Conveniently located across the street from the Metrodome, the Original Baseball Hall of Fame Museum offers baseball wanderers the opportunity to immerse themselves in a unique memorabilia collection that was assembled over parts of four decades by a former Washington Senators and Minnesota Twins employee. The museum's name is, however, a bit misleading. With its slightly surreal collection of oddball items, the museum is a one-of-a-kind attraction, so in that sense it is an "original," but it does not predate the National Baseball Hall of Fame, nor does it aspire to provide the comprehensive range of baseball artifacts that fans find in Cooperstown.

This museum is mainly dedicated to displaying items related to the Twins franchise, which is not surprising since it's tucked in the back of a 3,000-square-foot souvenir store that sells Twins and Minnesota Vikings apparel. For what it is, though, this is an excellent stop along any fan's tour of baseball landmarks; it's just not a rival to the National Baseball Hall of Fame. As long as visitors approach it with this in mind, they'll almost certainly find their ventures rewarding.

An elderly gentleman by the name of Ray Crump, who joined the Senators as a batboy in the 1950s, runs this interesting shop and museum. During his early days with the team, Crump began collecting any baseball-related items to which his part-time job allowed him access. Then, when the Senators moved to Minnesota to become the Twins in 1961, Crump moved, too, as a full-time employee for the team. Before long, he had worked his way up to the position of team equipment manager. And by the time Crump retired from the game in 1984, he had amassed a lifetime's worth of baseball mementos. In 1986 he opened the museum to share his collection with fans.

The self-guided museum tour offers chances to sit in stadium seats from old Metropolitan Stadium and to walk on a swath of the old park's artificial turf; a wall covered with baseballs autographed by not only players but pop icons too, featuring the likes of Harmon Killebrew, Casey Stengel, Elvis Presley, and Frank Sinatra; a Kirby Puckett exhibit; more than two hundred photos of Crump posing with ballplayers and celebrities he met through his position in the game; mannequins dressed in various incarnations of the Twins uniform; old team photos and yearbooks; autographed bats and baseball cards; and other odd little trinkets, like a Minnesota Twins pocketknife that apparently was quite popular back in the 1970s and "Domer Hankies," which Crump invented for the 1987 World Series, only to see the *Minneapolis Star Tribune*'s "Homer Hankies" get all of the press.

The museum's most fascinating attraction, though, is its benefactor, Mr. Crump, who enjoys sharing with fans the inside information he gleaned through his years of interacting with players, team executives, umpires, sportswriters, and fans. He is a very approachable man who is full of interesting stories. One story Crump will tell involves a revolutionary type of batting helmet he helped create for the Twins in 1962. After Twins slugger Earl Battey was twice struck in the face by pitched balls, Crump attached a metal flap to the left side of his helmet so that it hung down over his cheek. Reassured by the added protection, Battey went on to hit a career-best twenty-six homers in 1963. And the helmet flap Crump invented for him eventually became standard issue for players throughout the game.

Although the museum focuses mostly on baseball, there are also exhibits displaying items from Crump's pop-culture collection, including ones related to Elvis and the Beatles. The museum is open Monday through Friday from 9:00 A.M. to 4:00 P.M. and Saturday from noon to 3:00. When the Twins are playing, it stays open late. Admission is free.

Phoenix Municipal Stadium

=71=

PHOENIX MUNICIPAL STADIUM

5999 East Van Buren Street | Phoenix, Arizona

Some of the sites detailed in this book are accessible to visitors 365 days a year, while others offer more limited opportunity for exploration. Phoenix Municipal Stadium falls into the latter category, as it is open only during March, when the Oakland A's call it their Cactus League home, and October and November, when the Phoenix Desert Dogs of the Arizona Fall League use it. During either season the ballpark is worth visiting because it offers

stunning outfield views of red rock formations and because it offers an informative timeline on its concourse that provides a history lesson in Arizona baseball.

Immediately behind the fence in left and center, cacti grow on a sandy embankment. Looming a bit farther away, the red rocks of Papago Park rise dramatically above the field. These iron-rich sedimentary formations are between 6 and 15 million years old. One formation is particularly distinctive because of a circular hole in its center that has earned it the nickname "Hole in the Rock." The hole has eroded over the course of millennia as the result of rainwater and wind but looks pretty much the same today as it did when the Ho-HoKam Indians used the ray of sunlight that filters through it to mark the summer and winter solstices. Just as the game is enhanced by stunning water views in big-league cities like San Francisco and Pittsburgh, these rock formations, in their own way, create an utterly unique and pleasing backdrop that makes the baseball games played at Phoenix Municipal Stadium special.

As for the timeline, its sixteen entries are engraved in the concrete slabs on the walkway behind the seating bowl. They read:

- March 26, 1929: The first spring training game in Phoenix, Arizona was hosted by the Detroit Tigers. Immediately after the Ty Cobb era, the Tigers looked for inspiration and change for rebuilding, so therefore chose Phoenix for a portion of their spring training schedule. The Tigers hosted the Pittsburgh Pirates on an ideal Arizona baseball afternoon.

- 1930s and World War II: During the 1930s spring training was played in California and Florida. At the onset of World War II, Commissioner Kenesaw Mountain Landis, in cooperation with the Department of Defense, barred teams from traveling west of the Mississippi and south of the Potomac in order to save the railway lines for troops and supplies. These four years of cold springs created a desire to reestablish spring training in warmer climates.

- 1946: A league of two is formed when the Cleveland Indians persuaded the New York Giants to join them in Arizona for spring training. The Giants chose Phoenix to train for the spring while the Indians adopted Tucson.

- Spring of 1948: The relaxed sociopolitical climate of Arizona helped to further the integration of African Americans into the major leagues after Jackie Robinson broke the color barrier playing for the Brooklyn Dodgers. The Giants and Indians each acquired two African American players to their rosters.

- Spring 1951: New York Yankees co-owner and Phoenix resident/developer Del Webb trades spring training sites with the New York Giants in order to show off his talented team to Phoenix family and friends. This brought the Yankees to Phoenix for one year with a talented 19-year-old rookie named Mickey Mantle.

- Spring of 1952: New York Yankees owner and Phoenix resident/developer Del Webb convinced the Chicago Cubs to make the "Valley of the Sun" home for spring training. They ultimately settled in Mesa, Arizona.

- 1954: The "Cactus League" officially began, comprising of four teams, after the arrival of the Baltimore Orioles and the Chicago Cubs to the state. Both teams joined the New York Giants in the Phoenix Valley, playing at Scottsdale and Mesa, while the Cleveland Indians remained in Tucson.

- 1964: Phoenix Municipal Stadium, often referred to as "Muni," opened for its first spring training season as the home of the Giants who brought with them the lights from the Polo Grounds which illuminated the night skies of New York until September 18, 1963.

- March 8, 1964: Willie Mays hit the first home run at Phoenix Municipal Stadium, 420 feet to left-center field, in the stadium's inaugural game. The Giants defeated the Cleveland Indians 6-2 in front of an opening crowd of 8,502 people.

- Spring of 1972: The Oakland A's return to spring training as the defending World Series champions and the first Cactus League team to bring a World Series championship to the Valley.

- Spring of 1984: The Oakland A's make Phoenix Municipal Stadium their home.

- 1986: A study deemed Phoenix Muni as a viable temporary solution in attracting an MLB team to the Valley. The plans included expanding the stadium by more than four times its original size. This plan was not implemented, as instead Bank One Ballpark was constructed prior to the Diamondbacks' first season in 1998.

- Fall of 1989: As a result of the devastating earthquake in the San Francisco/Oakland Bay area during the World Series, the A's returned to Phoenix Municipal Stadium for practice. Before resuming the series, the A's played against their minor league players in an exhibition game at Phoenix Muni, with all proceeds going to the earthquake relief fund.

- 1994: The Oakland A's make Phoenix their home for all operations with renovations at Phoenix Municipal Stadium and construction of a training complex atop a former World War II German prisoner of war camp in Papago Park.

- Summer of 1996: The Arizona Diamondbacks called Phoenix Muni home with their first ever professional team which competed in the Arizona Rookie League. The Rookie League is a player development league, which plays in June through August of each year.

- 2004: The Cactus League celebrates its 50th year and new Phoenix Municipal Stadium renovations are completed.

★ ★ ★

=72=

PINK'S HOT DOGS

709 North La Brea Boulevard | Los Angeles, California

If the hot dog is *the* quintessential ball-park food, then no baseball pilgrimage would be complete if it didn't devote proper time, attention, and belly space to sampling the best of the ballpark weenies the big leagues and bush leagues have to offer. At the major-league level, the meaty Fenway Frank, snappy Miller's dog in Oakland, and spicy Nathan's Famous dog at Yankee Stadium stand above the rest. In the minors, strong cases can be made for both the White Hots—veal, ham, beef, and milk within a firm casing—at Frontier Field in Rochester and the Smokehouse Dogs—topped with barbecue sauce, bacon, and onions—at Riley Park in Charleston as the best frankfurters still waiting to be called up to the Show.

To taste the most scrumptious hot dog of all, though, baseball fans must stray a few miles from their ballpark touring and head for Hollywood. Here, hungry seamheads and legions of other tourists find America's premier destination for sampling that special culinary treat that has been married to the American Game ever since legendary concessionaire Harry Stevens began doling out franks to Giants fans at the Polo Grounds in the early 1900s.

Pink's embraces a Hollywood motif more than it does a sports or baseball one, but if you look carefully at the wall of glossy celebrity photos adorning this Tinsel Town landmark you'll notice a few famous baseball faces who have stopped by to sate their pre- or postgame appetites. While baseball lore offers multitudinous examples of historically big eaters within its ranks—a canon that extends from the days of the ravenous Babe Ruth to the modern era, when ample-bodied pros like David Wells and Ryan Howard carry the mantle—none of the ballplayers who have visited Pink's ever devoured as many hot dogs as a certain science-fiction writer.

According to legend, Orson Welles once consumed eighteen chili dogs during a visit to Pink's—a record that still stands. There's no word on whether the subsequent rumblings within his bloated belly inspired him to write *War of the Worlds* or if he found his muse elsewhere. But this much is certain: the Pink's stand that visitors flock to today still looks much the same as when Welles was a guest in the 1940s and 1950s.

The humble hot-dog cart that Betty and Paul Pink first began operating in 1939 had

PINK'S HOT DOGS

163

evolved into a hot-dog shack by 1946, and that's the same shack that still stands at the corner of La Brea Boulevard and Melrose Avenue today. And while Betty and Paul have since moved on to what are no doubt meatier pastures in the sky, Pink's is still family owned and still serves the same hot dogs it did in 1939. Manufactured by Hoffy since those earliest days when Pink's was a cart-and-carry operation, the all-beef Pink dog has a firm texture, a spicy flavor, and a snappy natural casing. It comes grilled to perfection and served in a soft steamed bun.

The menu features more than twenty different frankfurter variations, including ones that make use of such nontraditional toppings as pastrami, guacamole, chopped tomatoes, mayonnaise, and Swiss cheese. The number-one seller, though, is that tried-and-true American favorite, the chili dog, which comes topped with Pink's secret homemade sauce, mustard, and onions.

Pink's is open from 9:30 A.M. to 2:00 A.M. from Sunday through Thursday and from 9:30 A.M. to 3:00 A.M. on Friday and Saturday. On a typical day Pink's serves more than 2,000 hot dogs, and during peak lunchtime and evening hours the lines outside can grow quite long. But Pink's is worth the wait, especially for the hot-dog connoisseur who realizes that just because he can't find a hot dog this delicious at an American ballpark, he shouldn't deprive himself of one . . . or two . . . or eighteen, if he wants to go for the house record . . . on his once-in-a-lifetime baseball road trip.

★ ★ ★

=73=

THE BASEBALL RELIQUARY

Exhibits at Various Locations | Los Angeles County, California

The most eclectic collection of baseball artifacts fans will find anywhere in the baseball universe resides not in one home location but at several exhibit spaces throughout Los Angeles County. With a stated mission to display objects that "more conservative, timid, or uninformed baseball museums have failed to bring to the public's attention," the Baseball Reliquary is truly a one-of-a-kind establishment that has built a collection that ranges from the sublime to the surreal to the just plain silly.

Among the Reliquary's most prized possessions are a half-smoked stogie that Babe Ruth left on the nightstand of a Philadelphia brothel in 1924; the sacristy box that a priest from New York's St. Patrick's Cathedral used to administer the Bambino's last rites on the

Spitter painting by Ben Sakoguchi at the Baseball Reliquary

evening of July 21, 1948 (Ruth felt better by the next morning and lived nearly another month); a trophy presented to "Humanitarian of the Year" Ty Cobb after he made a donation toward the building of a hospital in his hometown of Royston, Georgia, in 1950; the jock strap that Bill Veeck's diminutive pinch hitter Eddie Gaedel wore in his lone at bat for the St. Louis Browns in 1951; a pair of skimpy thong panties worn by Wade Boggs's mistress Margo Adams during the 1986 season; a singed vinyl record from Bill and Mike Veeck's infamous "Disco Demolition Night" at Comiskey Park in 1979; a collection of humorous baseball-themed orange-crate paintings created by Southern California artist Ben Sakoguchi; and a soil sample that was taken from the batter's box of Hoboken, New Jersey's Elysian Fields less than a month after the first baseball game was played on that site in 1846.

True to form, the Baseball Reliquary does not offer a traditional hall of fame that celebrates its members' statistical achievements but rather its "Shrine of the Eternals" honors individuals acclaimed for "the distinctiveness of play (good or bad); the uniqueness of character and personality; and the imprint that the individual made on the baseball landscape." Each year, members of the Reliquary elect three new inductees and hold an induction ceremony at the Pasadena Central Library. The event, which usually takes place in July, attracts a couple of hundred people.

Among the baseball luminaries who have been enshrined are Jim Abbott, who pitched in the big leagues despite having been born with only one functional hand; Moe Berg, who served overseas as a spy for the United States during World War II after his catching career ended; Ila Borders, who became the first woman to play in a men's professional game when she toed the pitcher's rubber for the St. Paul Saints in 1997; Jim Bouton, who authored the most controversial and best-selling baseball book yet written, *Ball Four*; Dummy Hoy, the turn-of-the-century player whose hearing impairment catalyzed the invention of baseball's now-ubiquitous hand signals; Minnie Minoso, who played big-league ball in parts of five different decades and even collected a hit for the White Sox at the age of 53 in 1976; Jimmy Piersall, who endured mental illness to succeed in the big leagues during the 1950s and 1960s; Jackie Robinson, who broke baseball's color barrier; and Bill Veeck, whose promotional antics made the game eminently more interesting.

Monrovia resident Terry Cannon founded the Reliquary in 1996. It is a nonprofit organization that derives a portion of its funding from the Los Angeles County Arts Commission. Throughout the year, the Reliquary sponsors an ever-changing slate of exhibits that the public may view for free at places like the **Los Angeles Trade-Tech Library**, the **John F. Kennedy Memorial Library** on the campus of California State University, **Pasadena Central Library**, and Pasadena's **Jackie Robinson Center**. For information about the Reliquary's current exhibits, consult www.baseballreliquary.org.

★ ★ ★

=74=
THE BOB FELLER MUSEUM

310 Mill Street | Van Meter, Iowa

It didn't take Bob Feller long to become a household name. The farm boy from Van Meter made his major-league debut as a seventeen-year-old in 1936. After skipping the minor leagues entirely, Feller struck out fifteen St. Louis Browns in his very first big-league start. Later that season he established a new American League record by striking out seventeen Philadelphia Athletics in a nine-inning game. In 1938 he broke his own record when he whiffed eighteen Detroit Tigers. By 1939 he had embarked on a string of three straight seasons in which he would lead the American League in wins—or five straight if you discount the 1942 through 1945 campaigns when Feller missed all but nine games to serve as an antiaircraft gunner on a World War II battleship.

Feller had already won 109 games for the Cleveland Indians by the time he enlisted in the Navy at age twenty-two. By then he was known throughout the game as "Rapid

Bob Feller Museum

Robert." Alliterative though it may have been, this nickname was not the first one that had been crafted to pay tribute to Feller's blazing fastball. Back in his early teenage days, when he was playing American Legion and semipro ball and was not yet a national phenomenon, he was known as "the Heater from Van Meter."

Feller grew up in Van Meter, doing chores on his family farm and throwing baseballs on a diamond that his father made for him and during the colder months inside his father's barn. Today, Feller's hometown celebrates the accomplishments of its most famous son at the Bob Feller Museum. Steve Feller, a local architect who just happens to be the Hall of Fame pitcher's son, designed the stately brick building that opened on June 10, 1995, to house the museum. More than

800 townsfolk visited on the day of the grand opening, and ever since a steady stream of baseball fans and baseball luminaries has flowed to this landmark twelve miles west of Des Moines.

The museum displays old uniforms bearing Feller's number 19; collectible pennants, plates, and posters dedicated to Feller; trophies that Feller won during his playing days; signed bats and balls from Feller; photographs of Feller from his time in the game; and vintage newspapers marking Feller's greatest accomplishments—like his three no-hitters, his 1946 season when he returned from war to strike out a then-record 348 batters and lead the Indians to the World Series, and his Hall of Fame induction ceremony in 1962. The museum also showcases visiting baseball exhibits from the Hall of Fame and from the Negro Leagues Baseball Museum. Cooperstown, for example, recently loaned the Bob Feller Museum all three balls that Feller threw to clinch his three no-hitters, while the Negro Leagues' shrine recently sent to Van Meter a display honoring the life and career of the great Buck O'Neil.

Though he no longer lives in Van Meter, Mr. Feller is a frequent visitor to the museum. On these occasions the bristly octogenarian charges $25.00 for his autograph. Other baseball personalities who have visited Van Meter to sign their names for fans include Don Larsen, Bruce Sutter, Tony La Russa, Yogi Berra, Ozzie Smith, and Brooks Robinson. An on-site gift shop sells autographed memorabilia from these and many other baseball notables. The museum is open Tuesday through Saturday from 10:00 A.M. to 4:00 P.M. and from noon to 4:00 on Sunday. Admission costs $5.00 for adults and $3.00 for children and senior citizens.

=75=

DISTANT REPLAYS

Cumberland Festival Shopping Center | 2980 Cobb Parkway | Atlanta, Georgia

As the retro-stadium trend swept across the United States during the 1990s, outfitting major-league and minor-league cities from sea to shining sea with brand-new ballparks designed to look like old-time ballparks, a new market was born that similarly capitalized on the idea that baseball fans are by nature nostalgic creatures who carry within them deep-rooted memories of the game they knew and loved when they were younger. By the time the 1990s were drawing to a close, many of the fans who were flocking to the throwback ballparks were doing so while donning throwback hats and jerseys. This new type of gear was designed to reflect the long-abandoned logos and styles that teams fashioned decades earlier: a black-and-yellow-striped Pirates cap like the one we remember atop Willie Stargell's head, a Braves cap with a cursive "a" on it like Hank Aaron's, a brown and yellow Padres jersey like Dave Winfield's, a bright orange and yellow Astros jersey like Nolan Ryan's.

Buried deep in the recesses of every team's closet was at least one old uniform that in the modern era brought instant smiles to fans' faces, no matter how goofy it might now appear. What the new old-time ballparks did for the atmospheres in which the games were played, the new old-time gear did for the people turning out at those parks

Hat wall at Distant Replays

to watch. Both helped make the game seem innocent again. Both allowed grown fans to watch the game through children's eyes.

While this high-end fashion trend enabled scores of sports retail stores nationwide to either open their doors for the first time or reinvent themselves, the store that emerged as the industry bellwether was Distant Replays. Today its super store in Atlanta provides fans with the finest assortment of retro gear they'll find anywhere in the country. What began as a small stand operated by company founder Andy Hyman at a local shopping mall has grown into a large store that features items paying homage to the great teams and players from all four major American sports.

The list of Distant Replays' celebrity clients includes entertainers like Billy Crystal, Faith Evans, Trick Daddy, Big Boi, and Busta Rhymes; star athletes like Evander Holyfield, Allen Iverson, Randy Moss, and LeBron James; and baseball legends like Phil Niekro, Tony Perez, and Gaylord Perry. The store also welcomes a steady stream of current big leaguers during the season when members of visiting teams arrive in Atlanta to play the Braves and stop by to freshen up their wardrobes.

The baseball section includes jerseys, hats, jackets, and other gear related not only to the current big-league teams but also to extinct ones like the St. Louis Browns and Montreal Expos, minor-league teams, Negro

Leagues teams, Japanese league teams, and Caribbean league teams. It is enlightening to paw through the woolen jerseys of teams from the distant past and to associate a logo with a familiar name like the Homestead Grays or New York Black Yankees. It is also pretty neat to finger a White Sox jersey like the one Joe Jackson was wearing in 1919 when he and his teammates threw the World Series or a Boston Braves jersey like the one Babe Ruth was wearing when he hit his last big-league home run in 1935, or a Cleveland Indians jersey like the one Larry Doby was wearing when he broke the American League's color barrier in 1948.

Browsing through the racks of jerseys from teams from not quite so long ago is also thoroughly pleasant, as fans take their own personal trips down memory lane, their brains firing dormant synapses: a white and blue White Sox jersey, for example, suddenly conjures the bloated image of Greg Luzinski wearing the oversized pajamas that constituted his team's uniform in the early 1980s.

Perhaps most impressive of all, Distant Replays carries more than 400 different styles of baseball caps, including ones that feature the emblems of all of the major-league teams, as well as most minor-league, Negro Leagues, and international teams. The best-selling caps are displayed on a massive wall that is as colorful as it is interesting to browse.

For any fan who possesses an appreciation of the game's history, an hour spent browsing the racks at Distant Replays is a mesmerizing experience, even if plunking down two or three hundred dollars for a piece of clothing isn't really an option. The store is open Monday through Saturday from 10:00 A.M. to 7:00 P.M. and Sunday from noon to 6:00.

* * *

= 76 =

THE NATIONAL COLLEGE BASEBALL HALL OF FAME

Southwest Special Collections Library | Texas Tech University
15th Street and Detroit Avenue | Lubbock, Texas

Many of the places profiled in this book are landmarks that have helped shape baseball's identity over time, while others are not quite so well known or well established but hope to be one day. The National College Baseball Hall of Fame belongs to the latter category, as an emerging baseball location that shows a lot of promise and will hopefully develop into a site of increasing baseball importance in the years to come. While the hall currently consists of an exhibit in a library on the campus of Texas Tech University, efforts are under way to design and construct a separate building for it that could open as soon as 2009.

The additional space that a stand-alone building will provide will certainly be put to good use. It would be an understatement to say that the College Baseball Foundation—the nonprofit group founded in 2004 to document and promote the history of the college game—has some catching up to do. Although college baseball has been played in the United States for more than a century, until the foundation formed and its Hall of Fame inducted its first class of five former players and five former coaches in 2006, no comparable effort had ever been made on a national scale to honor the legends of the college baseball ranks. To make up for lost time, for the foreseeable future the hall will not only induct a class of recently retired players and coaches each year but also a class of "veterans," defined as individuals who left their mark on the college game prior to 1947, when the first All-America team for college baseball was chosen.

As the hall welcomes what promises to be a large crop of new members each year over the three days of ceremonies it orchestrates during Lubbock's annual Fourth of July celebration, the 4th on Broadway Festival, the impressive collection of portraits and memorabilia it displays should continue to grow quickly.

The inaugural class of 2006 included players Will Clark, Bob Horner, Brooks Kieschnick, Robin Ventura, and Dave Winfield and coaches Skip Bertman, Rod Dedeaux, Ron Fraser, Cliff Gustafson, and Bobby Winkles. The portrait of Winfield captures the future big-league star wearing his Minnesota Golden Gophers uniform. Rather than showing him in the batter's box. where he would spend his big-league career and bash his way into the National Baseball Hall of Fame, it depicts him on the pitcher's mound, where he excelled as a collegian. Winfield led the Golden Gophers to the College World Series in 1973, then jumped straight to the major leagues without playing a single game in the minors the next year.

The portrait of Clark shows a softer side of the player who would come to be known for his fiery intensity during his major-league career. Wearing his crimson Mississippi State Bulldogs cap and plenty of eye black, the 1984 and 1985 All-America smiles broadly. Ventura, who racked up a remarkable fifty-eight-game hitting streak while at Oklahoma State, is captured in the midst of a picture-perfect left-handed swing.

The second class, inducted in 2007, included Pete Incaviglia of Oklahoma State fame, Fred Lynn of Southern California, John Olerud of Washington State, Phil Stephenson of Wichita State, and Derek Tatsuno of Hawaii.

In addition to the portraits, the hall displays old press clippings, photographs, team pennants, player jerseys, and other items related to the enshrinees. Another display honors the winners of the Brooks Wallace Player of the Year Award, which since 2004 the College Baseball Foundation has presented to the nation's top collegiate player.

Display at National College Baseball Hall of Fame

The three finalists for the award each year are invited to the Hall of Fame ceremonies, and the winner is announced at a special event the night before the induction.

Players who have spent at least one season at a four-year college or university become eligible for enshrinement in the hall five years after they play their final game as a collegian, unless they go on to play professional baseball, in which case they do not become eligible until their retirement from the sport. Players who fit these criteria must also have made at least one All-America team to earn a place on the hall's ballot. Then it is up to a panel of more than eighty voters to decide whether they are worthy.

The separate Veterans and Historical Committee nominates and chooses the pre-1947 players and coaches. The inaugural class of old-timers included Jack Barry (Holy Cross), Lou Gehrig (Columbia), Christy Mathewson (Bucknell), and Joe Sewell (Alabama). As for coaches, they must also be retired from the game before they become eligible and must have won at least 300 games or 65 percent of their games during their time in the college ranks.

While it continues to occupy its spot at the Southwest Special Collections Library, the National College Baseball Hall of Fame is open Monday through Friday from 9:00 A.M. to 5:00 P.M. and Saturday from 9:00 to 1:00. As it grows and eventually moves into its own space, these particulars will change, so baseball travelers would be wise to check out the National Baseball Foundation Web site at www.collegebaseballfoundation.org for the latest visitor information before planning their trips to Lubbock.

★ ★ ★

= 77 =

THE ST. LOUIS WALK OF FAME

Delmar Boulevard | St. Louis, Missouri

In the Far West the most renowned American walk of fame of all, the one in Hollywood, honors just a handful of former baseball players and personalities, and even then the individuals memorialized are famous for reasons other than their associations with the game. Yes, Chuck Connors played first base for the Dodgers and the Cubs, for example, but he earned his place in America's heart and his star in Hollywood as TV's *Rifleman*. And yes, Gene Autry owned the Angels for nearly four decades, but in our memories he will always be the "Singing Cowboy" first and foremost. And Ronald Reagan, who spent his early days as a radio broadcaster for the Chicago Cubs? Well, he's better remembered as "the Gipper," not to mention as the fortieth president of the United States.

Although the Hollywood Walk of Fame isn't baseball-centric, baseball fans shouldn't fret. That's because the walk of fame in the city that bills itself as the "Gateway to the West," the one in St. Louis, goes above and beyond the expected call of duty to celebrate a whole bunch of former baseball players and baseball personalities. A stroll through the St. Louis Loop Neighborhood is

as interesting as it is educational and should rank high on any baseball fan's to-do list. The St. Louis Walk of Fame was founded in the late 1980s by Joe Edwards, the owner of a popular Loop restaurant named **Blueberry Hill** (6504 Delmar Boulevard). The project's mission in embedding stars and accompanying informational plaques in the sidewalks along Delmar Boulevard was to celebrate "St. Louisans past and present who have made significant contributions to life in America." Consequently, the more than one hundred stars found in the Loop honor people from a wide variety of fields. Visitors can find stars celebrating the contributions of actors like Redd Foxx and Kevin Kline; writers like Maya Angelou, T. S. Eliot, and Tennessee Williams; musicians like Tina Turner and Miles Davis; civil rights activists like Dred and Harriet Scott; and journalists like Elijah Lovejoy and Joseph Pulitzer. But most important of all, as far as traveling baseball fans are concerned, there are stars honoring baseball players, executives, and broadcasters who left their mark on the game.

The notable players whose names appear along the walk include Yankees legend Yogi Berra, who grew up with fellow honoree

Ozzie Smith, Bob Costas, and Chuck Berry at the 2003 St. Louis Walk of Fame induction ceremony

Joe Garagiola in southwest St. Louis, in the Italian-American neighborhood known as The Hill; Negro Leagues star Cool Papa Bell; and Cardinals immortals Lou Brock, Bob Gibson, Rogers Hornsby, Stan Musial, Red Schoendienst, and Ozzie Smith. Former St. Louis Browns star George Sisler is also represented, as is former Browns manager and front-office pioneer Branch Rickey. Famous broadcasters Jack Buck, Harry Caray, and Bob Costas have stars, too. All of the stars are located between 6200 and 6600 Delmar Boulevard on either side of the street. While the walk's official

Web site—www.stlouiswalkoffame.org—lists the exact location of each star, part of the fun in taking the walk lies in discovering each star for oneself, so readers are encouraged not to overprepare for this adventure.

To be eligible for a star, individuals must have been born in St. Louis or lived a significant portion of their life in the city, and they must have made a far-reaching contribution to America's cultural heritage. Each May an induction ceremony is held outside Blueberry Hill to honor the individuals for whom new stars have been added. But tourists needn't arrange their travel plans to visit during this one special time of year. The great thing about this unique civic and baseball attraction is that not only is it absolutely free, but it can be enjoyed twenty-four hours a day, seven days a week, all year-round, except when there's snow on the sidewalks. And any fan who wants to take a little piece of St. Louis history home with him or her need only bring some paper and charcoal to make chalk rubbings of favorite stars and plaques along the way.

★ ★ ★

= 78 =

MICKEY MANTLE MEMORIAL EXHIBIT

Hollywood at Home Video Store | Lakeview Shopping Center
536 West Third Street | Grove, Oklahoma

In his later years, as he finally sought treatment for his alcoholism and began to reconsider the live-fast, die-young attitude that had characterized his approach to life throughout his several decades in the public eye, Mickey Mantle allowed the world to see a more vulnerable side of himself that was as endearing as it was surprising. A nation was suddenly reminded that one of its mythic figures was not just a legend but, in fact, also a human being.

While the greater baseball universe may have needed to see a chastened Mantle pleading with schoolchildren not to be like him and encouraging adults to be organ donors, the folks back in Oklahoma, where "the Mick" grew up, never forgot. In the Sooner State, Mantle was always known as "the Commerce Comet," owing to his humble beginnings as

a miner's son in the northwest Oklahoma town of Commerce. Mantle made a sincere effort to return to his roots in his later years, and one of the new friends he made during that process today honors Mantle's memory with a remarkably comprehensive memorial located just 35 miles south of Commerce in the town of Grove.

What began as a sidelight to the video store that Terry Hembree owns has grown to claim more and more floor space and to become the site's primary attraction. You can pick up a movie at any old place or even through the mail or online these days, but you won't find a baseball shrine like this one anywhere else. Hembree and Mantle were introduced through their mutual interest in the Make-A-Wish Foundation and became friends. When Mantle began to slip away soon thereafter, it occurred to Hembree that he might put to use some extra display space in his store. Scores of donations and acquisitions later, the Mickey Mantle Memorial Exhibit now offers a plethora of unique Mantle artifacts, presented within the structure of a well-organized time line that traces the Mick's life from his birth in Spavinow, Oklahoma; to his family's move to Commerce when he was four years old; to his salad days in New York, when he smashed 536 home runs and played in twelve World Series; to his later years as a living legend trying to come to terms with a reckless past.

The most interesting artifacts include Mantle's old locker from Commerce High School; old schoolboy photos and yearbooks; a stretch of the fence from his boyhood home on South Quincy Street in Commerce; Mantle-endorsed products like Mickey Mantle Triple Crown Pound Cake, Wheaties boxes, and Mickey Mantle's Western blue jeans; dinnerware from Mickey Mantle's Country Cookin' Restaurants; baseball gloves and bats; lots of baseball cards; Mantle's golf bag; his Rolex; his cuff links; his sunglasses; his No. 7 Yankees jersey; and the jacket Mantle wore with the Yankees as a rookie in 1951. Mr. Hembree himself painted the mural of Mantle that appears at one end of the store, while television screens offer glimpses of Mantle's grace on the diamond and interviews with him. An audio attraction allows visitors to conjure up Mantle's voice at the push of a button.

The Mickey Mantle Memorial has been praised by such prominent Americans as former president Bill Clinton and Oklahoma governor Frank Keating, who in 2002 awarded Mr. Hembree the Governor's Commendation, IN RECOGNITION OF YOUR EFFORTS TO PROMOTE AND PRESERVE THE LEGACY OF MICKEY MANTLE. . . . Such accolades are certainly well deserved. This exhibit is clearly a labor of love for Mr. Hembree, who doesn't charge visitors for admission and who is always happy to share his memories of Mickey with those who come to see his collection. The exhibit is open Monday through Thursday from 1:00 P.M. to 9:00 P.M. and Friday and Saturday from 1:00 to 10:00.

★　★　★

=79=

AT&T BRICKTOWN BALLPARK

2 South Mickey Mantle Drive | Oklahoma City, Oklahoma

After forward-thinking major-league teams began replacing their aging and nondescript stadiums with fan-friendly models designed to replicate the magical cathedrals of baseball's Golden Era, the minor leagues caught the retro wave in the late 1990s. Among the first throwback parks to open in the bush leagues was Oklahoma City's Bricktown Ballpark, and it was immediately hailed as one of the finest minor-league facilities ever crafted. And while many other cities have since built their own old-timey minor-league yards, a decade later a strong case can still be made for the gem in Oklahoma City as the best minor-league venue in the land. Because it reflects the essence of its downtown neighborhood so well, and because it offers the type of decorative nods to its region's baseball past that you just don't find anywhere else, "the Brick" is a ballpark every traveling fan should put at the top of his or her minor-league list.

Similar to many of its big-league throwback cousins, the home of the Pacific Coast League Oklahoma City RedHawks was designed to blend into a preexisting neighborhood that was in need of revitalization. And as was the case in big-league cities like Baltimore, Cleveland, and Denver, where new ballparks breathed new life into once-blighted downtown districts, the new park in Oklahoma City fulfilled its charge and then some. By the time the $34 million publicly funded ballpark opened in 1998, what was once a sagging warehouse district east of downtown was already well on its way to becoming a vibrant entertainment district. And you probably thought the publicly funded stadium project was simply Corporate America's latest way to stick it to the taxpayer, right?

Approaching the ballpark, fans follow streets with names like Mickey Mantle Drive, Joe Carter Avenue, and Johnny Bench Drive to sports bars, steak houses, authentic Mexican eateries, and microbreweries. The highlight of this festive pre- and postgame scene is **Mickey Mantle's Steakhouse** (7 Mickey Mantle Drive), which, while not affiliated with the Mickey Mantle's in Manhattan, offers lots of great memorabilia, ranging from trophies to childhood photos to old Yankees caps and jerseys, to honor the most famous Sooner State slugger of them all.

Throughout the streets of Bricktown, colorful mosaic murals render uniquely Oklahoman scenes dating back to the early 1900s. Fans find murals in this same tradition decorating the exterior of the ballpark, along with lifelike statues at the ballpark of Bench, Mantle, and Warren Spahn and busts of Allie Reynolds and Bobby Murcer. The Bench statue stands, appropriately, just outside the home-plate entrance on Johnny Bench Plaza. It depicts the legendary backstop, who was born in Oklahoma City and grew up in Binger, wearing his catching gear. The Mantle statue, which stands outside the third-base entrance, catches the "Commerce Comet" in the midst of a mighty swing from the left-handed batter's box. Inlaid in its base are a set of the Mick's handprints and autographs from some of his friends and family members. The Spahn statue, which sits beyond the right-field fence, honors the winningest lefty ever, the pride of Broken Arrow, Oklahoma, who is depicted in the midst of one of his famously high leg kicks.

Mickey Mantle statue outside AT&T Bricktown Ballpark

As for the ballpark itself, as its name suggests, it offers an attractive redbrick facade. Inside, the Brick is large by minor-league standards—with slightly more than 13,000 seats—but maintains a cozy atmosphere, thanks to its low-to-the-field first level and to its minimal foul territory. The upper level also offers excellent sight lines, thanks to seats that hang out over the wraparound concourse atop the first-level seats down below. This excellent design, combined with the festive neighborhood around the park and the local interest fans have in seeing the Texas Rangers' top prospects, make the Brick a popular destination during the summer months. The RedHawks draw more than 500,000 fans per season, which usually places them among the top fifteen or so minor-league clubs in the country. The Brick also hosts two of the three games played each May between the Oklahoma State Cowboys and the University of Oklahoma Sooners. The Bedlam Series games attract sold-out crowds. And the park also hosts the annual Triple-A World Series, a one-game winner-take-all showdown between the Pacific Coast League and International League champions that airs on ESPN in mid-September.

★ ★ ★

= 80 =

LOS ANGELES MEMORIAL COLISEUM

3911 South Figueroa Street | Los Angeles, California

Although most fans who sat in its seats back in the late 1950s and early 1960s, as well as most of today's baseball historians, seem to agree that it provided one of the worst Major League Baseball environments ever—for fans and players alike—Los Angeles Memorial Coliseum did much to stamp its presence in the annals of baseball lore during its short life as a big-league facility, and for that reason it is worthy of the traveling fan's attention. And even though it currently exists as a football gridiron—the cavernous home of the University of Southern California Trojans, there are plaques on either side of the entry gates that celebrate its baseball past.

The coliseum was originally constructed in the early 1920s and then underwent an expansion so that it could accommodate the 1932 Olympics. During the next few decades it served as one of the early professional-football venues, hosting the National Football League LA Rams and American Football Conference LA Dons. Then in the mid-1950s, when Brooklyn Dodgers owner Walter O'Malley and New York Giants owner Hor-

Los Angeles Coliseum entrance

ace Stoneman began eyeing a move west to tap into a fertile but yet-to-be-developed baseball market, the coliseum emerged as a leading candidate to temporarily house one of the two migrating teams. Ultimately, it came down to a choice for O'Malley between the Rose Bowl in Pasadena, Wrigley Field in Los Angeles—where the American League–expansion Los Angeles Angels would wind up in 1961, or the coliseum.

After O'Malley chose the venue in the heart of the West Coast's largest population center, work began in 1957 to retrofit the 94,000-seat single-level coliseum for baseball. Three light banks were added, as well as dugouts, a press box behind what had previously been an end zone, a backstop, a home-run fence across the "10-yard line," and a 42-foot-high metal screen that extended from the leftfield foul pole—which stood just 251 feet from home plate—all the way into centerfield. Balls that hit the towering screen were in play. At one time there was talk of also adding a second screen some 80 feet behind the first one to serve as the home-run fence, the thinking being that pop flies that landed between the two fences would count as ground rule doubles, but California earthquake laws prevented such a Wiffle Ball–style second screen from ever being built. As a result, the coliseum was a right-handed pop-fly hitter's paradise.

The stadium's first year as a baseball park, 1958, saw the Dodgers break not only their single-season attendance record, as they drew more than 1.8 million fans, but also saw them combine with their opponents to challenge the single-season record for the most home runs at a stadium. In seventy-seven games, the Dodgers and their rivals hit 193 homers: 182 to left field, 3 to center field, which measured 425 feet from home plate, and 8 to right field, which measured 390 feet. While the record 219 home runs that the Reds and their foes had amassed at Crosley Field just the year before survived for a few more seasons, ultimately it would be broken when the Angels and their opponents hit 248 "long" balls at Wrigley Field in Los Angeles in 1961.

The Dodgers finished with a disappointing 71–83 record in their first year in LA, but by the next season they were back on top of the baseball world. The large crowds that continued to turn out at the coliseum—even though some seats were more than 700 feet from home plate—were treated to an exciting pennant race. After finishing the 1959 season with a record of 88–68 to edge the second-place Milwaukee Braves by two games, Gil Hodges, Duke Snider, Sandy Koufax, and Don Drysdale led the Dodgers to a six-game World Series win over the Chicago White Sox. The three games in Los Angeles drew more than 92,000 fans apiece, and the crowd of 92,706 that turned out for Game Five still stands as a World Series record.

By 1962, though, Dodger Stadium had been completed, and the Dodgers moved into their sparkling blue heaven in Chavez Ravine, as had been the plan all along. As for the coliseum, its baseball accoutrements would be dismantled, and it would return to its original function as a football field.

A visit to the coliseum today still offers the chance to see the same Roman entryway that stood in deep centerfield when the coliseum was a baseball diamond, as well as large bronze plaques that pay tribute to famous moments in stadium history. The 1958 and 1959 Dodgers receive their due on a plaque that reads in part, THIS PLAQUE PLACED TO COMMEMORATE A FINE TEAM EFFORT WHICH MADE POSSIBLE AN AUSPICIOUS START FOR LOS ANGELES IN MAJOR LEAGUE BASEBALL. Another plaque, which was added in 2005, pays tribute to Jackie Robinson, who, though he retired from the game after the 1956 season, before the Dodgers moved, had starred at the coliseum as a collegian on the UCLA track and football teams. The plaque lists Robinson's many accomplishments, both on and off the field, and describes him as AN ENDURING SYMBOL OF A STELLAR ATHLETE, A MAN OF COURAGE, AND A LIFE LIVED WELL.

★ ★ ★

=81=
THE MISSISSIPPI SPORTS HALL
OF FAME AND MUSEUM

1152 Lakeland Drive | Jackson, Mississippi

Heading into the 1937 All-Star Game, twenty-six-year-old Dizzy Dean had already won 134 games, a National League MVP award, and a World Series ring in just five-and-a-half big-league seasons. But more than just being the dominant pitcher of the previous half-decade, Dean had become one of baseball's most beloved figures. His seemingly endless reserve of "Ole Diz" stories and his playful country persona made him a fan and media darling not just in St. Louis but throughout the country. And that's why Dean never really left baseball after his career was cut short by an injury suffered in that fateful Mid-Summer Classic; he just transitioned into a new role as a national baseball broadcaster who doubled as the game's most vocal goodwill ambassador. It's also why the Dizzy Dean Exhibit, all these years later, is the most sought-out attraction at the Mississippi Sports Hall of Fame and Museum.

Dean was pitching during the third inning of the 1937 All-Star Game at Washington's Griffith Stadium when Cleveland Indians outfielder Earl Averill scorched a line drive up the middle. The ball struck Dean's right foot and broke his big toe. In the second half of the 1937 season, Dean rushed back to the mound before allowing his foot time to fully heal, and in overcompensating for the original injury, he changed his pitching delivery, which in turn caused irreparable damage to his right shoulder. Dean won just sixteen games over his final five seasons, then hung up his spikes and slid (or "slud," as he might have put it) into a seat behind a CBS microphone to serve as the play-by-play announcer for the *Game of the Week*. In this new role, alongside fellow baseball great Pee Wee Reese, Dean's creative misuse of the English language heightened his legend still further. Although grammar school teachers across the country no doubt shuddered to hear him, most fans could relate to the retired ballplayer who peppered his speech with words like "ain't" and sentences like "He weren't neither."

In 1953 Dean was elected to the National Baseball Hall of Fame, despite having won just 150 major-league games and having surpassed ten wins in only six seasons. For years there was also a Dizzy Dean Museum in Jackson; then in 1996 it was expanded to

Dizzy Dean kinetic sculpture at the Mississippi Sports Hall of Fame

honor Mississippi athletes from all sports. Today, the Dizzy Dean Exhibit, on the second floor of the Mississippi Sports Hall of Fame and Museum, does much to remember Dean's prolific, though short, career on the field, as well as his later years off it.

Thanks to a donation from Dean's widow, there are a great many photos of Dean, including ones of him posing alongside friends like President Dwight D. Eisenhower and Satchel Paige, and with his brother Paul—also a Cardinals pitcher—who teamed up with his big brother to win all four games (two apiece) of the 1934 World Series against the Tigers. Dean's World Series ring is on dis-

play, as is his Hall of Fame ring, some old gear, and one of his game-worn Cardinals jerseys. There are balls signed by players like Babe Ruth, Ty Cobb, and Cy Young. Perhaps best of all, the Museum's video footage includes an episode of the *Mel Tillis Variety Show* from the 1970s that features Ole Diz in a rocking chair singing "Wabash Cannonball," and a Falstaff Beer program in which Dean and Reese wrap up the 1961 season.

The museum also honors another Magnolia State diamond king, Cool Papa Bell. The fleet-footed Negro Leagues star, after whom a nearby street in Jackson is named, became the first Mississippi-born player to be enshrined in the National Baseball Hall of Fame in 1974. (Although Dean considered Wiggins, Mississippi, his home, he was, in fact, born in Lucas, Arkansas.) Among the twenty-five other baseball players enshrined in the Mississippi Hall are Bill Foster, the half-brother of Negro Leagues pioneer Rube Foster, who was himself considered the finest left-handed pitcher in Negro Leagues history; Boo Ferris, who helped pitch the Boston Red Sox to the 1946 pennant with a 25–6 record; and Joe Gibson, who starred on the baseball field and basketball court at Ole Miss and then won a World Series ring with the Pittsburgh Pirates in 1960.

The museum also honors Mississippi legends from other sports, like Jake Gibbs, Bailey Howell, Archie Manning, and Walter Payton. It features a Wall of Fame, where historic moments in Mississippi sports history are depicted; a theater, which plays a video history of Mississippi sports narrated by ESPN anchor Robin Roberts; and a Participatory Room, where visitors can try their hands and feet at virtual baseball, golf, football, and soccer activities. The museum is open Monday through Saturday from 10:00 A.M. to 4:00 P.M. Admission costs $5.00 for adults and $3.50 for students between the ages of six and seventeen and adults over the age of sixty.

= 82 =

JOE DiMAGGIO'S BOAT

Martinez Marina/Waterfront Park | North Court Street | Martinez, California

Long before he would become a baseball legend, Joe DiMaggio was born the eighth of nine children to Sicilian immigrants Giuseppe and Rosalie DiMaggio. He was born in Martinez, a small fishing village, but before his first birthday his family moved 30 miles southwest to San Francisco. While historically DiMaggio is remembered as San Francisco's son, it is in Martinez where today's fans will find a most unusual tribute to this iconic baseball figure. At the entrance to the city's marina, just off a road named Joe DiMaggio Drive, a restored antique powerboat named the *Joltin' Joe* pays homage to its one-time owner. The 22-foot Chris-Craft vessel has been mounted on a raised platform here since the early 1990s.

The boat was originally presented to the retiring slugger on Joe DiMaggio Day at Yankee Stadium on October 1, 1949. In addition, DiMaggio's haul that day included a new Cadillac, a Dodge, a Longines pocket watch, gold cuff links, a gold belt buckle, a gold tie pin, a gold money clip, a Westminster toaster, an air-foam mattress, 300 quarts of Cardini ice cream, a case of shoestring French fries, a case of Ventura County oranges, a case of frozen lima beans, and a cocker spaniel. DiMaggio, who remarkably managed to maintain his svelte waistline even during those early days of retirement when he had all of that cream in his freezer, kept some of the gifts that the Yankees and various businesses, civic organizations, and fans had given him, and other gifts he gave away. The Dodge, for example, he passed on to his mother. As for the boat, he used it a few times and then gave it to his brother Vince, who used it himself for a while, and then lent it to a cousin who was a fisherman.

The truth is that although baseball lore remembers DiMaggio as the son of an immigrant fisherman and although Ernest Hemingway portrayed him as a downtrodden fisherman's idol in his classic novella *The Old Man and the Sea*, DiMaggio was no fisherman or lover of the sea. The Great DiMaggio admitted as much within the pages of his autobiography when he wrote:

I was born in Martinez, but my earliest recollection was of the smell of fish at Fisherman's Wharf, where I was brought up. Our main support was a fishing boat, with which my father went crabbing. If you didn't help in the fishing, you had to help in cleaning the boat. . . . Baseball didn't have much appeal to me as a kid, but it was better than helping Pop when he was fishing, or helping clean the boat. I was always giving him excuses, principally that I had a weak stomach, but he insisted I was "lagnuso" (lazy) and to tell you the truth, I don't know which he thought was the greater disgrace to the family, that a DiMaggio should be lazy or that a DiMaggio should have a weak stomach.

In any case, after giving away the boat, DiMaggio presumably forgot all about it until several decades later when a man named Barry Wysling got in touch with him. A harbormaster in Martinez, Wysling knew that a boat there had once belonged to the Yankees legend, and when the DiMaggio cousin who had been using it passed away in the early 1990s, Wysling launched a campaign to restore it and transform it from a seafaring vessel into a monument to the city's most famous native son. A few weeks after receiving Wysling's request, DiMaggio stopped by the marina and signed over the title to the boat to the City of Martinez. Wysling, who described DiMaggio as a "quiet gentleman" in a *New York Times* article that ran on December 30, 1991, describing the unusual gift, even prevailed upon DiMaggio to sign a baseball for him.

Today, the *Joltin' Joe* not only reminds baseball fans who stop by its scenic waterfront location that Joe DiMaggio was born in Martinez and spent his earliest days there but perpetuates the legend that DiMaggio, as if by birthright, loved the sea and was drawn to the most honest and humble of avocations—fishing—like so many DiMaggio men before him. Yes, it is just a myth. But for a figure whose name was so liberally appropriated by an American culture that was always trying to define him but never quite succeeding, and whose inscrutable grace would come to symbolize a generation, this seems about right.

★ ★ ★

= 83 =
MIKE GREENWELL'S BAT-A-BALL AND FAMILY FUN PARK

35 Pine Island Road | Cape Coral, Florida

Shortly after finishing his career with the Red Sox in 1993, Mike Greenwell returned to his home on Florida's Gulf Coast and opened an amusement park. Not surprisingly, the park features an outdoor batting cage as one of its trademark attractions. Fans who remember the colorful slugger will also not be surprised to learn that one of his other passions is also reflected in the 10-acre park's offerings. No, there isn't an alligator-wrestling tank—Mike's gator-hunting days are over—but the park does have four different go-cart tracks. Boston fans will remember that midway through the 1991 season, Red Sox general manager Lou Gorman reprimanded Greenwell—who'd been advised by the team earlier in his career to curtail his barehanded alligator hunting—after a picture of the leftfielder sitting behind the wheel of a race car wound up splashed over the pages of the *Boston Herald*. Greenwell insisted he had only partici-

pated in a promotional lap around the track before a race in Seekonk, Massachusetts, and said that he drove *to* the track faster than he did *on* the track. Nonetheless, the Red Sox put the kibosh on any future racetrack rides for the slugger, adding a clause to his contract to prohibit them. After his retirement, Greenwell got a chance to do some real stock-car racing, participating in the Limited Late Model series at a speedway in Punta Gorda, Florida. Today, Mike can race all he wants at his own facility's junior track, slick track, Grand National track, or figure-eight track.

Besides the racetracks and batting cages, attractions at Greenwell's include a miniature-golf course, a video arcade, a fish-feeding dock, a paintball field, and a snack bar. As for baseball memorabilia, the main building displays more than fifty game-used bats signed by Mike's many friends in the game. These include models from Hall of Famers Wade Boggs, Cal Ripken Jr., and Carlton Fisk, as

Sign for Mike Greenwell's Bat-a-Ball and Family Fun Park

well as from Ellis Burks, Wally Joyner, Harold Baines, Sandy Alomar Jr., Tim Raines, and Juan Gonzalez. One bat is signed by every member of the 1991 Red Sox, and another is marked as the one Greenwell used on the day he hit for the cycle against the Orioles on September 14, 1988.

Greenwell batted .303 in his twelve-year career and finished second to a juiced-up Jose Canseco in the 1988 American League Most Valuable Player award balloting. He visits his amusement park regularly to take batting practice in the fast-pitch cage and to zip around the tracks with his children. The park is open year round, seven days a week, from 10:00 A.M. to 10:00 P.M. It's a favorite destination of Boston fans and players during spring training, when the Red Sox play their Grapefruit League games just a few miles up the road in Fort Myers.

=84=
NOLAN RYAN'S WATERFRONT STEAKHOUSE AND GRILL

Choke Canyon Reservoir | Highway 72 West | Three Rivers, Texas

Although those Advil ads he stars in may give viewers the impression that Nolan Ryan is a creaky-jointed old-timer doing little more than nursing his aches and pains in retirement, nothing could be further from the truth. In fact, Ryan has been remarkably active since his playing career ended. And while the man once trumpeted as the future governor of Texas has yet to throw his hat into the political arena, his successes in the private sector have demonstrated a keen head for business and an ability to get deals done. Ryan's larger victories in the business world include his part-ownership of two wildly successful minor-league baseball teams—the Double-A Texas League Corpus Christi Hooks and the Triple-A Pacific Coast League Round Rock Express, both of which play at beautiful new ballparks that Ryan's ownership group championed and both of which draw more than half a million fans per season.

Ryan, whose two teams are both Houston Astros affiliates, also finds time to serve as a special assistant to the Astros general manager, while also serving as the majority owner and chairman of the board of Express Bank and serving on the boards of directors of the Justin Cowboy Crisis Fund, the Texas Water Foundation, the Natural Resources Foundation of Texas, the Alvin Community College Baseball Fund, and the Nolan Ryan Foundation. He also owns several cattle ranches and is the owner of Beefmaster Cattlemen LP, which produces Nolan Ryan's Guaranteed Tender Aged Beef. Suddenly it becomes apparent why Ryan would find himself reaching for that bottle of Advil after a long day's work.

As if all of these ventures weren't enough to keep Ryan occupied, old No. 34 also owns a restaurant midway between San Antonio and Corpus Christi on the scenic shores of the Choke Canyon Reservoir. This is fishing country, *big* fishing country, and a trip to Nolan Ryan's Waterfront Steakhouse and Grill almost requires that visitors bring along their fishing gear and set aside some time for angling. Largemouth bass that grow as large as 10 pounds are the primary draw, but the reservoir also offers smallmouth buffalo that grow as large as 100 pounds and alligator gar that locals claim can grow to be nearly twice that size. As the story goes,

Choke Canyon had been a favorite fishing destination of Ryan's for years, so much so that he eventually decided to launch a restaurant in the area where he and his friends and fellow fishermen could enjoy a few drinks and a hearty meal after pulling in their lines.

As you might expect, the decor features Ryan memorabilia in a tasteful setting, and the menu features Nolan Ryan's Guaranteed Tender Aged Beef. The steaks really are to-die-for, as are the sweeping views of the gorgeous lake, which diners enjoy through the restaurant's wraparound windows. In addi-tion to the many cuts of fine beef, the menu includes such specialties as Fire Fries (fresh-cut French fries tossed in spicy seasoning), Sweet Potato Fries, and Southwestern Bar-becued Chicken. Although the chances of spotting Ryan during your visit may be slim, it's pretty neat to think that a Hall of Famer played a hand in raising the cow that eventually became the juicy rib eye on your plate. And it's pretty neat to visit a spot that a baseball legend—and a busy one, at that—considers one of his favorite places to catch a little R & R.

★ ★ ★

= 85 =

SCOTTSDALE STADIUM

7408 East Osborn Road | Scottsdale, Arizona

Thanks to the Arizona Fall League, fans who find themselves unable to let go of summer as the major-league playoffs come to an end can head to Greater Phoenix and prolong the season by a few more weeks before grudgingly accepting winter's grim reality. Major League Baseball founded the developmental league in 1992 to provide top prospects a place to further develop their skills while under the watchful eyes of their parent organizations.

The Fall League begins play in the second week of October and finishes in the third week of November, fielding six teams that each draw rookie and minor-league players from five major-league clubs. It utilizes five ballparks—Mesa's HoHoKam Park, Peoria Stadium, Phoenix Municipal Stadium, Scottsdale Stadium, and Surprise Stadium—all of which also see use during the Cactus League season in March. All of these facilities offer relaxed environments where scouts and hard-core fans enjoy up-close looks at baseball's best prospects, but Scottsdale Stadium is clearly the league's signature facility. In addition to serving as league headquarters, it is also the only Fall League facility with two home teams—the Scottsdale Scorpions and

Grand Canyon Rafters—and it is where the Arizona Fall League Hall of Fame is located.

Originally built in 1956 to serve as the spring park of the Baltimore Orioles, Scottsdale Stadium has been the Cactus League home of the San Francisco Giants since 1984. Its sightlines showcase the four peaks of the Camelback Mountains rising beyond the third-base line and a grassy berm across the outfield. The park underwent a major renovation prior to the 1992 spring season, following blueprints drawn by the architects at HOK, whose Oriole Park at Camden Yards was unveiled just a month later. The old-time effects at Scottsdale Stadium include antique light fixtures, primitive baseball gear on display on the concourse, and a facade of redbrick pillars and green iron gates that meshes well with the surrounding neighborhood. Cacti, desert flowers, jacaranda trees, and paloverde trees also appear throughout the stadium, contributing to a Southwestern flare.

Fans find the Fall League's Hall of Fame beneath the grandstand, where it offers bronze plaques displaying each inductee's name, year in the league, and Fall League team. Although more than 1,200 Fall League alumni have reached the major leagues, and 18 Fall League managers have succeeded to big-league managerial posts, the hall includes only 17 members. And it's no wonder there are so few. The hall charter sets the bar pretty high. It stipulates

To qualify for consideration for this prestigious honor, a player must have achieved recognition at the Major League level as a Rookie of the Year, a league MVP, an All-Star or a Gold Glove or Silver Slugger Award winner. Players meeting these criteria are placed on the AFL Hall of Fame ballot for consideration by the AFL Selection Committee, comprised of baseball executives who have participated in the Fall League's growth over the years.

Through 2007 the enshrinees included Garret Anderson, Dusty Baker, Terry Francona, Nomar Garciaparra, Jason Giambi, Shawn Green, Roy Halladay, Todd Helton, Derek Jeter, Grady Little, Jerry Manuel, Tony Pena, Troy Percival, Mike Piazza, Albert Pujols, Mike Scioscia, and Alfonso Soriano. The hall also provides a wall of plaques displaying the names of the annual Joe Black Most Valuable Player Award winners. Black, the 1952 National League Rookie of the Year and the first African-American pitcher to win a World Series game, spent his final three decades living in Phoenix and was a vocal proponent of the Fall League. He is also honored with a statue outside the regular-season home of the Arizona Diamondbacks in Phoenix.

Finally, not far from where the Hall of Fame is located on the concourse, fans find the Scottsdale Sports Hall of Fame, which honors more than thirty local athletes, including baseball great Jim Palmer.

While these two shrines are interesting places to peruse, undoubtedly it is the

Scottsdale Stadium

crack of the bat and the pop of rawhide smacking into leather that really draw fans to Scottsdale each autumn when the rest of the baseball world has suddenly gone silent.

And best of all, because there are two Fall League teams based at Scottsdale Stadium, this sweet music fills the air every day of the league's thirty-two-game season.

★ ★ ★

= 86 =
BOOG'S BEACH BARBECUE
401 Atlantic Avenue | Ocean City, Maryland

Boog Powell hit 339 home runs during a seventeen-year career that saw him play in four World Series. And yet the heavy hitter's biggest contributions to the game and its big-bellied fans may very well be the ones he's making right now at his barbecue joints in Maryland.

Any fan who has been to Oriole Park at Camden Yards can attest to just how delicious the hickory-smoked beef, pulled pork, and smoked turkey are at the Boog's Barbecue behind the rightfield fence on Eutaw Street. The smoky aroma of slow-roasting meat wafts into the stands all game long, beckoning hungry fans. Boog opened the original ballpark stand in 1993 and continues to appear there all summer long on game days.

But sadly, the Orioles play just eighty-one home games per year. So, happily, Boog opened a second summertime stand, this one in Ocean City. The satellite location offers the same great rotisserie-cooked smoked meats, slow-cooked barbecue beans, and homemade sauces as at the original stand. The Pork Sunday is a local favorite that layers barbecue beans, pulled pork, and coleslaw into one scrumptious concoction.

Boog's Beach Barbecue is part of a festive boardwalk scene that also includes seafood restaurants, watering holes, miniature-golf courses, and many other diversions for the kids and the kid in everyone. Boog stops by often on his way to the nearby fishing pier, to mingle with fans and to sign his name in barbecue sauce, so bring your baseball cards, as well as your appetite. There are other player-owned and operated barbecue stands out there in the baseball universe—including the ones run by Greg Luzinski (Philadelphia), Gorman Thomas (Milwaukee), Manny Sanguillen (Pittsburgh), and Randy Jones (San Diego)—but Boog's was the first and still is the best, and his Ocean City location is the only such stand operating just outside the bounds of a ballpark.

= 87 =

HANS L'ORANGE FIELD

94-1024 Waipahu Street
Waipahu, Hawaii

Baseball first arrived in the Hawaiian Islands in 1849, when Alexander Joy Cartwright, the man some consider the father of the game, relocated to Honolulu and became the fire chief of Waipahu, a thriving sugar-milling town. The islanders took to the game immediately, and over the next several decades, it became an increasingly important part of their lives. In the 1930s Babe Ruth, Jimmie Foxx, and Lou Gehrig headlined barnstorming tours of major leaguers who visited Honolulu. In the 1940s players like Joe DiMaggio, Phil Rizzuto, and Pee Wee Reese played in exhibitions on the islands.

By 1961 Honolulu was home to its own professional team, the Hawaii Islanders, who played in the Pacific Coast League. After twenty-seven seasons of shuttling back and forth to the mainland, however, the Islanders relocated to Colorado Springs following the 1987 season. But Hawaii's hardball drought did not last long. In 1993 the pro game returned to Honolulu in the form of the Hawaii Winter League. The unique circuit played for five consecutive seasons, offering fans the chance to see teams composed of minor leaguers from the United States, Japan, and Korea. Future major leaguers like Ichiro Suzuki, Jason Giambi, Tadahito Iguchi, A. J. Pierzynski, Todd Helton, Mark Kotsay, Preston Wilson, and Benny Agbayani all honed their skills in the league, but then

Hans L'Orange Field

the Hawaii League disbanded following the 1997 season.

Baseball has fortunately returned to the islands once again, though. The Hawaii Winter League was resurrected in 2006, when it breathed new life into one of the most charming little ballparks in all of baseball—2,100-seat Hans L'Orange Field. Today four teams play a forty-game schedule during October and November in the Hawaii League. The Waikiki Beach Boys and the Honolulu Sharks both call Les Murakami Stadium home, while the West Oahu Cane Fires and the North Shore Honu reside at Hans L'Orange Field.

The 4,306-seat Murakami Stadium has artificial turf but makes up for it by offering views of Diamond Head beyond its rightfield fence. Most fans agree, though, that "the Hans" is an even more impressive facility. It is about as cozy and inviting as a professional stadium can be, and from the stands around the infield, fans are treated to views of brilliant outfield sunsets that are made purple by the

"vog," or volcanic fog. Another distinctive feature on the outfield horizon is the old Oahu Sugar Company smokestack that rises beyond the fence in left-center. Given its proximity to the old mill, it is not surprising that this field saw its first use as a recreational diamond for Oahu Sugar Company employees or that it is named in honor of the sugar miller who convinced management to turn it into a permanent baseball stadium in the 1920s.

In addition to intimate environments and purple sunsets, fans of the Hawaii Winter League also enjoy unique ballpark menus that feature unusual items like teriyaki chicken, Portuguese bean soup, and sushi. Hopefully, this resurgent league will continue to operate for a good long time, now that it's up and running again. And even if it doesn't, the Hans's other home team, the Hawaii Pacific University Sea Warriors, will continue to offer fans the chance to enjoy the game that Mr. Cartwright brought to the islands so many years ago at this special venue.

★ ★ ★

= 88 =

THE CY YOUNG MUSEUM

Temperance Tavern | 221 West Canal Street | Newcomerstown, Ohio

During an illustrious playing career that spanned twenty-two seasons on either side of the turn of the last century, Cy Young was known as the most effective, efficient, and durable pitcher the game had yet seen. Young began his career with the Cleveland Spiders in 1890 at a time when pitchers stood just 55 feet from home plate at the back of the pitcher's box. Then in 1893 organized baseball took a tremendous evolutionary step forward when it moved the pitching rubber back 5 feet to its present location 60 feet, 6 inches from home plate. While the change bothered some veteran hurlers, it didn't faze Young all that much. Sure, his ERA rose from 1.93 in 1892 to 3.36 in 1893, but his record slipped only slightly, from 36–12 to 34–16. Young eventually adjusted, of course, and finished with an ERA under 3.00 in most of his remaining seasons. By the time he hung up his spikes for good, he had won twenty or more games in fifteen different seasons, and thirty or more in five seasons, while compiling a 2.63 ERA.

After Young's retirement and eventual death, when fans and players invoked the name of the man who had established "unbreakable" records, in categories like wins (511), losses (313), complete games (749), and innings pitched (7,357), they spoke in the reverent tones reserved for only a handful of select individuals among the upper echelon of baseball royalty. Young, Cobb, Ruth, and Robinson—these were the men who had transformed the game into something it might never have become without them.

Today, Young's name epitomizes pitching excellence, and while the association is an apt one, it also conveys a certain loss. To modern fans and players, Young is more an idea—pitching perfection—than someone who was an actual living, breathing person. The Cy Young Award, established by Commissioner Ford Frick in 1956 and presented to the best pitcher in each league each season, has appropriated the Young name so that whenever we refer to *the* Cy Young or to a *Cy Young–caliber season* we do so without really giving the man, Cy Young, much thought. This is not the case in the small town where Denton True Young spent his life before, during, and after baseball, however.

In Newcomerstown, Ohio, where Young picked rocks from his father's pasture in his childhood and threw them against the side of a barn until the structure looked as if a cyclone had hit it, where Young farmed in the off-season during his playing days, and where he hunted and fished with his many friends in retirement, he is still remembered first as a man and only then as a legend.

A pair of understated but well-maintained landmarks in Newcomerstown speak volumes to the affection that Young's contemporaries and their descendents felt and still feel for the humble farmer among them who just happened to also be the greatest pitcher to ever step foot onto a baseball diamond. The Cy Young Museum and the Young Monument both merit visits for any fan wishing to gain a greater understanding of Young.

The Cy Young Museum is located within Newcomerstown's ancient Temperance Tavern, which served as a stopover for travelers on stagecoach routes as early as the 1840s but has since been converted to house the local Historical Society. Among the items on display are Young's favorite rocking chair, his fedora hat, and one of his Boston Pilgrims uniforms. There is also an exhibit related to the town's other famous son, former Ohio State football coach Woody Hayes. The museum is open between Memorial Day and Labor Day, Tuesday through Sunday from 10:00 A.M. to 3:00 P.M. Admission costs $1.00.

Meanwhile, **Cy Young Memorial Park** (591 North College Street) offers visitors year-round access to the Young Monument behind the bleachers of a community field that was dedicated in the pitcher's honor in 1950. The eighty-three-year old Young was on hand for the ceremony and was deeply touched by the town's gesture. He frequently visited the park in his later years, before passing away in 1955. The cement monument features an engraved image of

Young, along with some words of praise.

Another popular location to visit is Young's gravesite at the **Peoli United Methodist Cemetery** (State Route 258) in the nearby town of Peoli. Young's headstone is adorned with a baseball sprouting angel's wings. His epitaph reads, FROM 1890 TO 1911, CY YOUNG PITCHED 874 MAJOR LEAGUE BASEBALL GAMES. HE WON 511 GAMES, THREE NO-HITTERS, AND ONE PERFECT GAME IN WHICH NO MAN REACHED FIRST BASE. It is a local tradition to decorate the grave with flowers and baseballs each Memorial Day, and local superstition holds that any youngster who places a ball on Young's grave will soon see his or her baseball skills improve.

★ ★ ★

= 89 =

RECREATION PARK

440 North Giddings Street | Visalia, California

The home field of the California League Visalia Oaks, Recreation Park presents baseball wanderers with a unique design. Counting the full- and short-season minor-league yards and the Indy-ball yards, there are more than 200 bush-league ballparks in America, but fans won't come across another one that looks quite like this. The stadium, which originally opened in 1946, owes its current appearance to a renovation that took place in 1967. At that

time the city used excess soil that had been excavated from the trench dug to lay U.S. Highway 198 to build a mound around the back of the preexisting seating bowl. After piling the dirt as high as possible, the city encased the mound with shot creek rock and slathered some mortar between the rocks. The result is a sloping rocky exterior that takes the ballpark-inside-a-hill design that fans have observed at Dodger Stadium in Los Angeles and at Grapefruit League

Fan dugout at Recreation Park

venues like Holman Stadium and Chain O' Lakes Park, to an entirely new level.

Even if your tour of the American Baseball West takes you through California in the off-season, it's worth stopping by Recreation Park to marvel at this distinctive exterior edifice. But should your trip to Visalia occur any time from April through early September, even better, because then you'll get to enjoy Recreation Park's ridiculously close-to-the-field seating. Amazingly, the first row of the grandstand is less than 20 feet from home plate, and offers fans a chance to calls balls and strikes unlike any other they'll ever have, unless of course they enroll at the Jim Evans' Umpiring School in Florida.

With a seating capacity of just a smidge over 1,600, Recreation Park owned for many years the distinction of being the smallest full-season minor-league yard in the country and the second-smallest professional-baseball stadium in the United States, exceeding in size only Joe O'Brien Field of the Appalachian League Elizabethton Twins. But a renovation scheduled to occur sometime in 2008 will add about 500 seats to the grandstand, as well as several luxury boxes that will likely take away this distinction. Visalia's ballpark will still be cozy, though. And it will continue to feature another baseball oddity—a third dugout, this one for the fans, that can be rented out by the game. Added in 2007, the fan dugout is a true replica of a player dugout, sunken and concrete, that places fans just 35 feet from third base.

= 90 =
THE HILO WALK OF FAME

71 Banyan Drive | Hilo, Hawaii

To discover the most mystical of all the wondrous baseball attractions America has to offer, travelers must set their compasses for the farthest reaches of the nation, Hawaii, where there grows a thriving banyan tree that was planted by none other than Babe Ruth. Ruth helped pile the rich volcanic soil of Hawaii's Big Island over the tree's delicate roots in 1933 when he visited the state as part of a barnstorming tour that would eventually lead him to Japan. At the time the tree was one of just a handful of saplings planted into a seaside grove on a peninsula that Hilo's town fathers envisioned would become a location of civic pride in future years.

And boy, were they right. Some seven decades later, Ruth's tree, which is clearly marked by a wooden plaque that bears his name, grows amidst more than forty other thriving banyans that were also planted by famous Americans and world leaders who have visited Hawaii through the years. And Banyan Drive, which traces the shores of the Waiakea Peninsula, has become a quintessential island tourist attraction.

Ruth's tree, which to baseball fans will surely seem more robust and vibrant than all the others, resides across the street from the Castle Hilo Hawaiian Hotel. Although it was just a twig when the aging slugger's two rough hands gently patted down the soil around its base, it now stands as an expansive monument to the Sultan of Swat.

The story of how the Hilo Walk of Fame and Banyan Drive came into existence dates back to 1933, when filmmaker Cecil B. DeMille arrived in Hawaii to film scenes for his stranded-adventurer movie *Four Frightened People*. The Hilo Park Commission asked DeMille and some of the actors from the movie to plant trees to commemorate their visit to the island, thinking that this might be a nice way to build civic pride. Ruth followed suit later in the year, then President Franklin Delano Roosevelt in 1934, then Amelia Earhart and King George V during separate visits in 1935, and so on. A road was added between the trees and before long hotels began sprouting up along it. Richard Nixon planted a tree in 1952, long before he became president, then after it was lost in a tsunami, First Lady Pat Nixon returned to the islands during his term in office to replace it. Supreme Court justice Earl Warren planted a tree, as did Chinese premier Sun Fo, musician Louis Armstrong, and a host of other famous people.

For the most part, the banyans have stood the test of time. Among all the types of trees Hilo might have banked on to withstand the decades and become increasingly visible parts of the local community, the banyan was a wise choice. Banyans are believed to live as long as a thousand years and can grow to more than 200 meters in diameter (that is not a typo!). There is something mystical and unusually reassuring about standing beside a living tree and knowing that a person you've read about in a history book, a person like Ruth, was responsible, at least in part, for its existence. Romantic baseball fans who hail from tropical climes can even pilfer some of the figs sometimes found scattered around the base of Ruth's tree, and take them home with them to plant in their own backyards, where they can cultivate a little bit of Ruth's legacy for themselves.

★ ★ ★

=91=
THE ALCOR LIFE EXTENSION FOUNDATION
7895 East Acoma Drive | Scottsdale, Arizona

In the wake of baseball immortal Ted Williams' death on July 5, 2002, a fierce controversy raged within the extended Williams family regarding what should be done with the Splendid Splinter's remains. The undignified squabble cast a dark cloud over what should have been a glorious time for a nation and its national game. Instead of focusing on the remarkable life of a true American hero, one who twice interrupted his career to go to war for his country, people opened their newspapers and turned on their televisions throughout the latter half of 2002 only to learn the latest revelations in a family feud that seemed to grow more vitriolic and more bizarre with each passing day. In short, immediately after Williams' death, John Henry Williams had his father's corpse shipped to the Alcor Life Extension Foundation, where it was cryogenically suspended in the hope that the slugger might be "reanimated" someday by virtue of future advances in medical technology. Meanwhile, John Henry's half-sister, Bobbie Jo Ferrell, said that it had always been her father's will to be cremated and have his ashes spread over the Florida Keys, where he fished for decades. Ms. Ferrell claimed that John Henry, who had made a career of selling his father's memorabilia and trotting his father around the country to promote his various business

Ted Williams with fans

interests, intended to one day sell Williams' DNA (perhaps to baseball teams that would clone second-generation Ted Williamses to dominate Major League Baseball the way the original had). Finally, after John Henry produced a scribbled contract signed by himself, his father, and his sister Claudia that stated the trio's desire to all be cryogenically suspended after their deaths, a judge declared that it had been within the younger Williams's legal right to oversee the handling of his father's remains.

Consequently, baseball travelers looking to pay their final respects to the man widely considered the greatest hitter who ever lived and the last man to bat over .400 in a major-league season find not a gravesite to visit but a large medical building that rises in the Arizona desert. Visitors are not allowed to see Williams' body or his reportedly severed head, but folks genuinely interested in arranging for their own cryopreservation one day can make appointments to visit Alcor and learn more about the company's services, which cost between $80,000 (brain only) and $150,000 (full body).

Williams is one of more than seventy patients currently preserved at Alcor, along with John Henry Williams, who died of leukemia in 2004. The ice-free cooling process, known as vitrification, begins immediately after death. Once a person is clinically and legally dead but not yet brain dead, the body is placed in ice water. Then, the body's blood circulation and breathing are restored by a heart and lung resuscitator. The body is then transported to Alcor, where the blood is drained and replaced with a special blend of chemicals as the body is cooled in nitrogen vapor to a temperature of minus 196 degrees Celsius. Finally, after the body reaches the desired temperature, it is placed in liquid nitrogen, and the long wait begins.

While many people contend that this type of medicine is the product of vivid imaginations that have been too heavily influenced by our culture's affinity for science fiction, Alcor, which has existed since 1972, boasts medical and scientific advisory boards rife with PhDs and MDs. So laugh now, if you'd like, but also acknowledge that the possibility exists, however small, that Ted Williams will visit his local library some time in the year 2105 or 2210, check out a copy of this book, and enjoy a hearty chuckle while the rest of us wither in our coffins or smile down on him from the grassy fields of baseball heaven.

= 92 =

BUCKY DENT'S BASEBALL SCHOOL

490 Dotterel Road | Delray Beach, Florida

Yankees fans wishing to relive one of the most exciting moments in Pinstripe history or Red Sox fans seeking to confront and perhaps finally come to terms with the haunting specter of one of the lowest moments in Boston baseball history should set their compasses for Bucky Dent's Baseball School, where there stands a replica of Fenway Park's famous leftfield wall. Dent, a light-hitting Yankees shortstop, permanently inscribed his name in the annals of Red Sox–Yankees lore in 1978, of course, when he lifted New York to victory in a one-game playoff at Fenway Park, delivering the American League East crown. The winning blow came in the seventh inning, when Dent lofted a Mike Torrez pitch into the screen above the Green Monster for a three-run homer. To this day, Dent is referred to throughout New England as "Bucky F—ing Dent," yet the number of New Englanders that visit the replica field at Dent's 23-acre baseball school easily exceeds the number of New Yorkers.

As long as classes aren't in session, fans are free to walk on the field, to have a game of catch, or to pose for pictures in front of the familiar black-and-white scoreboard that appears on the face of the Green Monster. Unlike the slate scoreboard in Boston, this board is painted onto the wall and is frozen in time so as to appear exactly as it did after Dent's dinger in the top of the seventh inning on that fateful October day in Boston. The line score shows that three runs have just crossed the plate for the visitors, that No. 21 (Torrez) is pitching for the Red Sox, and that No. 49 (Ron Guidry) is pitching for the Yankees.

Bucky Dent's Baseball School provides instruction to players from ages five through eighteen in the form of weeklong sessions. The school's roster of past and present guest instructors includes such baseball greats as Ted Williams, Pete Rose, Don Sutton, Alex Rodriguez, Ivan Rodriguez, Andre Dawson, Mike Piazza, Josh Beckett, and Ryan Howard. Howard, who lives nearby, in fact, takes batting practice at the school during the off-season to keep his swing sharp, while Juan Pierre is also a frequent visitor. And Dent himself is a daily presence at the school.

Since opening in 1974, four years before Dent would break New England's collective heart and a decade before a faux Green Monster would be erected on its grounds, the school has instructed tens of thousands of youngsters in the finer points of the game, while emphasizing a supportive learning environment. Among the impressive list of former Dent students who have gone on to enjoy careers in baseball are Yankees general manager Brian Cashman, former big-league first baseman Hal Morris, and longtime big-league pitcher Jamie Moyer.

In addition to serving Dent's school, "Fenway Park II," as the replica field is called, is home to the Atlantic High School baseball team.

★ ★ ★

= 93 =

THE BASEBALL MUD SITE

The Delaware River | Burlington County, New Jersey

As you've surely noticed, this book is devoted to detailing 101 places every baseball fan *should* visit, and in most cases your humble author has endeavored to provide a compilation of historically and culturally significant places that fans actually can visit if they choose to do so. In other words, the book doesn't offer entries like "Manny Ramirez's Son's Bedroom," which, however cool (it's modeled after Fenway Park) is not accessible to the rank-and-file fan unless he happens to be traveling with a crowbar and a good criminal defense attorney. This entry is a little bit different, though. While technically fans *could* visit the location where the mud that's used to "rub up" major-league baseballs is harvested, chances are that if they did, they wouldn't know for sure that they were there. That's because the exact location of the public riverbank where the Lena Blackburne Rubbing Mud Company dredges its silky till has been a closely guarded secret for more than seven decades.

Here are the details we do know. When the official major-league baseball that's made by Rawlings comes out of its box, its rawhide surface is slick and bright white. In this condition the ball doesn't allow pitchers to get a good grip on it, nor does it allow hitters to get a good look at it, owing to the glare on its surface created by the sun or ballpark lights. Thus, before each game the home-plate umpire is responsible for rubbing a smudge of mud that looks something like chocolate pudding onto several dozen game balls. This pregame rubbing ritual is nothing new. During the early part of the twentieth century teams rubbed Dead Ball Era horsehide with tobacco spit and shoe polish, substances that tended to mark balls inconsistently, or sometimes they used mud made from mixing the infield clay with water, which made the ball soggy and too easy for pitchers to illegally scuff. Then in 1938 former Chicago White Sox infielder Lena Blackburne, who was coaching third base for the Philadelphia Athletics at the time, happened

upon a special patch of mud while swimming in the Delaware River. It was dark but not too dark and exceptionally smooth. On a whim, Blackburne tried rubbing some of it onto a baseball, and he liked the result: a sphere that was easy to grip and that had surrendered its shine.

Blackburne returned to the river's edge with a couple of big buckets and the motivation to enter the mud-distribution business, and within a year every team in the American League was pretreating its balls with Lena Blackburne mud. An American Leaguer through and through, Blackburne initially demurred when National League teams expressed their interest in purchasing some of his special sludge, but finally in the early 1950s he relented and began supplying the Senior Circuit as well. Every major-league baseball since—including the one Don Larsen threw past Dale Mitchell to complete his perfect game in the 1956 World Series, the one Carlton Fisk swatted off Fenway Park's leftfield foul pole to win Game Six of the 1975 World Series, and even the one that Barry Bonds hit out of AT&T Park to pass Babe Ruth on the all-time home-run ledger in 2006—has been rubbed with Lena Blackburne Rubbing Mud.

Mr. Blackburne died in 1968, but before he did, he passed on the secret of the mud's location to his childhood friend John Haas. Haas managed the company for a while, then he passed on the secret to his son-in-law, Burns Bintliff, who has since passed it on to his son, Jim Bintliff, who is the company's present owner. Though inquiring minds have often pressed him for details, Jim Bintliff has guarded the secret as well as his predecessors did. All he's revealed to date is that he visits his mud hole once a year in July, at which time he collects enough mud to last an entire year. The site is believed to be somewhere on the New Jersey side of the Delaware River.

Major League Baseball rubs approximately one million balls per year with Blackburne Mud, while minor-league and amateur teams across the country rub up their own balls with the product as well. Fans wishing to rub up their balls at home may visit www.baseball rubbingmud.com, where an 8-ounce tub of mud sells for $17.25. A 32-ounce professional-size tub, big enough to last a major-league team for a year, sells for $51.75.

= 94 =

LAKEFRONT BREWERY

1872 North Commercial Street | Milwaukee, Wisconsin

If this were a book dedicated to not the most interesting baseball landmarks in the country but the best breweries, the old brick building on the banks of the Milwaukee River that houses Lakefront Brewery would deserve inclusion within these pages on the merits of its exceptional microbrews, which beer lovers enjoy across the Midwest. Milwaukee is the "Brew City," after all, and most sources (*Milwaukee Magazine, Maxim, Stuff*, etc.) that have looked into rating the better beers are in agreement that Lakefront belongs near the top of the list when it comes to ranking the Brew City's many breweries.

But this is not a book for beer lovers; it is a book for baseball lovers, and Lakefront Brewery earns inclusion within these pages for another reason. Lakefront, you see, is the place where Bernie Brewer's original chalet and slide have resided ever since the Brewers departed County Stadium for Miller Park in 2002.

Bernie Brewer, you may recall, has enjoyed several distinct incarnations as the Milwaukee mascot. The original "Bernie" was a sixty-nine-year-old man named Milt Mason, who famously mounted the County Stadium scoreboard in June of 1970 and refused to come down until the local fans started supporting the Brewers in greater numbers. He set his benchmark at a crowd of 40,000 and, true to his word, didn't descend until nearly two months later, when 44,000 fans turned out at the ballpark for a game. The Brewers, who had arrived in Milwaukee via Seattle just before Opening Day that season, went on to finish the season with a dismal 65–97 record, thirty-three games behind the first-place Minnesota Twins, but they placed a respectable seventh out of twelve American League clubs in home attendance, and they found a mascot their fans loved.

By 1973 a chalet had been erected for Bernie Brewer atop a three-story-high tower behind the centerfield fence at County Stadium. Whenever a Brewer hit a home run, the handlebar-mustached Bernie, who wore German lederhosen, would hop onto a slide and plummet into a big stein of foaming beer. It was quite a sight to behold and one that local fans just couldn't get enough of. In the mid-1980s, however, a renovation to County Stadium necessitated the removal of Bernie's chalet, slide, and tower, putting Bernie out of work for the better part of the next decade.

Finally, in the early 1990s, Bernie returned, when his chalet and slide were reassembled not far from their original location. It was at this time that Bernie became a more family-friendly and politically correct mascot. The sanitized Bernie wore a colorful costume rather than that greasy mustache and five o'clock shadow. And locals noted that the pleasant aroma of fermented hops no longer filled the ballpark concourses whenever Bernie walked by.

Later, when, the Brewers moved to Miller Park, they created a new perch and bright yellow slide for Bernie in the outfield rafters, but rather than having Bernie slide into a mug of beer, they built him a dry landing pad. As for the old slide, Lakefront Brewery moved quickly to purchase it from the team and happily installed it along its extremely popular brewhouse tour. Visitors will observe that many members of the Brewers have autographed the old apparatus, none more famous than the team's quartet of famous sausage racers. Their signatures, along with many others, appear beneath a Plexiglas cover. The brewery tour costs just $5.00, which includes three sample pints and a complimentary pint glass to take home. On Fridays Lakefront also offers a fish-fry dinner and polka dancing.

Through the years, Bernie has never been the most famous baseball mascot—that distinction has been passed back and forth between the likes of the San Diego Chicken, the Philly Phanatic, Don Zimmer, and other Johnny-come-latelies. And he has never been the hardest working, or the most loveable, or the best smelling, or the most kid-friendly mascot either. But he's always been the hardest drinking. And he embodies the unique personality of his home city in a way that that few of his fellow mascots do. Milwaukee is the land of brats and beer, and its residents—Bernie included—know how to enjoy both of these local treats and aren't ashamed to admit it. Bernie is to ballpark mascots what Homer Simpson is to cartoon characters—a lovable boozer who transcends the normal bounds of his medium to bring a whole new audience of devotees to his special genre of entertainment. And

Bernie's slide, the one that the rough-and-tumble original Bernie used to mount so nobly, is a fitting tribute to his legacy—one that couldn't be more appropriately placed than where it currently resides in Milwaukee's finest brewery.

★ ★ ★

= 95 =
THE DELAWARE SPORTS MUSEUM AND HALL OF FAME

Frawley Stadium | 801 South Madison Street | Wilmington, Delaware

In recent years several minor-league teams have incorporated a team hall of fame into their ballpark designs so that game-day fans and, in some cases, even fans who arrive on off days, can pay tribute to the local legends that have graced their diamonds through the years. The Wilmington Blue Rocks of the Class A Carolina League have taken the concept one step further, opening on their grounds a hall of fame that pays tribute to all of the great athletes who have excelled in a wide variety of sports in Delaware history.

For baseball fans, the museum's exquisitely detailed "Hallway of the Decades" chronicles the rise and fall of the original Blue Rocks, a team that played in the Interstate League from 1940 to 1952. The team played at old Wilmington Park, first as a Philadelphia A's affiliate and then as a Philadelphia Phillies farm club, starring future big leaguers like Robin Roberts, Curt Simmons, and Elmer Valo. The museum also honors familiar baseball names like Frank Coveleski, Dallas Green, and Delino DeShields, who are enshrined. The Hallway of the Decades also details the arrival of the new Blue Rocks, a Kansas City Royals affiliate, who arrived in 1993, and of Frawley Stadium, which debuted the same year.

But the highlight of the museum is the exhibit dedicated to Negro Leagues star Judy Johnson, perhaps the most unheralded and underrated Negro Leagues star of them all. Delaware remembers its lone native son to earn enshrinement in Cooperstown with a one-of-a-kind display. The Judy Johnson "talking exhibit" depicts a life-size Johnson mannequin sitting in a rocking chair and telling his own story in his own words. The recording conveys Johnson's passion for the game and the rich catalogue of baseball memories he carried with him throughout his life until he passed away in 1989. Also on display is the Hall of Fame plaque that Johnson received from the National Baseball Hall of Fame at the time of his induction in 1975.

Johnson, who is also honored with a statue outside the ballpark officially known

Judy Johnson Exhibit at the Delaware Sports Museum and Hall of Fame

as Judy Johnson Field at Daniel S. Frawley Stadium, played in the Negro Leagues from 1921 through 1938. A third baseman who consistently batted better than .300, he starred on the famed Philadelphia Hilldales teams of the 1920s, then later wore the uniforms of the Darby Daisies, the Homestead Grays, and the Pittsburgh Crawfords, playing alongside such fellow future Hall of Famers as Satchel Paige, Josh Gibson, and Cool Papa Bell. In retirement Johnson returned to Wilmington with his wife Anita and served as a baseball scout, first for the A's and then for the Phillies. He was so appreciative of being inducted into the National Baseball Hall of Fame that when he appeared in

Cooperstown he broke down in tears during his acceptance speech. The next year he was voted into the Delaware Sports Hall of Fame, which was then located at a different site. Johnson is also one of the twelve individuals honored with a statue on the Field of Legends at the Negro Leagues Baseball Museum in Kansas City.

To keep the memory of Johnson and the Negro Leagues alive, each year the Blue Rocks host an annual "Judy Johnson Night." The event raises money and awareness for the Judy Johnson Memorial Foundation, which was founded by local baseball historian Joe Mitchell, a close friend of Johnson's in his later years. The popular evening begins with a pregame ceremony that recalls the accomplishments of Johnson and of one other Negro Leagues star per year. Then, when it is time for the game to begin, the Blue Rocks and their opponents take the field in throwback uniforms that replicate the jerseys worn by famous Negro Leagues teams. Since they're a Kansas City Royals affiliate, the Blue Rocks wear Kansas City Monarchs uniforms. While Judy Johnson Night

educates the 6,500 fans that pack Frawley Stadium with an interesting and heartfelt history lesson, the museum also does its part to educate through the entire baseball season and even a bit beyond. It is open April through October, Tuesday through Saturday, from noon to 5:00 P.M. Admission costs $4.00 for adults, $3.00 for adults fifty and older, and $2.00 for teens; it is free for children twelve and younger.

★ ★ ★

= 96 =

ELYSIAN FIELDS

11th Street and Washington Street | Hoboken, New Jersey

As mentioned in the pages devoted to Cooperstown's Doubleday Field, baseball mythology offers two conflicting accounts of the game's origins—the one that credits Abner Doubleday with inventing baseball in 1839 and the other that credits Alexander Joy Cartwright with conjuring up the game at a park called Elysian Fields in Hoboken, New Jersey, in 1846. These are both myths, however. The truth is that neither man invented the game. Baseball historians agree that it evolved organically out of English precursors like cricket and rounders throughout the early 1800s, refining itself along the way and slowly incorporating many of the rules and subtleties by which it is today identified. Later in the

1800s, as modern means of transportation made the country a smaller place, the different versions of the game that had grown popular in different regions were slowly assimilated into one game with one set of accepted rules.

Just as it is an oversimplification to attribute the creation of the game to one divinely inspired father, it misses the point to label any one place the primordial field from which the game sprung up. In fact, scores of playing fields, some pastoral and idyllic, as the hopeless romantic in us all would like to believe, others cramped and cluttered and squeezed into urban centers, certainly all played roles in the game's development over several decades. While most of these venues

Elysian Fields, 1866

have long since faded out of existence and out of our national consciousness, the site of the Elysian Fields, where Cartwright made his contributions—however small they may have been—to the game, has long been viewed by some fans as holy ground. The once-expansive park has been reduced to a strip of lawn in the center isle between two lanes of traffic. On it, a monument is inscribed with the words: ON JUNE 19, 1846, THE FIRST MATCH GAME OF BASEBALL WAS PLAYED HERE ON THE ELYSIAN FIELDS BETWEEN THE KNICKERBOCKERS AND THE NEW YORKS. IT IS GENERALLY CONCEDED THAT UNTIL THIS TIME THE GAME WAS NOT SERIOUSLY REGARDED.

Readers will note that the inscription stops short of proclaiming Hoboken the birthplace of baseball. But that doesn't mean it's not worth visiting. Elysian Fields did play a role in the formalization of baseball's previously unwritten rules, even if the rules employed for the first baseball game there in 1846 bore only a shadowy resemblance to the ones that define the game we know today. The Elysian Fields story goes something like this: A Union Bank clerk named Alexander Joy Cartwright spent the early 1840s playing regular afternoon games of "base ball" at a vacant lot in Manhattan with other professionals who had spare time after work. Then in 1845 the lot they used as their field was marked for redevelopment, causing Cartwright and his friends to look elsewhere for a place to play. Enter Elysian Fields, a tree-lined park just across the Hudson River that Cartwright's newly formed club of "Knickerbockers" rented and traveled to regularly via ferry.

At the time of the move, in the winter of 1845–1846, Cartwright put pen to paper and outlined a set of fourteen rules that characterized the game he and his friends had already been playing in the city for several years. He was not inventing the rules of baseball, merely recording the parameters of the game that he and his friends had agreed upon over time at their old field. Most notably, the Cartwright rules stipulated that baseball be played on a diamond, not a square; that the distance between home plate and second base should measure 42 paces (which makes for approximately 75 feet between each base); that balls struck outside the baselines be declared foul; and that runners must be tagged out, as opposed to being struck by thrown balls as in rounders and town ball. The rules Cartwright recorded did not stipulate a distance between the pitcher's box and home plate, nor did they specify that there should be 90 feet between bases, nine players per team, or nine innings per game,

although Cartwright's plaque at the National Baseball Hall of Fame—hung in 1938—also credits him with establishing such modern baseball rules as these.

In any case, on June 19, 1846, a game closely resembling baseball was played following the rules that Cartwright had outlined. Cartwright's Knickerbockers faced a group of their old playmates from Manhattan who called themselves the New York Nine, and the home team lost 23–1 in four innings. Was it the only game involving four bases, a bat, and a ball played in the United States that spring day? Almost certainly not. Was it *the* evolutionary link between rounders and the modern game that would come to be known as baseball? No, probably not. But it was *one* of the early baseball games played that day, and it was *one* of the sport's evolutionary links, and in the absence of other memorable early games to celebrate it therefore qualifies Elysian Fields as someplace special.

★ ★ ★

= 97 =

THE PINK PONY STEAKHOUSE

3831 North Scottsdale Road | Scottsdale, Arizona

For a tasty steak served with a heaping side of baseball nostalgia, the traveling fan should visit the Pink Pony Steakhouse in Old Town Scottsdale. The

legendary player hangout is open for lunch and dinner year-round and is conveniently located just a few blocks from Scottsdale Stadium. The ballpark has been the Cactus

Pink Pony logo

League home of the San Francisco Giants since 1984 and before that served the Oakland A's, Chicago Cubs, Boston Red Sox, and Baltimore Orioles, dating all the way back to 1956. The bar has been a spring-training staple for even longer. The Pink Pony opened in 1949 and quickly became the March eating and drinking establishment of choice for baseball players, coaches, executives, scouts, writers, broadcasters, and just about anyone else connected to the game.

Dizzy Dean played a leading role in catapulting the Pink Pony to prominence. One spring Ole Diz, who by the 1950s was working as a national play-by-play announcer, struck up a conversation with owner Charlie Briley. The retired pitcher discovered that the friendly barkeep really knew his baseball, and the two men became good friends. They would hunt dove and quail together each year when Dean traveled to Arizona for spring training, and as Diz talked up the Pony to his many friends in the game, word spread. Soon the bar was opening its doors to players and retired players like Ty Cobb, Joe DiMaggio, Jimmie Foxx, Rogers Hornsby, Willie Mays, and Ted Williams on a nightly basis. On one memorable evening five Hall of Famers—Ernie Banks, Lou Boudreau, Bob Lemon, Mickey Mantle, and Eddie Mathews—all sat at the same table.

As one generation of players gave way to the next, baseball icons like Billy Martin, Don Sutton, and Reggie Jackson did their best to keep the Pony on baseball's "it" list; then Fergie Jenkins, Bob Uecker, and

Will Clark helped keep the Pony chic for the next generation. Today, the chances of bumping into any major-league stars during a visit to the Pink Pony are remote. Perhaps understandably, the modern player prefers the privacy of a night spent at his luxury condo to the experience of being mauled by well-intentioned but overzealous fans in a public setting. Minor leaguers, team executives, scouts, and writers still belly up to the bar at the Pony each spring, though, and the extensive collection of autographed jerseys and photos adorning the walls makes the restaurant a must-visit for anyone interested in baseball memorabilia.

The unique aspect of the decor is a series of caricatures mounted above the long bar. The colorful drawings pay tribute in a funny way to some of the Pony's more notable visitors through the years. Initially, these were the creation of Walt Disney animator Don Barclay, and then when Barclay passed away, Charlie Briley's wife Gwen continued the tradition. When it comes to the food, the Pink Pony offers an upscale menu highlighted by a juicy 28-ounce prime rib. Beef, beer, and baseball: what more could a fan want?

★ ★ ★

= 98 =
COOK COUNTY CRIMINAL COURTS BUILDING
54 West Hubbard Street | Chicago, Illinois

As increasingly damning information has come to light regarding baseball's recent steroid problem, pundits, historians, and others who have seen fit to comment on the saga have often invoked comparisons between today's crisis and the one that involved the Chicago "Black Sox" more than eight decades ago. That's because prior to the revelations that many of baseball's biggest stars were using performance-enhancing drugs, the most damning black eye the game had ever suffered involved the eight Chicago White Sox players who conspired with gamblers to fix the 1919 World Series.

Just as the steroid scandal has unveiled a far-reaching menace that threatens to undermine the legitimacy of the game, the case against Joe Jackson and his teammates illuminated a playing field that had often been anything but level during the first two decades of the twentieth century. In the wake of both scandals, fans were left to scratch their heads while trying to determine which of the games and performances they'd enjoyed were real and which were frauds. The similarities between the two scandals do not end there, however. In both cases, the trouble facing the game had been suspected by baseball's owners, writers, and fans for years but stubbornly ignored, before the offenses of certain players became so grievous that they could no longer be cloaked beneath a shroud of willful innocence any longer.

While the suspected continued use of human growth hormone among some of today's players leaves the contemporary observer with the distinct sense that the game has still not fully emerged from its Steroid Era, the Gamblers Era came to an end in Chicago in the early 1920s. Ground Zero for the revelations that exposed the so-called Black Sox was the Cook County Criminal Courts Building. While the building no longer serves as a courthouse, it still stands in Chicago, preserved as a National Historic Landmark. It represents the place where baseball lost its innocence. It was here that a horrified nation learned the details of the Black Sox Scandal and of the ensuing cover-up that involved signed confessions by three of the accused players—Jackson, Eddie Cicotte, and Lefty Williams—mysteriously disappearing. It was here that the growing rift between baseball's owners and players was revealed; here that the notion of the game as solely that, a game, and not a business, was finally dispelled once and for all; here that a jury ultimately found all eight accused players "not guilty" in the eyes of the State of Illinois, only to see the verdict "overruled" in the eyes of the baseball estab-

lishment by the game's first commissioner, Judge Kenesaw Mountain Landis, who banned the eight from the game for life.

Today a plaque beside the courthouse doors reads, THIS ROMANESQUE STYLE BUILDING, WHICH HOUSED THE COOK COUNTY CRIMINAL COURTS FOR 35 YEARS, WAS THE SITE OF MANY LEGENDARY TRIALS, INCLUDING THE LEOPOLD AND LOEB MURDER CASE AND BLACK SOX SCANDAL. . . . DEDICATED ON JUNE 9, 1993, RICHARD M. DALEY, MAYOR.

Baseball mythology holds that this is where a young fan implored Joe Jackson to "Say it ain't so," only to watch with tears in his eyes as his idol sadly said, "Yes, kid, I'm afraid it is." In fact, this exchange never took place. According to Jackson and others who watched him descend the courthouse steps after testifying before a grand jury that September day in 1920, there were no children present, just a few adults, including reporter Charley Owens of the *Chicago Daily News*, who later penned the article that included the details of this supposed encounter, perhaps as a way to personify the betrayal and hurt he felt himself upon learning that one of the game's brightest stars and one of his own heroes had conspired to purposefully lose the most hallowed of baseball events, the World Series.

What is true, however, is that the series of events that began that day at the courthouse in Chicago as Jackson followed Cicotte's lead and confessed, forced baseball to finally address its decades-old gambling problem. Over the next eleven months the courthouse provided the stage for a trial that deeply wounded the psyche of the nation but ultimately left the National Game on sounder footing than it had been before. Even though the missing confessions (years later they would turn up in the possession of White Sox owner Charlie Comiskey) helped ensure the players' acquittal, the undeniable connection the trial exposed between the players and many shady characters from the gambling underworld convinced Landis that they were guilty enough in his book. His unequivocal expulsion of them, and his subsequent refusal to consider their pleas for reinstatement during his remaining twenty-four years in office, discouraged other cheats and would-be cheats, while also helping to restore public faith in the game.

Today a visit to the Cook County Criminal Courts Building is a reminder that though the government can play a role in maintaining baseball's credibility, in the end the game must police itself. One can only hope that the current commissioner will visit this historic edifice someday soon, draw inspiration from Landis's definitive decree, and punish the current era's steroid transgressors, most of whom still have not been held accountable for their sins.

= 99 =

LASSITER BASEBALL COMPLEX

2601 Shallowford Road | Marietta, Georgia

101 BASEBALL PLACES TO SEE BEFORE YOU STRIKE OUT

Many high school ballparks across the country might have claimed a place within the pages of this book. In the big cities, small towns, and in all of the midsize communities in between, scores and scores of beautiful high school fields reflect their areas' commitment to providing youths with the best hardball diamonds possible. Perhaps nowhere better than at the high school level does the American love affair with the game sparkle quite so brightly. From the history teachers who double as coaches, hitting grounders until it's too dark to see on chilly March afternoons; to the moms and dads who sneak out of work early to sit knee to knee with other rooters on wooden bleachers; to the janitors, guidance counselors, and parents who take it upon themselves to make sure the chalk on the baselines is always fresh and perfectly straight; to the students who assume their positions in the field, at the end of the bench, or at the concession stand window; it really does "take a village" to run a high school baseball program successfully.

Lassiter Field

The Lassiter High School program in Marietta, Georgia, exemplifies this collaborative approach as well as any in the country, and the Trojans' home field shows it. Fans can certainly find high school parks with larger and flashier grandstands, but in a sense these yards are victims of their own success. The bigger and fancier they get, the more charm they seem to sacrifice. This is high school baseball we're talking about, after all, and at Lassiter the facilities seem just right. They reflect the innocence of the amateur game, as well as the sort of finishing touches that speak volumes about the pride supporters of the Lassiter team have developed since the school's inception in 1980.

The best time to visit the Lassiter Baseball Complex is in March or April, when the Trojans start their home games at 6:00 P.M. Approaching the diamond, fans find a 60-foot-long mural on the back of the visitors' first-base dugout that reads in gold letters against a maroon backdrop LASSITER BASEBALL. Also on the back of the dugout, the team logo—a larger-than-life ancient Greek warrior coiled in a left-handed batting stance—readies to swing. Across the diamond, the home dugout appears tucked beneath a wooden observation deck that extends off the Trojan House, a small building on the third-base line that offers four sliding glass doors through which fans can watch the action on the occasional rainy afternoon. The remainder of the seating takes the form of bleachers along the baselines.

A redbrick retaining wall between the field and two-story press box is a nice aesthetic touch, while the players' clubhouse and indoor batting cages down the leftfield line are the types of facilities that would make any high school team proud. Spanning the outfield, green trees seal in the ballpark, making the environment cozy. In right-center, the scoreboard bears the team logo and the words 1999 NATIONAL CHAMPIONS, remembering a season the Trojans finished ranked atop several national polls, including the ones that appeared in *Baseball America* and *Collegiate Baseball*.

Lassiter's fine facilities did not spring up overnight. Nor did they come about thanks to the generosity and hard work of just one or two individuals. Rather, this inviting ballpark has evolved over three decades as hundreds of people have played whatever roles they could to help. As Mickey McMurtry, the Trojans head coach since 1992, puts it, "We are proud of both our program and ballpark. As you can well imagine they are the product of a lot of hard work by a lot of people over the years."

Since his arrival at Lassiter, "Coach Mick"

has been astounded by the generosity displayed by members of the team's booster club, who have played prominent roles in supporting the program and field; by local contractors who have worked on the field and surrounding facilities; by East Cobb Baseball, a travel league that has partnered with Lassiter on many field improvements; and by parents and students who have volunteered their time. His players have done their part too, raising money in a variety of ways. The team's trademark event is an annual pancake-breakfast fundraiser in the school cafeteria. The coaches work the griddles, while the players provide wait service and bus the tables.

If the program at Lassiter sounds like one big family, and the ballpark like the family's backyard, then this chapter would be remiss not to also mention the family's beloved pet, Coach Mick's black Lab Jackson, who was a fixture at Lassiter games and practices for more than a decade before passing away in 2006. Whenever there was activity on the field, the faithful dog could be spotted trotting around with three or four baseballs in his mouth or hanging out near the concession stand waiting for a fellow fan to slip him a piece of hot dog. While Coach Mick and his family recently adopted a new black Lab, who is learning to play his own role in keeping the mood light and the fans entertained at Trojans games, Jackson will always hold a special place in the Lassiter community's collective heart.

= 100 =

THE BALCO LABS SITE

1520 Gilbreth Road | Burlingame, California

Fans wishing to visit the spot where government agents uncovered evidence of what so many baseball observers had suspected all along—that the game's offensive explosion of the 1990s and early 2000s was fueled by rampant steroid use among players—need look no further than the San Francisco suburb of Burlingame, where baseball's house of cards suddenly came crashing down in 2003. Here, fans will find the headquarters of the company formerly known as the Bay Area Laboratory Cooperative, or BALCO, as it is better known. While the biggest drug scandal in American sports history has continued to unfold, the nutritional supplement company has since reopened at its Burlingame location under a new name, Scientific Nutrition for Advanced Conditioning, but visitors will find the building looking much as it did on September 3, 2003, when a cadre of special agents from the IRS Criminal Investigations Unit, Food and Drug Administration, and San Mateo County Narcotic Task Force stormed its doors at high noon and seized documents related to the company's dealings with dozens of pro athletes, including the biggest baseball star of all, home-run king Barry Bonds.

The laboratory sits beside a toy store in an innocuous-looking strip mall that could be dropped into suburban-anywhere and fit in seamlessly. But behind the expansive storefront windows, a musician-turned-chemist named Victor Conte spent the 1990s developing an undetectable type of steroid precursor known as human growth hormone, or HGH, which he then distributed to athletes in the form of substances nicknamed "the clear" and "the cream."

In the days following the raid, the investigation was expanded to focus also on Bonds' personal trainer, Greg Anderson. Eventually, the list of athletes called to testify before the grand jury grew to include such baseball players as Bonds, Jason Giambi, and Gary Sheffield; football players Bill Romanowski, Dana Stubblefield, and Johnnie Morton; and track-and-field stars Marion Jones, Tim Montgomery, and Kelli White.

In exchange for immunity from prosecution and for the government's agreeing not to disclose their identities to the public, several of the baseball players implicated agreed to speak freely with prosecutors about their relationship with Conte. Eventually, however, two *San Francisco Chronicle* reporters came to possess "leaked" testimony that they published in the newspaper. These revelations prompted the U.S. House of Representatives to convene a Government Reform Committee to investigate steroids in baseball in March of 2004. And the Congressional action finally forced baseball, whose guardians had been in denial about steroid use among players for so long—and conveniently so, given the correlation between high-scoring games and increased ballpark attendance—to finally enact a steroid testing policy that made players somewhat accountable for what they put into their bodies.

In an ironic twist, however, baseball has still not begun to test players for human growth hormone, the substance that started the whole chain of events that exposed the game's problem. This is because baseball's testing program allows for urine testing only, not the type of blood testing required to detect HGH. Despite this and other imperfections in baseball's current steroid policy, few would disagree that the game is in better shape today than it was in the late 1990s and early 2000s. Home-run totals are down, players have begun to resemble baseball players again, not middle linebackers, and the statistical anomalies that characterized the previous decade have come to be viewed highly suspiciously.

A visit to the spot where the Steroid Era blossomed into previously unimaginable dimensions and then was exposed goes a long way toward helping fans come to terms with this regrettable period in the game's history, even if they are still waiting for the game to punish certain players and to strike from the record books certain achievements now known to have been steroid aided. As Barry Bonds so pointedly stated when speaking of Conte's "nutritional supplements" in an interview that appeared in *Muscle & Fitness* magazine three months prior to the BALCO raid, "I'm just shocked by what they've been able to do for me." Indeed, the entire baseball world was shocked. But we now know better.

★ ★ ★

=101=

LENNY DYKSTRA'S CAR WASH

1144 East Los Angeles Avenue | Simi Valley, California

While aging athletes have been known to open their own restaurants or sports bars after their playing days are through, former Mets and Phillies outfielder Lenny Dykstra chose a different path after hanging up *his* spikes. The gritty speedster known as "Nails" was rarely spotted with a clean uniform during a career that spanned 1985 through 1996, but in retirement he focuses on keeping Southern California automobiles shiny and clean. Lenny Dykstra's Car Wash, which opened in 1998, includes an ornate stucco exterior, a 150-foot-long conveyor that moves cars forward as they are hand-washed and hand-dried, a sixteen-bay auto-service center, a 10,000-gallon fish tank, an outdoor waterfall, TVs tuned in to sporting events, and baseball memorabilia from Lenny's private collection. On display are autographed photos, jerseys, and bats signed by Lenny and by his baseball friends, including Ryne Sandberg, Greg Maddux, Chipper Jones, Jeff Bagwell, Darryl Strawberry, and Tony Gwynn.

Lenny's employees wear dark red baseball caps and red and blue baseball jerseys that at first glance can easily be mistaken for Phillies garb. Upon closer inspection, though, it becomes apparent that these uniforms are adorned with Lenny's logo rather than the Phillies', to avoid any Major League Baseball licensing infringements. On busy days, the forty to fifty employees on duty at Lenny's wash more than a thousand cars and perform more than a hundred oil changes. Wash packages start at $12.95 for the "Double," and increase in price incrementally up to $24.95 for the "Grand Slam." Customers can add hand-waxing for $39.95 and opt for a $150.00 detailing service if they please. Lenny's is open 8:00 A.M. to 5:00 P.M. on weekdays and 7:00 to 5:00 on weekends and offers free shuttle service for anyone in Simi Valley who would like detailing service. An Orange County native, Dykstra is a hands-on owner who is often on-site to oversee operations and mingle with patrons.

During Dykstra's five seasons in New York and seven in Philadelphia, he made three All-Star teams and appeared in two World Series. He twice led the National League in hits and in 1993 finished second to Barry Bonds in the National League Most Valuable Player balloting and won the Silver Slugger Award. Today Lenny is baseball's undisputed "silver scrubber," and his luxurious car wash provides traveling fans with a great place to freshen up their road-trip cars while checking out some neat memorabilia before moving on to the next points of interest on their tours.

INDEX

PHOTO CREDITS

Introduction *Joe Jackson Statue*
Courtesy of the Greenville Chamber of
Commerce

1 *Hall of Fame, Plaque Gallery*
Photo by Milo Stewart Jr./National Baseball Hall
of Fame Library, Cooperstown, New York

2 *Field of Dreams Movie Site*
Photo by Kevin O'Connell

3 *Negro Leagues Museum, Field of Legends*
Courtesy of Negro Leagues Baseball Museum

4 *Monument Park, Lou Gehrig Monument*
Photo from Wikimedia commons free use page

5 *Little League, Lamade Stadium*
Courtesy of Little League International,
Williamsport, PA

6 *Rickwood Field Entry*
Courtesy of the Friends of Rickwood/Chris Frey

7 *Fenway Park, Green Monster*
Photo by Josh Pahigian

8 *Babe Ruth's Grave* Photo by Kevin O'Connell

9 *Rosenblatt Stadium* Courtesy of the College
World Series of Omaha, Inc.

10 *Dodgertown, Holman Stadium*
Photo by Josh Pahigian

11 *Cape Cod League, Cotuit Kettlers, Lowell Park*
Photo courtesy of Rick Heath

12 *Sluggers Exterior* Courtesy of Sluggers

13 *National Baseball Congress, Lawrence-
Dumont Stadium sign*
Courtesy of Wichita Baseball, Inc.

14 *Doubleday Field*
Courtesy Milo Stewart Jr./National Baseball Hall
of Fame Library, Cooperstown, New York

15 *Durham Athletic Park* Courtesy of the
Durham Convention & Visitors Bureau

16 *Mickey Mantle's Restaurant*
Courtesy of Mickey Mantle's Restaurant

17 *McCoy Stadium, Scott Cooper mural*
Photo by Nicole R. Morin and Jamie Pahigian

18 *Babe Ruth Birthplace and Museum*
Courtesy of Babe Ruth Birthplace and Museum

20 *Wiffle Ball Kid* Courtesy of Gene Kaiser and
the *South Bend Tribune*

21 *Jackie Robinson Center, Robinson Portrait*
Courtesy of the Baseball Reliquary, Inc.

22 *Midway Stadium, Trampoline Team*
Courtesy of the St. Paul Saints

23 *League Park today* Photo by Kevin O'Connell

25 *Canadian Baseball Hall of Fame*
Courtesy of the Canadian Baseball Hall of Fame
and Museum

26 *Ted Williams Museum and Hitters Hall of
Fame* Photo by Steven Kovich/Courtesy of the
Ted Williams Museum and Hitters Hall of Fame

27 *Baseball Boulevard, Al Lang Plaque*
Photo by Josh Pahigian

29 *McKechnie Field* Photo by Josh Pahigian

31 *Monument Park, Tampa, Ruth Monument*
Photo by Josh Pahigian

32 *Growden Park*
Courtesy of the Fairbanks, Alaska Goldpanners

35 *Louisville Slugger Museum, Giant Bat*
Courtesy of the Louisville Slugger Museum

36 *Joe Jackson Statue* Courtesy of the Greenville
Chamber of Commerce

37 *Joe Engel Stadium*
Photo by J. L. Francis, Director of Security,
Tennessee Temple University

38 *Crosley Field Replica, Scoreboard* Courtesy of
the City Manager's Office of Blue Ash, Ohio

39 *Ozzie's bat standings* Courtesy of Ray
Gallardo/Ozzie's Restaurant and Sports Bar

40 *Centennial Field, Scoreboard*
Photo by Josh Pahigian

42 *Braves Museum, Championship Lockers*
Courtesy of the Atlanta Braves

43 *Mavericks Stadium* Courtesy of Steve Saenz

44 *Ty Cobb Museum, Sign*
Courtesy of the Ty Cobb Museum

45 *Joe DiMaggio's, Booth with Monroe*
Photo by Mitch Tobias/Courtesy of DSE Corp.

47 *Cardinals Hall of Fame*
Courtesy of the St. Louis Cardinals Hall of Fame

48 *Ripken Center, Cal Sr.'s Yard*
Courtesy of the Cal Ripken Sr. Foundation

49 *Yogi Berra at the Yogi Berra Museum*
Courtesy of Yogi Berra Museum and
Learning Center

50 *Sports Legends Museum at Camden Yards*
Courtesy of Sports Legends Museum at Camden
Yards

52 *Huntington Avenue Grounds, Cy Young
Statue* Photo by Josh Pahigian

54 *Babe Ruth Photomosaic, ESPN Zone*
Courtesy of Photomosaic® by Robert Silvers

55 *Heroes of Baseball Wax Museum*
Courtesy of Tim Greer

56 *McCovey Cove* Courtesy of City Kayak

57 *Forbes Field Flagpole and Fence*
Photo by Kevin O'Connell

58 *Big League Dreams Wrigley Field Replica*
Peter Rogers Photography

59 *Reds Hall, Rose Exhibit*
Courtesy of the Cincinnati Reds

61 *Jackie Robinson Ballpark*
Courtesy of the Daytona Cubs

63 *House of David*
Courtesy House of David Museum

65 *Mall of America, Metropolitan Stadium Seat*
Photo by Kevin O'Connell

66 *Samford Stadium-Hitchcock Field at
Plainsman Park* Todd J. Van Emst, Auburn
University Athletic Department Photographer

67 *McCovey's Restaurant*
Mitch Tobias/Courtesy of DSE Corp.

68 *Tiger Stadium* Public Domain

69 *Carroll B. Land Stadium*
Courtesy of Point Loma Nazarene University

71 *Phoenix Municipal Stadium, Rock Formations*
Photo by Josh Pahigian

73 *Baseball Reliquary, Spitter Painting
from Ben Sakoguchi*
Courtesy of the Baseball Reliquary, Inc.

74 *Bob Feller Museum*
Courtesy of the Bob Feller Museum

75 *Distant Replays, Hat Wall*
Photo by Miles Cliatt, Distant Replays

76 *National College Baseball Hall of Fame*
Courtesy of the College Baseball Foundation

77 *St. Louis Walk of Fame, Ozzie Smith, Bob
Costas, Chuck Berry, 2003 Induction*
Photo by Hope Edwards/Courtesy of the
St. Louis Walk of Fame

79 *Mantle Statue*
Courtesy of Oklahoma RedHawks/Wendy Eagan

80 *Los Angeles Memorial Coliseum Entrance*
Photo by Kevin O'Connell

81 *Mississippi Sports Hall of Fame, Dizzy Dean
kinetic sculpture* Courtesy of the Mississippi
Sports Hall of Fame and Museum

83 *Greenwell's Sign* Courtesy of Mike
Greenwell's Bat-a-Ball and Family Fun Park

85 *Scottsdale Stadium, Infield and Mountain*
Photo by Josh Pahigian

87 *Hans L'Orange Field*
Courtesy of the Hawaii Winter Baseball League

89 *Recreation Park, Fan Dugout, Action Shot*
Courtesy of Visalia Oaks

91 *Ted Williams with Fans* Courtesy of Boston
Public Library, Print Department

95 *Judy Johnson Exhibit* Courtesy of the
Delaware Sports Museum and Hall of Fame

96 *Elysian Fields, 1866* Courtesy of the Library of
Congress/in public domain

97 *Pink Pony Logo* Photo by Josh Pahigian

99 *Lassiter Field View*
Photo courtesy of Josh Mathews

Author Photo Photo by Heather Pahigian